Doctors, Patients and the Law

Edited by

CLARE DYER

Solicitor
Legal Correspondent, *The Guardian*
and
Legal Correspondent, *British Medical Journal*

OXFORD
BLACKWELL SCIENTIFIC PUBLICATIONS
LONDON EDINBURGH BOSTON
MELBOURNE PARIS BERLIN VIENNA

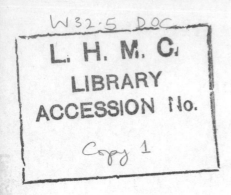

DISTRIBUTORS

Marston Book Services Ltd
PO Box 87
Oxford OX2 0DT
(*Orders:* Tel: 0865 791155
         Fax: 0865 791927
         Telex: 837515)

USA
Blackwell Scientific Publications, Inc.
3 Cambridge Center
Cambridge, MA 02142
(*Orders:* Tel: 800 759-6102
               617 225-0401)

Canada
Times Mirror Professional Publishing, Ltd
5240 Finch Avenue East
Scarborough, Ontario M1S 5A2
(*Orders:* Tel: 800 268-4178
               416 298-1588)

Australia
Blackwell Scientific Publications
(Australia) Pty Ltd
54 University Street,
Carlton, Victoria 3053
(*Orders:* Tel: 03 347-0300)

British Library
Cataloguing in Publication Data

A Catalogue record for this book is
available from the British Library

ISBN 0–632–03442–4

Contents

List of Contributors

IAN DODDS-SMITH *Solicitor, Partner in McKenna & Co*

LAWRENCE GOSTIN *Professor of Health Law, Harvard University and Executive Director, American Society of Law and Medicine*

MICHAEL A. JONES *Senior Lecturer in Law and Dean, Faculty of Law, University of Liverpool*

IAN KENNEDY *Professor of Medical Law and Ethics, Head and Dean, School of Law and Director, Centre of Medical Law and Ethics, King's College, London*

ROBERT G. LEE *Director of Education, Wilde Sapte, Solicitors*

ALEXANDER McCALL SMITH *Senior Lecturer in Law, University of Edinburgh*

SHEILA McLEAN *International Bar Association Professor of Law and Ethics in Medicine and Director, Institute of Law and Ethics in Medicine, University of Glasgow*

J.K. MASON *Regius Professor (Emeritus) of Forensic Medicine, University of Edinburgh*

ROY PALMER *Secretary and Medical Director, the Medical Protection Society*

BRIAN RAYMOND *Solicitor, Partner in Bindman & Partners*

MICHAEL SPENCER *QC, Barrister*

Foreword

by Sir Douglas Black, MD, FRCP,
Past President, Medical Protection Society,
and Royal College of Physicians

The chapters of this book constitute a series of authoritative statements by distinguished lawyers on areas where the interests and responsibilities of doctors and lawyers meet, and may thus overlap or even conflict. But in these matters, the paramount interest must surely be that of the individual described in a medical context as 'the patient', and in a legal context as 'the client'. That interest is surely best served when doctors and lawyers most fully understand the similarities, and also the differences, between their respective professions.

The ideal of a profession, as set out for example in the Oath ascribed to Hippocrates, is that its members have a duty to set the interests of those who consult them even above their own. So, far from being a conspiracy against the laity, a profession should safeguard within the limits of its competence members of the public from harm and wrong. The greatest similarity between our two professions is that we share this ideal. As fallible individuals, we are certain to fall short of it from time to time. But simply to possess and acknowledge this common ideal can only improve our professional conduct. It may, for example, help members of our two professions to see in that shared obligation, that of helping people, an inducement to keep within the bounds of civilised discourse our statements on matters in which we may happen to differ. As was said by William Harvey, the uncanonised patron saint of doctors in this country, *Concordia res parvae crescunt, discordia res magnae dilabuntur* – with agreement small things grow, with discord large things slip away. (This may not be a matter in which our politicians – many of them lawyers, and a few of them doctors – set us the best example.)

There is one particular difference between our two professions which may be worth mentioning. It was well described by the late Sir Roger Ormrod, both a doctor and a lawyer, in an address to the Royal College of Pathologists. He pointed out that at the end of the road legal decisions have to be 'binary' – a clear-cut 'yes or no' – whereas in many medical matters, this type of decision may be unattainable, or even if attainable, may be undesirable. This sharper focus in the 'set' of those who practise in the law is something to be recognised by members of both professions. Towards understanding one another, in our attitudes as much as in our formal codes, these chapters must contribute.

The topic of each one of these chapters is of interest to lawyers and doctors in common; but for doctors, and for the Medical Protection Society, the one which comes closest to our business and bosoms must be that on medical negligence: for the practising doctor, only rarely as yet, but when it happens, very intensely; for the Society, constantly. 'If something goes wrong in the course of an illness, someone must be to blame' – there we have a proposition which does no justice to the complexity either of illness or of the patient's constitution, and which fails to recognise that sadly there remain many clinical situations in which the die is cast from the onset of the episode. But if for 'must' we substitute 'may', we have a proposition to which, as professional men and women, doctors must assent. There remains the hard task of relating the general possibility to the particular situation; that is the particular duty of the Society, and it is one in which doctors and lawyers must share in mutual understanding, so that justice and equity prevail.

Preface

One hundred years ago, when the Medical Protection Society was founded, medical law was still in its infancy. Few patients thought of suing their doctors for negligence, although the courts had already been called upon to make pronouncements on the standard of care the law expects from doctors. In 1838, in *Lanphier v Phipos*, Chief Justice Tindal said (and his words are still true today): 'Every person who enters into a learned profession undertakes to bring to the exercise of it a reasonable degree of care and skill. He does not undertake, if he is an attorney, that at all events you shall gain your case, nor does a surgeon undertake that he will perform a cure; nor does he undertake to use the highest possible degree of skill.'

In 1892, patients' access to their own medical records was still a century away. Surrogacy, artificial insemination and *in vitro* fertilisation were still in the realms of science fiction. Doctors were expected not to bring their profession into disrepute, but the idea that they should be accountable for the standards of their services was a long way off.

Doctors must now keep up not only with advances in medicine, but the response of the law to those changes. Some fields – for example, reproductive medicine, patients' access to records, product liability – have seen profound changes in the last decade. A book of this size cannot encompass the whole field of medical law. But we have attempted to choose the main areas of relevance to doctors, to paint a picture of where the law stands as the Medical Protection Society reaches its centenary, and to point to some future developments. Although the book has been commissioned by the Society, however, the views expressed are those of the authors alone.

The English language's failure to provide a unisex pronoun has forced us to adopt the Interpretation Act 1978, section 6, so that, unless the contrary intention appears, words importing the masculine gender include the feminine and *vice versa*.

The law is stated as at 31 January 1992.

Clare Dyer
London 1992

Table of Cases

Table of Statutes and Statutory Instruments

Italic page numbers indicate where the text refers to a statute by note number only.

Chapter 1

Medical Negligence

The possibility of a claim for professional negligence by a dissatisfied patient or client is a risk which confronts all professional people. The opportunities for human error are manifold, though this knowledge does not necessarily enable the professional to face the prospect with equanimity. Negligence is a multi-faceted term. To some it suggests not merely the single lapse, the error to which all individuals are prone, but a general inability to perform one's professional skills and carry out one's responsibilities. In this sense an allegation of negligence is an attack on the defendant's professionalism, which may be deeply felt. This was the view taken by Lord Denning in *Hatcher v Black* [1] when he suggested that an action for negligence against a doctor was comparable to having a dagger plunged into his back, and in *Hucks v Cole* [2] where he said that a doctor should not be held negligent unless it could be said his conduct was deserving of censure or inexcusable. On the other hand, judges recognise that professionals are human and that, on that score alone, errors are inevitable. This can be seen in the commonplace assertion that not all mistakes should be regarded as negligence, but also in statements to the effect that in the real world everyone makes careless errors. In *Whitehouse v Jordan*,[3] for example, Lord Justice Donaldson commented:

'There are very few professional men who will assert that they have never fallen below the high standards rightly expected of them. That they have never been negligent. If they do, it is unlikely that they should be believed. And this is as true of lawyers as it is of medical men. If the judge's conclusion is right, what distinguishes Mr Jordan from his professional colleagues is not that on one isolated occasion his skill deserted him, but that damage resulted. Whether or not damage results from a negligent act is almost always a matter of chance and it ill becomes anyone to adopt an attitude of superiority.'

Some instances of negligence may be so glaring that they do warrant censure, but many acts of carelessness can be attributed to understandable human error, and some errors may be such that they do not amount to negligence. The courts have always taken into account the possibility of error. In 1838 Chief Justice Tindal said:

'Every person who enters into a learned profession undertakes to bring to the exercise of it a reasonable degree of care and skill. He does not undertake, if he is an attorney, that at all events you shall gain your case, nor does a surgeon undertake that he will perform a cure; nor does he undertake to use the highest possible degree of skill. There may be persons who have higher education and greater advantages than he has, but he undertakes to bring a fair, reasonable and competent degree of skill . . .'[4]

This statement of the law is as accurate today as it was 150 years ago. The medical practitioner has always been held accountable for a failure to exercise reasonable care in treating his patient, even in the absence of a contract with the patient. The surgeon, like the innkeeper or common carrier, exercised a 'common calling' which gave rise to a duty to exercise proper care and skill. Today the duty arises from the tort of negligence, but it does not depend upon the doctor's status, qualifications or expertise. Rather it is imposed by law when the doctor undertakes the task of providing advice, diagnosis or treatment. It is irrelevant who called the doctor to the patient or, in the case of private treatment, who pays his fee.[5]

In the case of private treatment a term will be implied into the contract that the treatment will be performed with reasonable care and skill. The standard of care required to satisfy this obligation is the same as in the tort of negligence, so for most practical purposes there is no difference between the position of a private patient who sues a doctor in contract and the NHS patient who sues in the tort of negligence. It is theoretically possible for a doctor to give a contractual warranty to achieve a particular result – for example, that a sterilisation operation will render a patient sterile. Such a warranty would amount to a guarantee that the procedure will be an unqualified success, but in the absence of a clear and unequivocal statement to this effect by the defendant the court will not infer a warranty, because medicine is an inexact science and it is unlikely that a responsible doctor would guarantee the outcome of any treatment.[6]

The meaning of negligence in law

The tort of negligence consists of a legal duty to exercise reasonable care, and breach of that duty by the defendant which causes damage to the plaintiff. In cases of medical negligence the existence of a duty owed to the patient is usually regarded as axiomatic, and attention normally focuses on whether there has been a breach of duty or whether the breach caused damage. Breach of duty is measured by reference to the conduct of a hypothetical 'reasonable man', sometimes referred to as the ordinary man, the average man, or the man on the Clapham omnibus. The reasonable man is clearly a fiction, but he is used as an objective measure of conduct, a standard by which the defendant's actions will be judged. In the case of professional liability the defendant will be judged not by the standards of the ordinary man but by those of his peers. The classic statement of the test for professional negligence is the direction to the jury of Mr Justice McNair in *Bolam v Friern Hospital Management Committee*.[7] Now widely known as the '*Bolam* test', it has been approved at the highest level on at least three occasions as the touchstone of liability for medical negligence.[8] Mr Justice McNair explained the law in these terms:

> 'But where you get a situation which involves the use of some special skill or competence, then the test whether there has been negligence or not is not the test of the man on the Clapham omnibus, because he has not got this special skill. The test is the standard of the ordinary skilled man exercising and professing to have that special skill. A man need not possess the highest expert skill at the risk of being found negligent . . . it is sufficient if he exercises the ordinary skill of an ordinary competent man exercising that particular art.'

Moreover, a doctor is not guilty of negligence if he has acted in accordance with a practice accepted as proper by a responsible body of professional opinion. The *Bolam* test recognises, however, that there may be more than one responsible practice. Accordingly, 'a doctor is not negligent, if he is acting in accordance with such a practice, merely because there is a body of opinion that takes a contrary view'. In the Scottish case of *Hunter v Hanley* [9] Lord President Clyde commented:

> 'In the realm of diagnosis and treatment there is ample scope for genuine difference of opinion and one man clearly is not negligent merely because his conclusion differs from that of other professional men, nor because he has displayed less skill or knowledge than others would have shown. The true test for establishing negligence in

diagnosis or treatment on the part of a doctor is whether he has been
proved to be guilty of such failure as no doctor of ordinary skill would
be guilty of if acting with ordinary care.'

This statement of the law has also been approved by the House of
Lords.[10] The medical practitioner is not an insurer, and so cannot be
blamed every time something goes wrong. Indeed, it is widely acknowledged that in medicine, in particular, things can go wrong in the
treatment of a patient even with the very best available care. This has long
been reflected in judicial statements of the law:

'A surgeon does not become an actual insurer; he is only bound to
display sufficient skill and knowledge of his profession. If from some
accident, or some variation in the frame of a particular individual, an
injury happens, it is not a fault in the medical man.'[11]

The practitioner is not judged by the standards of the most experienced,
most skilful, or most highly qualified member of the profession, but by
reference to the standards of the ordinarily competent practitioner in that
particular field. Nor is the doctor to be judged by the standards of the least
qualified or least experienced. It is not a defence that he acted in good faith
to the best of his ability if he has failed to reach the objective standard of
the ordinarily competent and careful doctor.

Degrees of risk

When assessing whether a defendant is in breach of a duty of care the
courts normally engage in a balancing exercise to determine whether a risk
which was foreseeable was justified in the circumstances. This involves
weighing the magnitude of the risk of damage to the plaintiff (which is a
combination of the likelihood that the harm will occur and its potential
severity if it should materialise) against the defendant's purpose or
objective and the practicability of taking precautions against the risk. In
cases of professional negligence, however, this judgment is largely
subsumed within the court's assessment of the expert evidence. If the court
is persuaded by the expert witnesses' views as to whether a particular
course of conduct was reasonable in the circumstances, it is unlikely to
make a separate determination of whether the risk was justified or
unreasonable. Cases of professional negligence, and particularly medical
negligence (unlike, say, cases involving road or work accidents) almost
invariably turn on the expert evidence.

Common practice

As a general rule, a person who acts in accordance with the general or commonly accepted practice of others in similar circumstances will not be held to have been negligent. So, for example, in *Vancouver General Hospital v McDaniel* [12] Lord Alness said that a defendant charged with negligence can 'clear his feet' if he shows that he has acted in accordance with general and approved practice. Following a common practice is only *evidence*, however; albeit strongly persuasive evidence, it is not conclusive. The court may find that the practice is itself negligent.[13] There may be many reasons, such as convenience, cost or habit, which have nothing to do with reasonable prudence against potential harm to others, why a particular practice is commonly followed.[14] The willingness of the courts to condemn a common practice as negligent has been most apparent in cases of employers' liability, but it is also evident in some cases of professional liability involving bankers, solicitors, and ships' masters.

An important feature of the *Bolam* test is the significance that is attached to compliance with common or accepted practice. A doctor is not guilty of negligence 'if he has acted in accordance with a practice accepted as proper by a responsible body of medical men skilled in that particular art'. There are many cases in which actions for medical negligence have been dismissed on the basis that the doctor conformed to an accepted practice of the profession. The *Bolam* test also leaves room for the possibility that there may be more than one 'responsible' practice. In *Maynard v West Midlands Regional Health Authority* [15] Lord Scarman expressed the position in these terms:

> 'It is not enough to show that there is a body of competent professional opinion which considers that [the defendants'] was a wrong decision, if there also exists a body of professional opinion, equally competent, which supports the decision as reasonable in the circumstances . . . Differences of opinion and practice exist, and will always exist, in the medical as in other professions. There is seldom any one answer exclusive of all others to problems of professional judgment. A court may prefer one body of opinion to the other: but that is no basis for a conclusion of negligence.'

Some judicial statements appear to suggest that in cases of alleged medical negligence compliance with a common practice is conclusive and will always exonerate the defendant.[16] The better view, however, is that the same rule applies to the medical profession as to all other professions: that even where no expert in the relevant field condemns the defendant's conduct it is still open to the court to conclude that no reasonably prudent doctor would have ignored an obvious risk.[17] In other words, the court may condemn even a universally followed practice as negligent. If this were not the position, it would give the impression that the profession was above the law. In a Canadian 'swab' case, *Anderson v Chasney*,[18] for example, Justice Coyne commented that if general practice were a conclusive defence 'a group of operators by adopting some practice could legislate themselves out of liability for negligence to the public by adopting or continuing what was an obviously negligent practice, even though a simple precaution, plainly capable of obviating danger which sometimes might result in death, was well known'.

Nonetheless, it is extremely rare for a commonly accepted practice to be condemned as negligence. Only where it can be said that the risk was, or should have been, obvious to the defendant, so that it would be folly to disregard it will the courts take this drastic step.[19] This may be easier for the court to contemplate where the conduct in question does not involve difficult or uncertain questions of medical treatment, or highly technical scientific issues, but is concerned with whether obvious and simple precautions could have been taken, such as counting the swabs used in a surgical operation or guarding against sparks in an operating theatre.[20]

Moreover, before any question of complying with accepted practice can arise the court must be satisfied on the evidence presented that there is a responsible body of professional opinion which supports the practice. It is always open to the court to reject expert evidence applying the ordinary principles of credibility that would be applied in any courtroom – for example, that the evidence is internally contradictory, or that the witness was acting as an advocate rather than an impartial and objective expert.

Departing from common practice

Just as compliance with accepted practice is good evidence that the defendant has acted with reasonable care, a departure from accepted practice may be evidence of negligence, but in neither case is the evidence conclusive. Thus, a slight departure from the standard textbook treatment is not necessarily negligent, since a doctor has to treat a particular patient, whereas the textbooks deal with a subject generally.[21] If deviation from a common professional practice were considered proof of negligence then no doctor could introduce a new technique or method of treatment without facing the risk of a negligence action if something went wrong. As Lord President Clyde commented in *Hunter v Hanley* this 'would be disastrous . . . for all inducement to progress in medical science would then be destroyed'.

Sometimes a departure from accepted practice may provide overwhelming evidence of a breach of duty, particularly where a practice is specifically designed as a precaution against a known risk and the defendant has no good reason for not following the normal procedure. If the risk materialises the defendant will have great difficulty in avoiding a finding of negligence, unless there is evidence which would justify the departure. Some instances of departure from accepted practice are quite clearly negligent even where they are performed consciously and routinely. For example, in *Chin Keow v Government of Malaysia* [22] a doctor was held negligent for giving a patient an injection of penicillin without making any enquiry about the patient's medical history. Had he done so he would have discovered that she was allergic to penicillin. The patient died as a result of an allergic reaction to the drug. The doctor was aware of the remote possibility of this risk but he carried on with his routine practice of not making any enquiry because he had had no mishaps before. All the medical evidence was to the effect that enquiries, which would have taken no more than five minutes, were necessary.

Keeping up to date

There is an obligation to keep up to date to take account of changes in professional practice. As Mr Justice McNair put it in *Bolam v Friern Hospital Management Committee* a doctor cannot 'obstinately and pig-headedly carry on with some old technique if it has been proved to be contrary to what is really substantially the whole of informed medical opinion'. Although this is clearly common sense, in practice it may be more difficult to state precisely when a new development will make adherence to old practices negligent. Mr Justice McNair was probably on safe ground when he illustrated the point by suggesting that a surgeon was not entitled to apply the surgical methods of the eighteenth century, by ignoring anaesthetics or antiseptics.

In *Crawford v Charing Cross Hospital* [23] the plaintiff developed brachial palsy in his arm following a blood transfusion, as a result of the position in which the arm was placed. The Court of Appeal held that the anaesthetist, who had failed to read an article published in *The Lancet* six months earlier warning about this risk, was not negligent. It was unreasonable to expect a doctor to read every article appearing in the medical press. A similar conclusion was reached in the Australian case of *Dwan v Farquhar* [24] in which it was held that there had been no negligence when a patient contracted AIDS from a blood transfusion, although an article identifying this risk had been published two months earlier. Even where an article warning of a risk and suggesting an alternative procedure has been read, it is not necessarily negligent to omit to implement the change immediately, though there might come a time when the new procedure was so well proved and widely accepted that it should be adopted.

Practices followed in other countries are not necessarily evidence of the appropriate standard in the UK. In *Whiteford v Hunter* [25] the defendant mistakenly diagnosed prostate cancer without performing a biopsy or using a cystoscope, procedures which were both standard practice in the United States. The instrument was rare in England at the time and the defendant did not have one. Moreover, the evidence indicated that it was against approved practice in England to use a cystoscope in cases like the plaintiff's where there was acute urinary retention. The House of Lords held that the defendant was not negligent.

Innovative treatment

There is an inevitable tension between the obligation to keep up to date, and the need to prove new ideas effective and safe before adopting them. Patients should not be subjected to untried methods of treatment unless the traditional approach has proved ineffective and the anticipated benefits are justified by the risks. On the other hand, despite the emphasis in many medical negligence actions on complying with common practice, the courts are careful to avoid the danger that findings of negligence may stifle innovation. In *Wilsher v Essex Area Health Authority*,[26] for example, Lord Justice Mustill said that where the doctor embarks on a form of treatment which is still comparatively untried, with techniques and safeguards which are still in the course of development, 'if the decision to embark on the treatment at all was justifiable and was taken with the informed consent of the patient, the court should . . . be particularly careful not to impute negligence simply because something has gone wrong'. Similarly, in *Sidaway v Bethlem Royal Hospital Governors* [27] Lord Diplock commented:

'Those members of the public who seek medical or surgical aid would be badly served by the adoption of any legal principle that would confine the doctor to some long-established, well-tried method of treatment only, although its past record of success might be small, if he wanted to be confident that he would not run the risk of being held liable in negligence simply because he tried some more modern treatment, and by some unavoidable mischance it failed to heal but did some harm to the patient. This would encourage "defensive medicine" with a vengeance.'

This statement recognises the public interest in allowing the medical profession to develop new and more effective methods of health care, without the fear of claims for negligence simply for trying something different from established practice. The legal issue remains whether the doctor acted reasonably in all the circumstances, which will depend to a large extent on the relative risk of the treatment in comparison to the alternative treatments and the nature of the illness for which it is prescribed. Where the patient's condition is very serious and the standard treatment is ineffective, a doctor will be justified in taking greater risks in an attempt to provide some effective treatment. A degree of care is expected which is commensurate with the risk involved. When undertaking an experimental procedure it is no defence to claim that the risks were unknown and so unforeseeable. There is an obligation to think things through and to assess the dimensions of the 'venture into the unknown'.[28]

Unforeseeable harm

The question of negligence is determined by the standards and knowledge of the profession at the time of the allegedly negligent act. It is not a matter of judging the defendant with the 20/20 vision of hindsight (the 'retrospectoscope'). This is illustrated by the famous case of *Roe v Minister of Health* [29], where anaesthetic which was kept in glass ampoules stored in disinfectant became contaminated by the disinfectant which had seeped through cracks in the glass. The cracks were invisible to the naked eye. The plaintiff suffered permanent paralysis as a result of being given the contaminated anaesthetic during an operation. This risk was not known at the time of the accident in 1947. The Court of Appeal held that there was no negligence because the danger was not reasonably foreseeable, and a reasonable man cannot take precautions against an unforeseeable risk. Lord Justice Denning commented that the court 'must not look at the 1947 accident with 1954 spectacles', although it would have been negligence to adopt the same practice in 1954 when the risk was more widely known.

Specialists

A specialist is expected to achieve the standard of a reasonably competent specialist in that field. This is inherent in the *Bolam* test itself. So, for example, in the field of neurosurgery it would be necessary to substitute for the phrase 'no doctor of ordinary skill' the phrase 'no neurosurgeon of ordinary skill'. References to 'a doctor' in the *Bolam* test are shorthand for 'a doctor undertaking this type of procedure'. Thus, although a general practitioner must be judged by the standards of other general practitioners and not specialists, if the general practitioner undertook a specialist task he would be judged by the standards of that specialty. Within a specialist field the standard of care is that of the ordinary competent specialist, not that of the most experienced or highly qualified, nor that of the least experienced. Even a 'novice specialist' must achieve the standard of the reasonably competent specialist.

Inexperience

The objective nature of the test for negligence means that inexperience is not a defence. The defendant's subjective reasons for failing to achieve the objective standard are irrelevant. A learner driver, for example, must come up to the standard of a reasonably competent and experienced driver. His 'incompetent best' is not good enough. This principle applies with as much force to an inexperienced doctor as it does to an inexperienced motorist. Thus, in *Jones v Manchester Corporation*,[30] in which a patient died from an excessive dose of anaesthetic administered by a doctor who had been qualified for five months, the Court of Appeal made it clear that it was no defence to an action by a patient to say that the doctor did not have sufficient experience to undertake the task, or to say that the surgeon in charge was also to blame. The patient was entitled to receive all the care and skill which a fully qualified and well-experienced anaesthetist would possess and use, and it was irrelevant that the hospital authorities knew that doctor did not have sufficient experience for the task and were also to blame for failing to provide proper supervision.

In *Wilsher v Essex Area Health Authority* a premature baby in a special care baby unit received excess oxygen due to an error in monitoring its supply of oxygen. An inexperienced junior doctor inserted the catheter by which the blood oxygen pressure was to be measured into a vein rather than an artery. This in itself was not negligent, since it was the sort of mistake that any reasonably competent doctor might have made in the circumstances. The doctor failed to spot that the catheter was mispositioned on an X-ray, though he did ask a senior registrar to check the X-ray. The registrar also failed to notice the mistake. The baby was subsequently discovered to be suffering from retrolental fibroplasia, possibly as a result of the exposure to excess oxygen (the medical evidence was conflicting on this issue). Sir Nicolas Browne-Wilkinson, the Vice-Chancellor, in a dissenting judgment, considered that it was unfair to hold a junior houseman in his first year after qualifying or someone who has just started in a specialist field in order to gain the necessary skill in that field to be at fault if, at the start of their time, they lack the very skills which they are seeking to acquire. The majority of the Court of Appeal, however, applied the objective standard because the effect of applying a subjective test would be that the standard of care that a patient would be entitled to expect would depend upon the level of experience of the particular doctor who, by chance, happened to treat him. Lord Justice Glidewell commented that if the law did not require the trainee or learner to be judged by the same standard as his more experienced colleagues 'inexperience would frequently be urged as a defence to an action for professional negligence'. Lord Justice Mustill created some confusion by adding that the standard of care should be related, not to the individual, but to the post which he occupies, distinguishing 'post' from 'rank' or 'status'. If applied, this would have the effect of introducing variable standards of care by reference to the 'posts' occupied by different doctors.

The objective test is the correct and long-established approach. A single standard of care for patients can only be achieved by relating the reasonableness of the defendant's conduct to the task that is undertaken, and what is objectively reasonable does not change with the experience of the defendant or, for that matter, the post he holds. This would be most obvious if a doctor in a specialist post were to undertake some procedure which was completely outside the sphere of that specialty. He would be required to achieve the standard of the reasonably competent doctor in performing that procedure, and if it were a specialised procedure he would have to achieve the standards of the specialty. This has nothing to do with his post or level of experience. Undertaking work which is beyond one's competence constitutes negligence.[31] As a matter of practice and common sense the inexperienced doctor will normally undertake less complex tasks than his experienced colleagues, and he can discharge his duty of care by seeking the assistance of more experienced colleagues to check his work, even though he may himself have made a mistake. It was on this basis that the junior doctor was found not to have been negligent in *Wilsher v Essex Area Health Authority*, although the registrar was held negligent. So a house surgeon who acts on the instructions of a consultant orthopaedic surgeon is not negligent,[32] and a dentist is entitled to rely on a doctor's opinion about a patient's response to antibiotics unless that opinion is clearly inconsistent with the observed facts.[33]

This principle is not limited to actions against newly qualified doctors. It can apply at any stage where a doctor gets in above his head. The specialist will be held to the standards of a reasonably competent specialist, 'even if he is a novice specialist'.[34] In *McKeachie v Alvarez*,[35] for example, a surgeon was held liable for severing a nerve which could have been seen and avoided, and of whose existence he should have been aware, even though this was the first occasion on which he had done this type of operation. A doctor must recognise his limitations and where necessary seek the advice or supervision of more experienced colleagues, or refer the patient to a specialist.[36]

The objective standard of care in negligence also applies to factors such as stress, overwork, tiredness or ill-health. A defendant who is unable to measure up to the objectively required standard for any reason will nonetheless be found negligent. In *Barnett v Chelsea and Kensington Hospital Management Committee*[37] it was held that a hospital casualty officer, who was himself unwell, had been negligent when he refused to see three nightwatchmen who presented themselves in the casualty department, telling them to go home and call in their own doctors, although the action failed because the evidence was that the plaintiff, who was suffering from arsenic poison, would have died anyway.

Whatever the position of the inexperienced doctor, it is likely that a health authority would be in breach of a primary duty of care to the patient if it allowed inexperienced staff to practise without adequate supervision. In *Jones v Manchester Corporation* a majority of the Court of Appeal held that the hospital board was liable to contribute to the damage for the death of a patient caused by an inexperienced doctor's negligence. Indeed, the board bore the brunt of the blame (80 per cent). This point was reiterated in *Wilsher v Essex Area Health Authority*, where the Vice-Chancellor, Sir Nicolas Browne-Wilkinson said that 'a health authority which so conducts its hospital that it fails to provide the doctors of sufficient skill and experience to give the treatment offered at the hospital may be directly liable in negligence to the patient'. The health authority would be directly liable if its organisation was at fault.

Arguably, this proposition applies with equal, if not greater, force to other organisational failures which expose patients to serious risk of injury, such as requiring junior hospital doctors to work excessive hours, with the result that they become so fatigued that their judgment or competence becomes impaired. While a claim that the doctor was overworked would not provide a defence for the doctor in an action by the patient, it is a good reason to place the burden of responsibility upon the health authority; indeed, it is possible that a health authority could be liable to the overworked doctor in its capacity as an employer, for breach of its duty of care for the employee's health and safety, if excessive hours and stress affected the doctor's health.[38] Since 1 January 1990 health authorities have assumed responsibility for new and existing claims of medical negligence against NHS hospital staff and no longer require their medical and dental staff to subscribe to a defence organisation.[39] This means that in practice the health authority will pay the compensation whether the injury was caused by its own fault or the doctor's. From the patient's point of view it is therefore irrelevant whether the doctor or the health authority is held to have been negligent, but from the individual doctor's perspective the issue may be extremely important.

Emergencies

The court will make due allowance where a doctor has acted in an emergency. The fact of the emergency will be taken into account as part of 'all the circumstances of the case' when determining what was reasonable care. A defendant who had to act on the spur of the moment will not be judged too critically simply because with hindsight a different course of action might have avoided the harm. In *Wilsher v Essex Area Health Authority* Lord Justice Mustill said:

'Full allowance must be made for the fact that certain aspects of treatment may have to be carried out in what one witness . . . called "battle conditions". An emergency may overburden the available resources, and, if an individual is forced by circumstances to do too many things at once, the fact that he does one of them incorrectly should not lightly be taken as negligence.'

If the error is one which a reasonably competent doctor could have made in the circumstances the defendant is not negligent. Conversely, if a reasonably competent doctor would not have made that error the defendant will be liable, even though it occurred during an emergency. Furthermore, where an emergency is foreseeable it may be negligence to have an inadequate system for dealing with the known risks that the emergency is likely to create,[40] in failing to have an essential piece of equipment readily available or in failing to have a system to check the safety of equipment.[41]

Errors in diagnosis

As with any type of error, an error of diagnosis is not necessarily negligent: this is measured by the standard of the *Bolam* test – whether the defendant acted as a reasonable doctor in all the circumstances, including the difficulty of making the diagnosis given the signs and symptoms, the diagnostic techniques available, and the dangers associated with alternative diagnoses. Errors in diagnosis can arise from various causes, including inadequate history-taking, errors in conducting an examination, failing to perform appropriate tests or refer the patient for specialist consultation, or failing to monitor treatment and revise the initial diagnosis if the condition is not responding to treatment. The doctor should not acquire 'tunnel vision' about a diagnosis.[42]

The need for adequate inquiry into the patient's medical history is graphically illustrated by *Chin Keow v Government of Malaysia* where the patient died from an allergic reaction to an injection of penicillin after the defendant failed to make any inquiry because he had not had any mishaps before. Taking a history includes *listening* to what the patient has to say. In the Australian case of *Giurelli v Gurgis* [43] an orthopaedic surgeon formed the view that the plaintiff was a 'difficult patient', with a propensity for histrionics and exaggeration. As a result he dismissed his complaints of serious pain and inability to put weight on his leg following an operation to repair a fractured tibia. He was held liable for the subsequent fracture when the plaintiff attempted to put weight on the leg, because he had failed to take into account the possibility that the fracture was not uniting satisfactorily and had dismissed the plaintiff's complaints without any proper investigation.

In some instances, although the practitioner cannot be faulted for failing to identify the specific illness or disease from which the patient is suffering, the condition is so serious that the doctor ought to appreciate that further tests are required or that the patient should be referred to a specialist who is capable of making an accurate diagnosis. In *Langley v Campbell* [44] for example, a general practitioner was not negligent in failing to diagnose malaria, but the patient's symptoms were such that he should have realised that it might be a tropical disease of some kind, given that he knew that the patient had just returned from Uganda and that he had suffered from malaria in the past. The defendant was held liable for the patient's death, since he should have been alerted to the possibility that the illness was not caused by an indigenous disease.

Communication errors

A lack of communication is often said to be at the heart of many medical negligence actions. This may refer to the breakdown in the doctor/patient relationship which can occur after a medical accident when health care professionals refuse to discuss the circumstances of the accident frankly with the patient. A patient who believes that something is being withheld may conclude that the only way to find out what happened is to resort to the courts, even where the doctors are completely blameless. However, failures of communication, whether between doctor and patient or between practitioners, may be the cause of the initial injury.

Patients will normally need some information about the nature of their medical condition and the form of treatment proposed in order to give a valid consent to treatment. Moreover, it is possible that a doctor has a duty to inform a patient what has been done when something goes wrong with the treatment;[45] although in practice it would be rare for breach of such an obligation to cause any additional harm to the patient. This could occur, however, if the patient takes a risk that he should otherwise have avoided, or if his ignorance leads to delay in diagnosis if an emergency should subsequently arise as a result of the damage of which he is unaware.

A doctor often requires the patient's co-operation in performing an examination or administering treatment. This may be as simple as requiring the patient to keep still,[46] giving instructions about taking medication, or giving a warning about any 'danger signs', with instructions as to what should be done if they occur. The duty is to give the patient instructions in comprehensible terms, making sure that he understands both the instructions and the importance of adhering to them. Thus, it can be negligence to give no warning about the dangerous side-effects of a drug nor any instruction to report the symptoms of such side-effects to a doctor immediately.[47] If the treatment has not been completed the patient should be advised to return for further treatment. The doctor has a responsibility to bring home to the patient the importance of obtaining further treatment and the dangers of failing to do so.[48]

The other area where communication may break down is between the health care professionals with responsibility for the patient. Such errors may be the product of isolated acts of carelessness or the result of an organisational failure, such as an inadequate system for summoning expert assistance,[49] or for communication between hospitals (or hospitals and general practitioners) about the treatment that the patient has received.[50] A doctor who fails to read the nursing notes will probably be held negligent,[51] and relying too much on casual exchanges about a patient, in hospital corridors for example, can create problems.[52]

Communication errors may be the result of simply mishearing or misreading an instruction, and the question may then arise as to whether there was any system for checking for such errors. In *Collins v Hertfordshire County Council* [53] a patient died after being injected with cocaine instead of procaine as a local anaesthetic. The word 'procaine' had been misheard as 'cocaine' by a junior doctor. The pharmacist dispensing the drug at the hospital pharmacy did not question the request for an 'unheard of dosage' of a dangerous drug, and the surgeon did not check before injecting the solution that he was injecting what he had ordered. Both the surgeon and the junior doctor were held liable, as was the hospital authority for having an unsafe system of dispensing. Similarly, a written prescription must be reasonably legible. In *Prendergast v Sam and Dee Ltd* [54] a general practitioner wrote a prescription for 'Amoxil' for the patient's chest infection. The pharmacist read the prescription as 'Daonil', a drug used to control diabetes. Both the general practitioner and the pharmacist were held to have been negligent. The doctor had a duty to write a prescription clearly. On its own the prescription could reasonably have been read incorrectly, although there were other factors which should have alerted the pharmacist to the possibility of an error. Liability was apportioned 25 per cent to the doctor and 75 per cent to the pharmacist.

'Wrongful life'

Before 1976, it was assumed that there was no legal liability for negligently injuring a fetus. For births occurring on or after 22 July 1976 this was rectified by the Congenital Disabilities (Civil Liability) Act 1976, though it has been subsequently held that a common law duty does indeed exist.[55] The Act applies only to children born alive, and, moreover, only where the injuries were inflicted by the defendant. If the child has congenital disabilities which, as a result of the defendant's negligence, were not detected during pregnancy so that the mother was not given the opportunity to have an abortion there can be no claim *by the child* against the defendant. The defendant has not caused the disabilities; rather, he has failed to detect them, and the child's action would amount to a claim that it should not have been born at all, because if informed about the disabilities its mother would have undergone an abortion. This type of claim is known as 'wrongful life' and is specifically excluded by the Act. The Court of Appeal has also held, in *McKay v Essex Area Health Authority*, that such an action should not be available in the common law tort of negligence.[56] A claim by the child over negligent genetic counselling would normally take the form of a wrongful life action, and so be excluded.

This does not mean that negligent genetic counselling or a negligent failure to detect fetal abnormalities is of no consequence, since the parents would have a claim where they can establish that with the correct information they would not have conceived the child, or the mother would have undergone an abortion (provided that she would have been entitled to one under the Abortion Act 1967[57]). In *McKay* the Court of Appeal accepted that the doctor owed a duty of care to advise the mother of her right to an abortion. A claim by parents in these circumstances may be characterised as an action for 'wrongful birth', although this term has been applied to a much wider range of circumstances such as failed abortion operations,[58] failed sterilisation operations,[59] and even actions involving the non-disclosure of the risk that a sterilisation operation may not succeed in achieving sterility.[60]

Proof of negligence

The burden of proving that the defendant was negligent rests with the plaintiff. It is not for the defendant to show that he was not negligent. The standard of proof required is the normal civil standard, 'on the balance of probabilities' – in other words, more likely than not – not the criminal standard of 'beyond reasonable doubt'. The standard of proof tends to conceal the fact that the cogency of the evidence that the courts require in order to satisfy the 'balance of probabilities' test can vary with the issues at stake. It is more difficult, for example, in civil proceedings to establish that a defendant has behaved fraudulently than to prove that he was negligent. It has been suggested that cases of professional negligence create particular problems for the courts and, in practice, this may result in what is effectively a higher standard of proof than for 'ordinary' cases of negligence. Thus, in *Dwyer v Roderick* [61] Lord Justice May said:

> 'Professional men . . . are entitled to no special preference before the law, to no rule requiring a higher standard of proof on the balance of probabilities than any other. But it is to shut one's eyes to the obvious if one denies that the burden of achieving something more than that mere balance of probabilities is greater when one is investigating the complicated and sophisticated actions of a qualified and experienced lawyer, doctor, accountant, builder or motor engineer than when one is enquiring into the momentary inattention of the driver of a motor car in a simple running-down action.'

In an appropriate case a plaintiff may be able to rely on an inference of negligence where the circumstances are such that the injury of which he complains does not normally happen in the absence of negligence. This may be referred to by the Latin tag *res ipsa loquitur* ('the thing speaks for itself'). This requires the defendant to provide some reasonable explanation of how the accident could have occurred without negligence by him.

In practice it is comparatively rare for the principle of *res ipsa loquitur* to apply in medical negligence cases, although in *Cassidy v Ministry of Health* [62] the plaintiff's claim succeeded where, having gone into hospital for the treatment of Dupuytren's contracture with two stiff fingers, he came out of hospital with four stiff fingers; and in *Saunders v Leeds Western Health Authority* [63] it was held that *res ipsa loquitur* applied where a healthy child suffered cardiac arrest lasting 30 to 40 minutes under general anaesthetic. *Res ipsa loquitur* has been held not to apply when a dentist left part of the root of a tooth behind during an extraction and broke the plaintiff's jaw;[64] nor when a dental drill broke and was left embedded in the jaw resulting in a fracture.[65] On the other hand, though it may not be negligent to break a patient's jaw during an extraction, a dentist who fails to notice that he has dislocated the patient's jaw, either at the time of the extraction or at a subsequent visit, may be liable.[66]

Causation

There must be a causal link between the defendant's breach of duty and the damage sustained by the plaintiff. In medical malpractice litigation this issue is largely a matter of medical and scientific evidence, for example, about the pathology of a particular disease and the prospects for successful treatment with proper care. The issue is normally dealt with by the 'but for' test. If damage to the plaintiff would not have occurred 'but for' the defendant's negligence then the negligence is *a* cause of the damage. It is not necessarily *the* cause, however, because there may well be other events which are causally relevant. Putting this another way, if the loss would have occurred in any event, the defendant's conduct is not a cause. Two cases illustrate this point. In *Barnett v Chelsea Hospital Management Committee* three nightwatchmen attended hospital, clearly appearing ill, and they informed a nurse that they had been vomiting. The casualty officer did not see the men, but they were advised to go home and see their own doctors. They left, and about five hours later one of the men died from arsenic poisoning. Mr Justice Nield held that the casualty officer was negligent in failing to have seen and examined the deceased. It could not be said, however, that but for the doctor's negligence the deceased would have lived, because the medical evidence indicated that even if the patient had received prompt treatment it would not have been possible to diagnose the condition and administer an antidote in time to save him. Thus, the negligence did not cause the death.

Similarly, in *Robinson v Post Office* [67] a doctor was found to have been negligent in the manner in which he administered a test dose to test for an allergic reaction to an anti-tetanus vaccination. The plaintiff subsequently suffered a serious allergic reaction to the vaccine, causing brain damage. It was held that the failure to administer a proper test did not cause the damage, because the test was not a complete guarantee against a subsequent reaction, and the circumstances of the plaintiff's reaction were such that even if the correct procedure had been employed it would probably not have produced a reaction in time to alert the doctor to the danger.

Where the defendant has made an error in diagnosis, but the correct diagnosis would not have produced any difference in the treatment or management of the patient, the error has not caused any damage for which the defendant is responsible, even if he was negligent. For example, in *Fish v Kapur* [68] a dentist who failed to diagnose a patient's broken jaw was held not liable because there was no treatment that could have been given in the circumstances, and so the plaintiff did not suffer any additional pain or discomfort as a result of the error.

The burden of proving that the defendant's negligence caused the plaintiff's injuries lies with the plaintiff. In some cases this can be an insuperable burden for the patient to discharge, simply because the state of scientific knowledge is such that it is impossible to say with any degree of conviction, let alone on the balance of probabilities, how the causal mechanism works. The Pearson Commission reported that:

> 'The Medical Research Council said that while future research was likely to establish more causal relationships it would also reveal increasingly complex interactions which would heighten the problems of proving causation in the individual case.'[69]

In *Loveday v Renton* [70] the plaintiff failed to show, on the balance of probabilities, that pertussis vaccine could cause brain damage in young children, although it was 'possible' that it did because the contrary could not be proved either. Medical and expert opinion was deeply divided on this issue. Similarly, in *Kay v Ayrshire and Arran Health Board* [71] the plaintiff was unable to prove that an overdose of penicillin could ever cause deafness. Even where it is possible in principle to establish a connection between the type of harm suffered by the plaintiff and a specific hazard, it may be very difficult to show that the individual plaintiff's condition was caused by exposure to that hazard rather than some other factor for which the defendant was not responsible. The plaintiff does not have to establish that the defendant's breach of duty was the main cause of the damage provided that it materially contributed to the damage.[72] That is, inevitably, a matter of drawing inferences from the known facts, but the courts have not been willing to assist plaintiffs in medical negligence actions to overcome evidential difficulties by drawing an inference of a causal connection where the plaintiff can only point to an increased risk of harm created by the defendant's negligence. If the defendant has merely added to the existing risk factors which could have caused the plaintiff's injury this is not evidence that in fact the defendant did cause the injury.[73]

A patient who had a less than even chance of a successful medical outcome may well face problems in proving that negligent treatment or an omission to provide suitable treatment caused his damage. On the balance of probabilities, proper treatment would not have prevented the ensuing damage which can be attributed to the initial injury or disease for which the patient sought treatment. In *Hotson v East Berkshire Area Health Authority* [74] the plaintiff suffered an accidental injury to his hip in a fall which created a 75 per cent risk that he would develop a permanent disability through avascular necrosis of the femoral epiphysis. Due to negligent diagnosis the hip was not treated for five days, and the delay made the disability inevitable. The plaintiff contended that the doctor's negligence had deprived him of a 25 per cent chance of making a good recovery, whereas the defendant argued that the plaintiff had failed to prove that the negligence caused the disability. The House of Lords accepted the defendant's argument that the high probability, put at 75 per cent, that even with correct diagnosis and treatment the plaintiff's disability would have occurred, amounted to a finding of fact that the fall was the sole cause of the disability. The plaintiff could not claim for 'loss of a chance' of a successful outcome in these circumstances.

The future

The problems with the present system of compensating patients for medical injury through the action for negligence are well-documented and widely acknowledged. It is slow and expensive, with only a limited range of plaintiffs having access to the courts – those poor enough to qualify for legal aid or those rich enough to be able to risk the costs of losing. The action for negligence can be capricious in its results, depending as it does on proof by the plaintiff of both negligence and causation, and the system of lump sum awards of damages, in which the amount of compensation is fixed once and for all without possibility of review, can produce both over-compensation and under-compensation. (The possibility of reaching a 'structured settlement' whereby damages can be paid in the form of an annuity does not necessarily remove this difficulty, since the 'structure' of the award is determined at the outset and is not reviewed if unforeseen contingencies arise.) These problems apply to all personal injuries actions, no matter how the plaintiff sustained the injury, although in practice the victims of medical injury generally have greater difficulty in establishing negligence and causation.

Dissatisfaction with the present system of compensating patients for medical injuries has led to calls for the introduction of a no-fault compensation scheme specifically for the victims of medical accidents. The British Medical Association now favours such a scheme, as does the Royal College of Physicians. A no-fault compensation scheme, under which claimants would receive compensation for their injuries without having to resort to law, and without having to prove negligence, would provide a quicker, more efficient method of compensation. There would be wider access to compensation, since the cost to the patient would be minimal in comparison to potential legal costs, and some patients who currently fail to prove negligence would succeed in obtaining some compensation. But 'no-fault' compensation should not be seen as a panacea. The first report of the BMA's No Fault Compensation Working Party, in 1987, rightly drew attention to the fact that patients with similar disabilities may receive different benefits under the tort system. A child may sustain brain damage following (a) encephalitis, (b) vaccine inoculation, or (c) traumatic birth delivery, but the available compensation will range from none at all for the first child, to £20,000 for the second child (under the Vaccine Damage (Payments) Act 1979, provided causation can be proved), to some hundreds of thousands of pounds for the third child if it can prove negligence and causation. A no-fault compensation scheme, however, would probably not change the outcome of this particular example. The child with encephalitis would not be compensated under any current no-fault scheme since illness or disease and congenital disability are excluded, and even the child with vaccine damage would probably not receive compensation under some no-fault schemes (if the damage is considered to be an inherent and unavoidable risk).

This illustrates an important issue with any no-fault compensation scheme which is not comprehensive in its eligibility rules. A scheme limited to medical accidents is by definition non-comprehensive, and the problem centres on just what is meant by a 'medical accident'. The New Zealand no-fault compensation scheme, for example, which applies to all cases of 'personal injury by accident', has experienced some difficulty in identifying what constitutes 'medical misadventure'. An unsatisfactory outcome which is within the normal range of medical or surgical failure does not amount to medical misadventure. This excludes many injuries which in the true sense of the word are 'accidental'. An adverse reaction to a drug may be a known side-effect, in which case it is an inherent risk of the treatment, and so not medical misadventure. The scheme also has considerable difficulty in dealing with omissions to treat, because the damage or death resulting from errors of diagnosis and the consequent non-treatment may be characterised as attributable to disease or infection, and thus outside the definition of 'personal injury by accident'. The Swedish Patient Insurance Scheme is probably more comprehensive than the New Zealand scheme, although it has a number of specific exclusions including: injury or disease resulting from necessary risk-taking when diagnosing or treating a life-threatening injury or disease or one which entails a risk of severe disability; injury or disease which has its origin in or is caused by a disease in the patient (unless due to misdiagnosis); unavoidable side-effects of a drug (which are covered by a separate insurance scheme funded by pharmaceutical companies); injury caused by infection, if the treatment creates an increased risk of infection or is in an area which is bacteriologically unclean; and 'minor' injuries.

While the Royal College of Physicians' report did not identify any eligibility criteria, the proposed BMA scheme excludes significant categories of accidental medical injury: (a) injuries which are a consequence of the progress of the disease under treatment; (b) diagnostic error which could have been avoided only by hindsight; (c) unavoidable complications, however carefully and competently the procedure was carried out; (d) infections which were difficult to avoid; and (e) complications of drug therapy carried out in accordance with the drug manufacturer's instructions. These restrictions would mean that, in practice, the scheme would apply only to 'avoidable' medical injury which could well be interpreted to mean avoidable with the exercise of reasonable care. In other words, a patient would be eligible for compensation where he could show that there had been carelessness in the treatment. As the Pearson Commission recognised, there is a danger that this would simply:

'. . . convert the negligence test into a statutory formula, thereby making it easier for the victims of negligence to obtain compensation, but doing nothing for those suffering medical injury from other causes.'

Any no-fault compensation scheme which is not comprehensive enough to cover disease and congenital disability must distinguish between eligible beneficiaries on the basis of how the claimant's injuries were caused. This is a major criticism of the present tort system, which selects its beneficiaries on the basis that the claimant's injuries were caused by someone else's fault. A no-fault scheme limited to medical accidents must inevitably distinguish between injuries which are *caused* by medical accident, and if it is limited to 'avoidable' medical accidents then, again, it will select its beneficiaries on the basis that the injury was caused by someone else's fault. This would be unfortunate in a scheme that is intended to remove the connection between compensation and proof of fault.

The levels of compensation for patients under a no-fault scheme would probably have to be lower than under the tort system. The Swedish scheme provides the same levels of compensation as tort damages, but payments are comparatively modest because social security benefits are high and the scheme is usually topping up the patient's pecuniary losses. The New Zealand scheme does not attempt to replicate tort damages, but concentrates on compensating economic losses subject to capping the loss of earnings element. Non-economic losses are compensated at a very low level in comparison to tort. The BMA No Fault Compensation Working Party Report, 1991 suggests compensation for loss of income up to a limit of twice the national average wage, though overall the report envisages awards of about 'half the size of those which a court would make in a successful action'.

In practical terms the present tort system favours defendants in medical negligence litigation. The Pearson Commission found that some payment is made in 30 per cent to 40 per cent of claims for medical negligence compared with 86 per cent of all personal injury claims. Figures from the King's Fund Institute suggest that only 25 per cent of plaintiffs in medical negligence cases succeed in obtaining some compensation,[75] and in the United States, where it is said that medical malpractice actions are at crisis level, it has been found that while 1 per cent of patients in the state of New York suffered injury as a result of negligence, over 90 per cent of these patients went uncompensated.[76] It is, perhaps, surprising then that the pressure for reform should be coming from organisations representing potential defendants. The evidence from the medical profession to the Pearson Commission in the 1970s was overwhelmingly in favour of retaining the tort action. It was argued that tort liability maintained the profession's sense of responsibility, and so enabled doctors to claim professional freedom. It was also argued that the traditions of the profession were not sufficient in themselves to prevent all lapses which, though small in number, might have disastrous effects. Some penalty helped to preserve the patient's opportunity to express disapproval and obtain redress.

The profession's changed perspective on the subject has almost certainly been conditioned by the substantial increase in medical malpractice litigation that has occurred since the Pearson Commission reported. Whatever one's views about the accuracy of claims that there is a malpractice 'crisis', with a corresponding growth of 'defensive medicine', this is clearly the backdrop against which the debate about no-fault compensation has so far been conducted. If the law, and lawyers, are seen to be bad for the practice of medicine and the health of patients, the solution must be to remove the source of the problem, or at least make it largely irrelevant, by introducing a no-fault compensation scheme. If compensation were the only issue raised by malpractice litigation, 'no-fault' represents a reasonable, if limited solution. A no-fault compensation scheme would almost certainly provide (lower) compensation for more patients, more quickly and more efficiently than the present tort system. But the tort action also creates a form of accountability. The worst cases of negligence never get to court, because they are settled, but accountability is not simply about a plaintiff's having his 'day in court'. Rather it is a mechanism or process whereby a professional person's conduct is subject to scrutiny under the independent authority of the law. The tort action is not ideally suited to this function, for all the reasons that make it a poor method of obtaining compensation, but other mechanisms of accountability currently available to patients are not much better. The Health Service Commissioner, for example, is specifically precluded from investigating complaints about the exercise of clinical judgment. The procedure for hospital complaints that involve the exercise of clinical judgment is generally limited to complaints which are 'substantial' but which are not likely to be the subject of legal action, and the investigation is conducted by two independent consultants. General practitioners may be disciplined by the family health services authority only where the subject of the complaint amounts to a breach of the doctor's terms of service, which may or may not cover a particular question of clinical judgment. A persistent criticism of the way in which the General Medical Council exercises its disciplinary powers is that it fails to deal with what by any standard is culpable conduct in the treatment of patients because it cannot be categorised as *serious* professional misconduct.

Andrew Morrison, a surgeon and council member of the Medical Defence Union, has suggested that by removing the deterrent effect of the potential action in tort the introduction of a no-fault compensation scheme would tend to lower rather than raise health care standards, and in New Zealand there has been concern about the lack of accountability of doctors in the absence of tort litigation. The Royal College of Physicians has recommended that a no-fault compensation scheme should be accompanied by a separate mechanism for the scrutiny of each claim in which doctors were involved to ensure that appropriate professional standards of care had been observed. If not, questions of professional discipline should be pursued.[77] This would be essential to avoid any impression that the medical profession was seeking to protect its own interests rather than those of patients.

Moreover, a combination of no-fault compensation and greater accountability should not change doctors' 'defensive' reactions to medical errors. The present tort system has no direct financial effect on a doctor, since damages are paid by the health authority or a defence organisation, and a negligent doctor is not penalised financially. Thus, the deterrent effect of tort must be linked to the consequences of litigation on professional reputation. Separating compensation from the proof of fault does not reduce the risk to a doctor's reputation if there is to be a genuine mechanism of accountability. A system of accountability, in which doctors who have been guilty of blameworthy conduct are held responsible for their actions, would presumably have a deterrent effect (indeed, if there were no deterrent effect this would bring into question the adequacy of the system). Doctors would still be inclined to practise 'defensively' in order to protect their reputation and avoid disciplinary proceedings. Nor can it be assumed that 'defensive' practice is necessarily bad practice. Greater caution may have the effect of reducing accidental injuries. It is widely acknowledged that, in the context of road safety, lowering speed limits reduces both the number and severity of accidents. Clearly, comparing the practice of medicine with driving a motor car is not an exact analogy, but the general point remains that greater caution reduces the potential for inflicting accidental harm. Deterrence is not necessarily a bad thing; the real issue is what is the optimum level of deterrence. The tort of negligence provides the bottom line: it sets the minimum standard of acceptable professional conduct for all professions. In practice, medical negligence is a failure to live up to proper medical standards, and those standards are set by the medical profession.

Ultimately, it is likely that there will be some change to the present system of compensating patients who suffer medical injury. In February 1991 there was an unsuccessful attempt to introduce a scheme of no-fault compensation through a private member's bill, the National Health Service (Compensation) Bill 1991.

Improving the injured patient's chances of obtaining compensation through the tort system is, in the long run, likely only to increase the pressure for reform, which appears to be driven by the increasing costs of compensating the victims of medical accidents. On the other hand, an adequate no-fault compensation scheme would almost certainly cost more overall than the current tort system.

Notes

1   (1954) The Times, 2 July. See also Lord Denning's comments in *Roe v Minister of Health* [1954] 2 QB 66, 86–7; *Whitehouse v Jordan* [1980] 1 All ER 650, 658; *Hyde v Tameside Area Health Authority* (1981) reported at (1986) 2 PN 26.
2   (1968) 112 SJ 483, 484.
3   [1980] 1 All ER 650, 666.
4   *Lanphier v Phipos* (1838) 8 C & P 475, 479. See also *Greaves & Co. (Contractors) Ltd v Baynham Meikle and Partners* [1975] 3 All ER 99 at 103–104, *per* Lord Denning MR.
5   *Gladwell v Steggal* (1839) 5 Bing (NC) 733; *Pippin v Sheppard* (1882) 11 Price 400.
6   *Thake v Maurice* [1986] 1 All ER 479; *Eyre v Measday* [1986] 1 All ER 488 (CA).
7   [1957] 2 All ER 118.
8   *Whitehouse v Jordan* [1981] 1 All ER 267; *Maynard v West Midlands Regional Health Authority* [1984] 1 WLR 634; *Sidaway v Bethlem Royal Hospital Governors* [1985] 1 All ER 643.
9   1955 SC 200, 204–5.
10 *Maynard v West Midlands Regional Health Authority* [1984] 1 WLR 634, 638; *Sidaway v Bethlem Royal Hospital Governors* [1985] 1 All ER 643, 660 *per* Lord Bridge.
11 *Hancke v Hooper* (1835) 7 C & P 81, 84, *per* Tindal CJ; *Mahon v Osborne* [1939] 2 KB 14, 31, *per* Scott LJ.
12 (1934) 152 LTR 56, 57–8. See also *Morton v William Dixon Ltd* 1909 SC 807, 809; *Morris v West Hartlepool Steam Navigation Co. Ltd* [1956] AC 552, 579.
13 See, e.g., *Lloyds Bank Ltd v E.B. Savory & Co.* [1933] AC 201; *Cavanagh v Ulster Weaving Co. Ltd* [1960] AC 145. In *Bank of Montreal v Dominion Gresham Guarantee and Casualty Co.* [1930] AC 659, 666 Lord Tomlin observed: 'Neglect of duty does not cease by repetition to be neglect of duty'.
14 See, e.g., the comments of King CJ in the Australian case of *F v R* (1982) 33 SASR 189, 194.
15 [1984] 1 WLR 634, 638.
16 *Marshall v Lindsey County Council* [1935] 1 KB 516, 540, *per* Maugham LJ. Lord Scarman, in particular, seems to have taken this view in *Maynard v West Midlands Regional Health Authority* [1984] 1 WLR 634 and *Sidaway v Bethlem Royal Hospital Governors* [1985] 1 All ER 643.
17 *Sidaway v Bethlem Royal Hospital Governors* [1985] 1 All ER 643, 662–663. See also Sir John Donaldson MR in *Sidaway v Bethlem Royal Hospital Governors* [1984] 1 All ER 1018, 1028; *Hucks v Cole* (1968) 112 SJ 483, 484, *per* Sachs LJ; *Clarke v Adams* (1950) 94 SJ 599, where the defendant physiotherapist was held to have been negligent even though he was using the very technique he had been taught to use; *O'Donovan v Cork County Council* [1967] IR 173, 193 *per* Walsh J; *Albrighton v Royal Prince Alfred Hospital* [1980] 2 NSWLR 542, 562–563 *per* Reynolds JA.
18 [1949] 4 DLR 71, 85 (Manitoba CA); affd [1950] 4 DLR 223 (SCC).
19 *Paris v Stepney Borough Council* [1951] AC 367, 382; *General Cleaning Contractors v Christmas* [1953] AC 180, 193; *Morris v West Hartlepool Steam Navigation Co. Ltd* [1956] AC 552, 579; see also *O'Donovan v Cork County Council* [1967] IR 173, 193 *per* Walsh J.

20 *Anderson v Chasney* [1949] 4 DLR 71, 86–87; affd [1950] 4 DLR 223 (SCC); *Crits v Sylvester* (1956) 1 DLR (2d) 502, 514; affd (1956) 5 DLR (2d) 601.

21 *Holland v The Devitt & Moore Nautical College* (1960) The Times, 4 March.

22 [1967] 1 WLR 813. See also *Landau v Werner* (1961) 105 SJ 257 and 1008 (CA) – a psychiatrist who engaged in social contact with a female patient who had developed a strong and obsessive emotional attachment to him was held negligent, because it was a departure from recognised standards of psychiatry.

23 (1953) The Times, 8 December.

24 [1988] Qd R 234.

25 [1950] WN 553.

26 [1986] 3 All ER 801, 812.

27 [1985] 1 All ER 643, 657.

28 *Independent Broadcasting Authority v EMI Electronics Ltd and BICC Construction Ltd* (1980) 14 BLR 1.

29 [1954] 2 QB 66.

30 [1952] 2 All ER 125.

31 *R v Bateman* (1925) 94 LJKB 791, 794.

32 *Junor v McNicol* (1959) The Times, 26 March.

33 *Tanswell v Nelson* (1959) The Times, 11 February.

34 *Poole v Morgan* [1987] 3 WWR 217, 254 Alberta QB.

35 (1970) 17 DLR (3d) 87 BCSC.

36 *Payne v St Helier Group Hospital Management Committee* (1952) The Times, 12 July.

37 [1968] 1 All ER 1068.

38 *Johnstone v Bloomsbury Health Authority* [1991] 2 All ER 293.

39 HC (89) 34, HC (FP) 22.

40 *Bull v Devon Area Health Authority* (1989) unreported, CA.

41 *Meyer v Gordon* (1981) 17 CCLT 1 (BCSC); *Denton v South West Thames Regional Health Authority* (1980) unreported QBD (not a case involving an emergency).

42 As is illustrated by the Canadian cases of *Layden v Cope* (1984) 28 CCLT 140 and *Bergen v Sturgeon General Hospital* (1984) 28 CCLT 155.

43 (1980) 24 SASR 264.

44 (1975) The Times, 6 November.

45 See the comments of Sir John Donaldson MR in *Lee v South West Thames Regional Health Authority* [1985] 2 All ER 385, 389 and *Naylor v Preston Area Health Authority* [1987] 2 All ER 353, 360.

46 *Stamos v Davies* (1986) 21 DLR (4th) 501.

47 *Crichton v Hastings* (1972) 29 DLR (3rd) 692; *Sheridan v Boots Co. Ltd* (1980) unreported, QBD.

48 *Coles v Reading and District Hospital Management Committee* (1963) 107 SJ 115.

49 *Bull v Devon Area Health Authority* (1989) unreported, CA.

50 *Coles v Reading and District Hospital Management Committee* (1963) 107 SJ 115.

51 *Holmes v Board of Trustees of the City of London* (1977) 81 DLR (3d), 67, 94.

52 A practice criticised as 'curbstone consultation' in the Canadian case of *Bergen v Sturgeon General Hospital* (1984) 28 CCLT 155, 175.

53 [1947] 1 KB 598.

54   [1989] 1 Med LR 36.
55   *B v Islington Health Authority* [1991] 1 All ER 825; *De Martell v Merton and Sutton Health Authority* [1991] 2 Med LR 209. These decisions apply only to births before 22 July 1976.
56   [1982] QB 1166.
57   *Rance v Mid-Downs Health Authority* [1991] 1 All ER 801.
58   *Scuriaga v Powell* (1979) 123 SJ 406, affd (1980) unreported, CA.
59   *Emeh v Kensington and Chelsea Area Health Authority* [1984] 3 All ER 1044.
60   *Gold v Haringey Health Authority* [1987] 2 All ER 888; *Thake v Maurice* [1986] 1 All ER 479; *Eyre v Measday* [1986] 1 All ER 488.
61   (1983) The Times, 12 November.
62   [1951] 2 KB 343.
63   (1984) 129 SJ 225.
64   *Fish v Kapur* [1948] 2 All ER 176.
65   *Fletcher v Bench* (1973) 4 BMJ 17 CA; *Keuper v McMullin* (1987) 30 DLR (4th) 408.
66   *Lock v Scantlebury* (1963) The Times, 25 July.
67   [1974] 2 All ER 737.
68   [1948] 2 All ER 176, 178.
69   Pearson (Chairman) *Royal Commission on Civil Liability and Compensation for Personal Injury* (1978) (Cmnd 7054) Vol I, para. 1364.
70   [1990] 1 Med LR 117. The Ontario High Court came to the same conclusion on pertussis vaccine in *Rothwell v Raes* (1988) 54 DLR (4th) 193.
71   [1987] 2 All ER 417.
72   *Bonnington Castings Ltd v Wardlaw* [1956] AC 613.
73   *Wilsher v Essex Area Health Authority* [1988] 1 All ER 871, HL.
74   [1987] 2 All ER 909.
75   C. Ham, J. Dingwall, P. Fenn and D. Harris *Medical Negligence: Compensation and Accountability* (1988) King's Fund Institute.
76   Report of the Harvard Medical Practice Study to the State of New York: *Patients, Doctors and Lawyers: Medical Injury, Malpractice Litigation and Patient Compensation in New York* (1990).
77   See the report of the BMA Working Party on No Fault Compensation (1991), which questions whether a system of no-fault compensation 'importantly diminishes the accountability of doctors'.

Chapter 2

Confidentiality and Medical Records

Doctors have a duty, long recognised by the law, not to disclose information about their patients learned in the course of their practice.[1] This includes not only information supplied by the patient but data from other sources, for example social services departments or other doctors treating the patient. The duty to keep such information secret is not absolute, however. Apart from cases where the doctor has the patient's express or implied consent, disclosure may be justified by a court order or statutory obligation or in the public interest. Good medical practice depends upon openness between doctor and patient. The Hippocratic oath, the International Code of Medical Ethics and the Declaration of Geneva all begin with the premise that secrecy is vital as between doctor and patient. It follows that any disclosure contrary to a private interest is also potentially damaging to the public interest, because it inhibits open disclosure to medical practitioners.

An example of this may be found in the case of *X v Y*.[2] Employees of an unnamed health authority divulged to a national newspaper the fact that two practising doctors were being treated for AIDS. In an action to restrain publication, the court accepted that there was a public interest in disclosure. The public interests claimed were the freedom of the press and the right of the public to informed debate about the problems of doctors with AIDS. However, the court held that these were substantially outweighed by the public interest in the confidentiality of AIDS-related information. If such information were to be released from hospital records, this might deter patients from attending hospital for investigation or treatment for fear of wide discovery of their condition. In the case of doctors with HIV infection, fear of disclosure might deter them from seeking counselling on ways of practising safely. In the words of Mr Justice Rose: 'In the long run, preservation of confidentiality is the only way of securing public health'.

In other contexts, the courts have weighed up conflicting public interests and come down against disclosure. The House of Lords upheld the National Society for the Prevention of Cruelty to Children's right not to reveal the name of an informant sought for the purpose of bringing a defamation action.[3] The law held that the wider public interest that people with information indicating possible child abuse should be able to volunteer it freely outweighed the right to information vital to pursuing what could be a legitimate legal action. In *AB v Scottish Blood Transfusion Service* [4] the court refused to order the service to disclose the identity of a blood donor to a patient claiming to have been infected with HIV from a blood transfusion and wishing to sue for negligence.

But the Court of Appeal approved a doctor's disclosure of confidential information in *W v Egdell* [5] which raised 'in an unusually stark form the question of the nature and quality of the duty of confidence owed to a patient'. A patient had been detained in a secure hospital without limit of time having killed five people and wounded two others. His application, 10 years later, to a mental health review tribunal for discharge or transfer to a less secure unit had received some support from the hospital authorities. Following opposition from the Home Secretary, W's solicitors approached Dr Egdell, a consultant psychiatrist, for a report in support of the application. He formed the opinion that W was suffering from a paranoid psychosis and pointed to the possibility that he might have a psychopathic deviant personality underlying the mental illness. In view of this, Dr Egdell strongly opposed the application and expressed concern at the possibility of a release or transfer.

This report was sent to W's solicitors, and Dr Egdell apparently assumed that it would be placed before a tribunal. Instead, the solicitors withdrew the application to the tribunal. When Dr Egdell discovered this, he sought the solicitors' agreement to forward a copy of the report to the hospital authorities. The solicitors, acting on W's instructions, refused. Nonetheless Dr Egdell forwarded a copy of the report to the medical director of the hospital, who in turn, at Dr Egdell's prompting, forwarded a copy to the Home Secretary. He referred W's case back to the tribunal, providing a copy of Dr Egdell's report. W issued a writ against Dr Egdell seeking an injunction restraining the use of the report in the tribunal proceedings and damages for breach of confidence.

In the High Court Mr Justice Scott refused the application and claim for damages, holding that the duty of confidence owed to the patient was subordinate to the public interest in ensuring that there was a proper assessment of W's mental condition. At one point in his judgment, he says: 'I readily admit that W had a strong private interest in barring disclosure of the Egdell report to the Home Office . . .'. Yet later, in a crucial passage, he states that 'the interest to be served by the duty of confidence . . . is the private interest of W and not any broader public interest. If I set the private interest of W in the balance against the public interest served by disclosure of the report . . . I find the weight of the public interest prevails'. An appeal by W was dismissed by the Court of Appeal. However, the court based its decision on competing public interests. A mental patient ought to be free to seek advice and assistance from an independent doctor and to speak without reservation. But the countervailing interest was the safety of the public. In view of the number and nature of the killings it was vital that those responsible for W's treatment were provided with the fullest relevant information concerning his condition.

Although the Egdell case is instructive, its value is limited by its particular and unusual facts. To begin with, W's past medical history clearly raised immediate concerns for public safety. The court accepted that to justify disclosure there must be 'a real risk' of danger. Clearly, this was easier to establish in view of the medical history in this case. Even so, it must be noted that all that could be pointed to was a possibility of danger, with which other medical assessments disagreed. More problematic cases can be envisaged where a psychiatrist forms a view that a patient without any history of violence is a genuine danger to the public. It would seem to follow from the 'real risk' formulation that disclosure could nonetheless be appropriate. However, it will be important, as the Court of Appeal noted, for the court to remain the final arbiter of the medical assessment. This is particularly so since medical opinion may not be unanimous.

Egdell illustrates that the law will pay serious regard to the ethical guidelines governing the conduct of doctors. Great weight was placed upon the General Medical Council's 'Blue Book' (*Professional Conduct and Discipline: Fitness to Practise*), notwithstanding its lack of formal legal status. The GMC's latest guidance on disclosure, to be incorporated in the 1992 edition of the Blue Book, states: 'Rarely, cases may arise in which disclosure in the public interest may be justified, for example a situation in which the failure to disclose appropriate information would expose the patient, or someone else, to a risk of death or serious harm'.[6] The judges made it clear, however, that disclosure must be limited to the proper authorities. They stated that Dr Egdell's disclosure of his findings to a Sunday newspaper would have amounted to a breach of the duty of confidence. There is a problem here, however, which bedevils the whole law of confidentiality. Once confidence is broken, it is impossible to restore the information to the precious status of a secret. This is well illustrated by a post-*Egdell* case, *R v Crozier*.[7] A psychiatrist whose report on a defendant who pleaded guilty to attempted murder was not disclosed at trial drew it to the attention of counsel for the Crown. Although compiled at the request of the defendant, the report was influential in the sentence of detention without limit of time under the Mental Health Act 1983.

Although the Court of Appeal accepted that 'at first blush' the doctor's conduct seemed 'entirely wrong', it found that he acted 'responsibly and reasonably' in approaching lawyers for the Crown. The court added that even if the doctor's disclosure was improper and in breach of confidence 'the judge could do no other than act upon it as he thought right in the public interest'. In such instances the confider is at risk of losing his liberty for an unlimited time. Yet medical opinions on his condition may vary – as indeed they did in *Egdell* and, initially, in *Crozier*.

A duty to disclose?

Clearly doctors can be justified in some circumstances in releasing information about patients without their consent. But can there be a duty to disclose a patient's confidential information to third parties?

There may be statutory duties to disclose, for example, information involving notifiable diseases or controlled drugs. Clearly there may be duties to disclose where this is necessary for patient care. This will generally encompass disclosures to other practitioners, although it may be necessary, on occasions, for the welfare of the patient to pass information over to a relative, or other carer. Note, however, that the ethical and juridical basis of such disclosure is the consent, if only implied, of the patient.

A more difficult problem, however, arises where the disclosure which the health professional would wish to make does not concern the patient's care, but takes the form of information which the doctor believes ought to be disclosed to an interested third party. If in the *Egdell* type of case, the persons at risk are not the public at large, but a small identifiable group of people, ought that to influence the outcome of that type of case? Should we, in this situation, blame the doctor for informing the relevant authorities? At least one commentator argues that there is no distinction between the real risk to the public at large, and a risk to a single identifiable person.[8] Suppose further that, rather than informing the relevant authorities, the doctor chose to inform the at-risk group themselves. Assume that there was no immediate emergency, but that the group were relatives of the mentally ill patient, and patients of the same doctor. Some would regard disclosure by the doctor as a justified breach of the duty of confidence. Might we go further than this and say that the doctor owes a duty to the persons at risk to disclose to them the fact of the danger which they unwittingly face?

Take the converse situation in which the patient is being exposed to danger at the hands of a third party, say by domestic violence. Where a patient fully capable of taking decisions decides to run a risk it seems the doctor must be powerless to disclose information without the patient's consent to those in a position to take preventive action. But where a doctor develops a strong suspicion of abuse following the examination of a child patient, he would be justified in reporting this to the local social services department. Suggestions that a statutory duty to report abuse should be placed upon doctors have been generally rejected on the basis that 'the fact that health service personnel do not have coercive powers plays an important part in the establishment of relationships which allows them to investigate cases at a low level of suspicion without antagonising clients'.[9] The latest guidance from the GMC, however, states:

'Deciding whether or not to disclose information is particularly difficult in cases where a patient cannot be judged capable of giving or withholding consent to disclosure. One such situation may arise where a doctor believes that a patient may be the victim of physical or sexual abuse. In such circumstances the patient's medical interests are paramount and may require the doctor to disclose information to an appropriate person or authority.'[10]

In the US, in the *Egdell* type of case, it has been suggested that a doctor may have a positive duty to warn a third party known to be a potential victim of a dangerous patient, to notify the police, or to take other action, depending on the circumstances.[11] Duties to warn of contagious diseases have been recognised also by courts in the US. Californian and Texan legislation permits disclosure to the spouse of an HIV positive patient. In New York this is extended to known sexual partners and needle-sharers even in the face of patient objection. In the UK, while the case law offers little or no guidance, it may be that the principles are obvious enough. The worst case for the doctor might be one in which a patient, A, is the known sexual partner of another patient, B, who is HIV positive. In this situation, it might be argued that the knowledge which the doctor has ought to be used to A's advantage to ensure that A does not contract a deadly infection. Here it might be argued that the wider benefits which arise from public health programmes based upon the confidentiality of AIDS-related information outweigh the benefit of informing individual patients of the danger which they face. In addition the private interest, indeed, right of the patient to impart information to a doctor in confidence should *prima facie* be respected.

Unless confidentiality between doctor and patient is asserted as an absolute value, we have to allow for exceptional disclosure. It may be necessary to allow that a doctor may become, against his wishes, party to information, for example, of a patient's intention, which is of such a nature that stronger moral reasons dictate the disclosure of the information rather than the preservation of a confidence. It is vital to understand what is at stake here. To begin with, a promise has been made which will be broken. Again it may be possible to suppose situations in which we should be prepared to release a promisor on moral grounds from a promise not to tell. But we might understand also if the promisor feels absolutely bound by the promise. Even more so when the promise was not a unilateral action but was an implicit part of some mutual agreement.

In the case of third party warnings we come close to allowing that a doctor may use the promise of confidentiality to secure otherwise inaccessible information, only to break the promise and violate the confidence once the information is obtained. Such a process is manifestly contrary to notions of fairness, not least because it was the assurance of fair dealing that secured the trust upon which the confider relied. If, in the face of all this, we should wish either to permit doctors to breach trust, or, more than that, order doctors to respect other loyalties which have been thrust upon them, then our reasons for so doing should be powerful indeed. In relation to AIDS-related disclosures, however, it is not easy to assess the weight of argument because issues surrounding the virus are not always debated rationally. Unlike the case of psychiatric disclosures, however, there is no reason to dispute the competence of the patient to consent to disclosure. Doctrines of consent must allow that patients may act against what doctors view as the patients' own best interests without being considered irrational. The law supports this view – if not always as forcefully as it might.[12] Equally, in view of the discrimination suffered by HIV positive patients, they can hardly be considered irrational if they insist on absolute secrecy concerning their health state. Thus they assert a strong private interest and it is against this that we must weigh any public interest in warning sexual partners and needle-sharers.

It follows that a doctor seeking disclosure to a third party should attempt to encourage the HIV positive patient to disclose or offer to make disclosure with that patient's consent. Problems arise only when faced with an adamant refusal. It seems that before disclosure can even be considered, the justifying risk would have to be one of death or serious injury to a known third party. In such a case, it is possible to argue that confidentiality may be overridden in order to eliminate the risk. This assumes that the third party will act upon the information and will reduce risk by, for example, not sharing a needle in the future.

Grubb and Pearl argue that the doctor has a right to disclose to known sexual partners and needle sharers if a patient refuses to consent.[13] In a statement on ethical problems associated with AIDS and HIV infection, issued in May 1988, the General Medical Council says: 'The council has reached the view that there are grounds for such disclosure only where there is a serious and identifiable risk to a specific individual who, if not so informed, would be exposed to infection'. Doctors must discuss with the patient the question of informing the spouse or sexual partner, but where consent is withheld, 'the doctor may consider it a duty to seek to ensure that any sexual partner is informed, in order to safeguard such persons from a possibly fatal infection'. The courts would be likely to regard such a disclosure as justified, provided it was strictly limited to those who might be at risk without the information.

Disclosure to medical practitioners

The spread of HIV infection has highlighted the issue of disclosure of information by one medical practitioner to another. It is usual to imply consent in cases where medical information is passed on to other practitioners responsible for the patient's care. But in the case of AIDS-related information, the patient may not agree, and cannot be assumed to agree, that information about the infection should be passed on. Consultants have been accused of being 'over-protective of confidentiality' when it comes to passing AIDS-related information on to general practitioners.[14] It is not clear, however, on what basis a general practitioner should have a right to know in the face of patient refusal. Refusal to pass on the information would not place the practitioner at risk in ordinary circumstances. It is true that restrictions on information may make it difficult to offer adequate treatment, but the patient must retain the right to decide this even at the risk of therapeutic disadvantage.

In the face of this disease, doctors have been willing to advocate departures from ordinarily accepted principles. For example, the Royal College of Surgeons has advised that members may test high risk patients for the HIV virus without consent. Such responses illustrate the fragile nature of ethical standards when faced with cases of HIV positive patients. It is therefore not inappropriate that the standard adopted is over-protective rather than under-protective of confidentiality.

The GMC advises that the specialist should point out to the patient that his GP cannot be expected to provide adequate care and management without full knowledge of his condition. However, where the patient insists on confidentiality, his wish should be respected. The only exception would be the rare case where failure to disclose would put a member of the health care team at serious risk.

The problems of third party disclosure arise not from the likelihood that physicians will seek to renege wholesale from the duties of confidentiality by which they have been traditionally bound. The danger is that pressures resulting from developments largely outside the control of the doctor force greater inroads into the confidentiality rule. These pressures are many and varied. They can arise from changing patterns of health care delivery, over which doctors assert increasingly less control. They may stem from the promotion of preventive medicine, or from action demanded in its name. Pressures may come too from the increasing commercial value of health-related information or from the interest shown in such information by providers of services or employment. The increasing complexity of medical procedures may generate significant problems of confidentiality, especially where such procedures involve donors.

PATIENTS' ACCESS TO MEDICAL RECORDS

Disclosure in legal proceedings

The Administration of Justice Act 1970 gave potential parties to High Court proceedings the right for the first time to seek court orders for disclosure of relevant documents before starting proceedings. This right of disclosure (which now exists under the Supreme Court Act 1981) is available against either a person likely to be a party to proceedings, or a third person who is not expected to be involved. Both powers are confined to actions involving personal injuries or fatal accidents, but both clearly cover records required in medical negligence cases. Prior to 1971 (when the 1970 Act came into force) it was impossible to compel production of medical records in advance of trial. The difficulties were obvious, as adjournments of trials to study medical evidence were common. Out of court settlements were clearly hindered. However, a solicitor, with the client's consent, might seek disclosure of the client's medical record by providing a guarantee not to proceed against the hospital, and by naming a medical expert to whom the records could be sent. In 1968, the Winn Committee on Personal Injury Litigation [15] suggested the formalisation of this process of pre-trial disclosure.

The Winn Committee had suggested that discovery of medical notes and records should be confined to a medical adviser. However, sections 31 and 32 of the 1970 Act spoke of disclosure 'to the applicant'. It was not long before this fundamental difference was the subject of litigation. In *Davidson v Lloyd Aircraft Services Limited* [16] Lord Denning offered a number of reasons why the statute should not be taken too literally and records and notes disclosed only to medical advisers. In his view, medical notes were difficult for a layman to interpret, and could contain information which would be distressing to the patient or embarrassing to relatives, and the possibility of diclosure to the patient could inhibit the doctor's keeping of full and frank records. The view taken in this case was later confirmed by the Court of Appeal in *Deistung v South Western Metropolitan Regional Hospital Board*,[17] and by the mid-1970s the law seemed well settled.

In 1978, however, in the case of *McIvor v Southern Health and Social Services Board* [18] the House of Lords found the wording of sections 31 and 32 too plain to confine disclosure to the medical adviser only. In a seemingly commendable judgment Lord Diplock said that such arguments against disclosure were not 'of general applicability or convincing'. However, on closer reading, much of Lord Diplock's argument seems to have assumed that disclosure would actually always be to the solicitor. On a number of occasions, he mentions the precautions that the legal adviser will take with the notes. Lord Diplock would also have allowed 'irrelevant parts of the document to be covered up', and stated that he would be prepared to offer court orders allowing the hospital to make the reports available in some manner other than straightforward disclosure to the solicitor or applicant. However, both Lord Edmund-Davies and Lord Scarman cast considerable doubt on the possibility of such procedures.

The Supreme Court Act 1981 is less favourable to the patient, allowing the court to limit disclosure to the patient's legal or medical adviser. But we have come a long way since *McIvor*, and it is now usual for pre-action discovery to be given without an application to the court. All that is generally necessary is that the defence solicitors are persuaded that a court order would be likely to be made. This is not to say that disclosure is never contentious. In *Davies v Eli Lilly & Co.*[19] the Court of Appeal allowed disclosure to a scientific co-ordinator. This case was part of the complex litigation surrounding the anti-arthritis drug Opren and the co-ordinator was a researcher, Charles Medawar, described by the then Sir John Donaldson, Master of the Rolls, as 'an unwelcome critic of the pharmaceutical industry'. The court was happy to accept that he would honour obligations of confidentiality and ensure that information was not misused.

Access to computer records

It was some years before there was any widening of access to records. When this came, it arose not out of a concern with medical records in particular, but from the Data Protection Act 1984, enacted to comply with an EC directive giving individuals a right to see information about them held on computer. The legislation gives 'data subjects' a right to see the records to ensure their accuracy. It applies to computerised records only, but as many medical practices and health authorities have computerised medical files, it does provide a potential route of access to information. However, under section 29(1) of the Act, the Secretary of State has power to exempt certain categories of data, including medical records. From the earliest stages of the Act, the Government made it known that this exemption would be used to restrict the disclosure of certain personal health data, and in 1987 this was done.[20] The exemption permits doctors to withhold data from medical records on the grounds that disclosure would be likely to:

(a)   cause serious harm to the patient's physical or mental health; or
(b)   lead the patient to identify another person, other than a health professional involved in his care, who has not consented to the disclosure of his identity.

Note that the first ground leaves it to the doctor's discretion to decide whether harm is likely to result and whether harm will be 'serious'.

Access to other reports and records

The 1984 Act provided the model, in part, for the Access to Personal Files Act 1987. This was a private member's bill, and the sponsor was persuaded, in return for Government support, to limit the scope of the bill to information held by local authority housing and social services departments. Thus medical records are exempt. Moreover, information held by a social services department which originates from health professionals is subject to special rules. The health professional must be consulted as to whether the information should be withheld on grounds similar to those under the Data Protection Act exemptions.

Support for the 1987 Act may have been influenced by the case of Graham Gaskin, who had been pursuing a case before the European Commission/Court of Human Rights since February 1983. Gaskin had spent most of his childhood in care and he passed through the hands of a number of foster parents. On leaving care, he formed the view that he had good grounds to sue the local authority's social services department in negligence for their handling of him while he was in their care. Unfortunately, however, his application for pre-action discovery of his personal file was rejected by the Court of Appeal, which upheld the High Court judgment that it was 'necessary for the proper functioning of the childcare service that the confidentiality of the relevant documents be preserved'.[21]

In view of Gaskin's failure to obtain a remedy before the English courts, he applied to the European Commission of Human Rights, alleging that the refusal of access to his case records constituted a breach of his right to respect for private and family life under article 8 of the European Convention on Human Rights, and of his rights to information under article 10. His claim under article 8 was upheld by the Commission, on a casting vote, although his claim under article 10 was decisively rejected. The European Court of Human Rights in turn found that there had been a violation of article 8.

It was clear that the traditional line of refusing patient access to health records in general terms would have had difficulty surviving in the aftermath of the European Court judgement in *Gaskin*. Although the decision was limited in scope, the case paved the way for wider access to records, notes and reports.

The Access to Medical Reports Act 1988, which came into force on 1 January 1989, covers all reports generated for insurance or employment purposes prepared by a medical practitioner responsible for the clinical care of the patient. It follows that not all reports are included within its scope, since it remains open for employers or insurance companies to delegate the preparation of the report to a doctor not responsible for a patient's clinical care (for example, a company doctor). The subject of the report would have no access to this.

The 1988 Act, like the 1987 Act, came about as a result of intense pressure from the freedom of information lobby, and the rights under the Act reflect their concerns with these reports. The Act gives rights to the individual to be notified of the application for a report and to consent to it. The individual has the right to see his report prior to its disclosure to the person commissioning it. If he disagrees with the report, he is entitled to ask for amendments to be made if he feels the report is inaccurate or misleading. Where the medical practitioner is not prepared to amend the report, it may be possible to attach a statement outlining the areas of disagreement.

There are exemptions which cover disclosure of information in the report which the doctor feels ought not to be revealed to the patient. These are similar to the exemptions under the Data Protection Act, considered above. A doctor who proposes to deny access to the whole report may not hand it over to the employer or insurance company without the patient's consent.

In the aftermath of a later statute widening access to medical records, the 1988 Act remains a vital piece of legislation. It would be unfortunate if patients could gain access to their own records, but still not know what was written to third parties about them. However, this still does happen in various other contexts. Medical reports are sought by many public authorities including vehicle licensing authorities, social security and housing departments. An inaccurate report in these contexts may have significant effects upon the individual's welfare, yet it may not be accessible under either the 1987 or 1988 Acts. An individual may eventually gain access to social security and housing reports under the 1987 Act, but this may be at too late a stage, and may not happen at all given the special rules for reports from health professionals.

The Access to Health Records Act 1990 completes the jigsaw by extending the right of access to records kept manually. The Act covers records containing information (including expressions of opinion) about the physical or mental health of an individual, kept by or on behalf of a health professional. The definition excludes records which have been anonymised – for example, for research purposes. Both NHS and private health records are covered.

Applications for access must be made in writing to the holder – the patient's GP or, for hospital records, the health authority or health board. For private practice records, applications go to the private practitioner concerned. There are three cases in which access to information may be denied. The first two are akin to the exemptions to disclosure under the Data Protection Act: that disclosure would be likely to cause serious harm to the physical or mental health of the patient or someone else, or to identify a third party. The third exclusion relates to health records made before the commencement of the Act on 1 November 1991. Here disclosure need not be made unless, in the opinion of the record holder, it is necessary to enable a later record to be understood. As with the Access to Medical Reports Act 1988, corrections can be made to the records if the holder agrees the information is inaccurate, or disagreements noted.

Where NHS hospital records are concerned, patients will be able to complain about non-compliance with the 1990 Act through the hospital complaints procedure. A similar right of appeal is planned for general practice records, but at the time of writing it had not been decided which body would deal with complaints. Patients who are still dissatisfied will be able to ask a court to order compliance.

Since the Data Protection Act 1984, the Access to Medical Reports Act

1988 and the Access to Health Records Act 1990 all give the record holder, as a matter of discretion, the right to exclude information, one might expect a number of challenges to such decisions under the Acts. However, since the applicant has no right to be told that information has been withheld, these rights of challenge may be extraordinarily difficult to pursue in practice.

Finally, it is worth considering the impact of the Access to Health Records Act. It lays down no guidelines for the medical practitioner on how records should be maintained or information disseminated. Nonetheless, one might imagine that doctors will take greater care in keeping records in the future, and this may enhance the treatment given to patients. Since the Act gives no specific remedies to patients who suffer as a result of inaccuracies, the remedy most likely to be pursued is an action in medical negligence, assuming some degree of damage or distress.

The impact of the legislation will not be immediate. Since it applies only to records kept after 1 November 1991, it will take some time before patients will gain meaningful information from these records, unless the holders of the records, in their discretion, give much wider access to records compiled before the commencement of the Act.

Access to the health records of a third party

The right of access in the 1990 Act is primarily to the patient. However, disclosures to third parties are possible within the framework of the Act. In the most obvious circumstance, the patient may authorise another person in writing to make an application. Where a patient has died, his personal representatives and others having a possible claim arising out of the patient's death may be able to gain access to the relevant health records. This is subject, however, to the release of this information by the holder, who may refuse if he believes that the patient gave the information or underwent the medical procedure in the expectation that the information would not be disclosed to the applicant. It may prove difficult for the holder to determine after the patient's death whether or not that patient would have allowed release and to whom. It follows that doctors may be advised to counsel their patients on such matters and solicit their views on eventual disclosure, where the circumstances make it obvious that there might be some sensitivity over disclosure.

There may be areas in which conflicts arise between duties of confidentiality towards a child patient and the exercise of parental rights. Children are entitled to access to their own medical records if, in the record holder's opinion, they are capable of understanding the nature of the application for access. Parents and others exercising parental responsibility will be able to see a child's records with the child's consent or, where the child is not capable of understanding the nature of the application, only if the holder believes that access would be in the child's best interests.

Parents will not be able to see information which, in the record holder's opinion, has been provided by the child in the expectation that it would be kept confidential from them. One commentator notes that 'a 15-year-old girl, having been prescribed contraceptives, could prevent her doctor from granting her parents access to her medical record even though the doctor considered access to be in the girl's best interests'.[22] This notion of 'best interests' creates unnecessary confusion, however. The question is more simply one of capacity. The case of *Gillick v West Norfolk and Wisbech Area Health Authority* [23] made the point strongly that parental authority had to yield before a child's right of decision-making at the point at which the child reached a sufficient understanding, and possessed sufficient intelligence, to be capable of making up his own mind. It would seem to follow that where the doctor formed the view that a young person possessed legal capacity to consent to contraceptive advice and treatment, that patient ought also to have sufficient understanding to control the disclosures of the relevant health records. In the face of a decision by such a patient, the doctor's own opinion as to what may or may not be in the best interest of that particular patient would be redundant.

Conclusion

Confidentiality in relation to medical practice gives rise to many and varied problems. The pressing problems for the future are likely to surround disclosure to third parties of patient-related information. With this in mind, the right of access for patients to information kept about them is particularly welcome. Access to individual records will increase patients' autonomy. Once patients are assured that records which are kept about them are accurate and uncontroversial, they should have less hesitation in allowing necessary disclosures. Thus many of the problems of third party information may be resolved by the ready consent of the patient to the disclosure of the medical record. At the very least, the resolution of the battle by patients for access to their own health records will allow us to focus, in the future, on the ethical dilemmas which surround third party disclosures.

Notes

1   *Hunter v Mann* [1974] QB 767.
2   [1988] 2 All ER 648.
3   *D v National Society for the Prevention of Cruelty to Children* [1978] AC 171.
4   1990 SCLR 263.
5   [1990] 1 All ER 835.
6   General Medical Council *Guidance for Doctors on Professional Confidence*, November 1991.
7   [1991] Crim LR 138.
8   M.A. Jones 'Medical Confidentiality and the Public Interest' (1990) 16 Professional Negligence 19.
9   J. Eekelaar and R. Dingwall *The Reform of Child Care Law* (1990) p. 66.
10 N.6, above.
11 *Tarasoff v Regents of University of California* (1976) 131 Cal. Rptr 14 and see also *Hedlund v Superior Court of Orange County* 34 Cal. 3d 695, 669 P. 2d 41, 194 Cal. Rptr 805 (1983).
12 See D.H.J. Hermann and R.D. Galiano 'AIDS, Therapeutic Confidentiality and Warning Third Parties' (1989) 48 Maryland LR 55.
13 A. Grubb and D.S. Pearl *Blood Testing, AIDS and DNA Profiling: Law and Policy* (1990).
14 N. Duncan 'GPs demand to be told results of AIDS tests' (1987) Pulse, 3 January, 1.
15 Winn (Chairman) Committee on Personal Injury Litigation (Cmnd 3691) (1968).
16 [1974] 3 All ER 1.
17 [1975] 1 All ER 573.
18 [1978] 2 All ER 625.
19 [1987] 1 WLR 428.
20 Data Protection (Subject Access Modification) (Health) Order 1987, SI 1987 No 1903.
21 *Gaskin v Liverpool City Council* [1980] 1 WLR 1549.
22 I. Cram 'Access to Health Records' (1990) 140 NLJ 1382.
23 [1985] 3 WLR 830.

Chapter 3

Consent to Treatment: The Capable Person

Why consent?

It is now so well accepted as hardly to merit consideration that doctors and dentists should ask their patients for consent before embarking on treatment. Commitment to gaining consent in any real sense was not, however, always so strong. It does not require a long memory to recall being instructed to roll up your sleeve and to find that you were having an injection or that your blood pressure was being taken. And still today, while lip-service may be paid to the idea of consent, the manner in which it is gained may vary greatly. One doctor may utter some generalised formula and then get on with things while the patient looks on inquiringly. Another may deliver a thoughtful explanation of what is going to be done and ask the patient whether he understands or would like to know more. Patients equally differ in the way they deal with their doctor. Some may present as nervous and anxious, some as self-possessed. Some may ask questions, some may not want to know, and some may simply want the whole affair over as soon as possible, preferably without having to think about it.

Against this background of varying realities, it is helpful, therefore, to begin any discussion of consent by asking what it is all about. Is it the great bulwark of 'patients' rights'? Is it a necessary nuisance granted as a concession to modish thinking? Is it simply a figment of some lawyer's (or – awful word – medical ethicist's) imagination which practitioners know is meaningless in practice? Is it just part of the rhetoric of 'patient power', sent to try doctors' patience and challenge their authority?

Perhaps the best way to understand what it is all about is to look at an example which has nothing to do with doctors or dentists. Imagine, if you will, that you were hungry and had decided to buy some food. Imagine that the shopkeeper at whose window your nose was pressed took you by the arm and smartly introduced a doughnut into your mouth. To your protest (once you had removed the doughnut) that he take his hands off you, the shopkeeper replied that he could see that you needed some food. Acting in your interests he had simply made sure that you were fed straightaway. That you may have gone to another shop, or that you did not like doughnuts was neither here nor there. You had been fed, hadn't you? What was there to complain of? You would begin, I suppose, by complaining that you were quite able to make your own decisions. You would go on to say that you found it unconscionable to be made to do something against your will. The shopkeeper should wait to be asked and should find out what you wanted.

It can be objected immediately that this is a somewhat far-fetched example. What does it have to do with the practice of medicine? It teaches us first of all that when we discuss abstract questions such as consent, we often use the technique of argument by analogy. We try to find situations with some similarity to the one under discussion and ask, what would you do? If you say you would do so and so, we then ask whether that offers any guidance as regards the situation we are interested in. In our example, your principal complaint would be that something was done without your permission. From that we deduce that you take your permission seriously, at least in the context of eating, however hungry you may be. Then we can ask whether what is true as regards eating is true in other contexts. The answer would be that it is. Your permission is critical in virtually all your dealings with others. Exceptions seem to exist only (assuming, as we do in this chapter, that you are capable of giving permission) when you have done something wrong, such that others are entitled to lay hands on you and, perhaps, detain you. Why is this so? Is it not because of the value we place on freedom, the freedom to act, to choose what we want, to go where we please, provided we do not interfere with others? Freedom, then, is the key. Permission, or consent, is the means whereby we assert our freedom. And if freedom is as important to us as we claim, it follows that consent, its guardian, is equally important.

Does this teach us anything about the relationship between doctor and patient? Unless you can argue in some way that freedom in the various forms we know it has no place in the relationship, we are driven to the conclusion that consent is not just important, but critically important. It is the crucial means whereby the patient can assert his freedom to choose and to act as he wishes. That is what consent is all about.

Of course, nothing in life is quite so simple. Freedom is all very well but it only has any real meaning when someone is capable of making choices and being free. The context in which people consult their doctors is often one of anxiety, illness or depression in which this capacity is somewhat impaired. We must be careful, therefore, that we do not embrace an over-abstract concern for consent. It would be the worst of all worlds if we compelled patients to suffer because of some misguided commitment to protecting their freedom. We must recognise that while consent is crucial, so is an awareness of its limits and limitations. Consent, in short, is a subtle and complex concept. Having established its significance, let us examine it in detail.

Why law?

Consent is, of course, primarily an ethical precept. Depending on the theory of ethics you find most convincing, it is the doctor's duty to obtain it or the patient's right to give it, or it is for the common good that it be obtained. But it also finds expression in the law. Some find this unfortunate. They would much rather that the law did not intrude (their word) into medicine. Law, it is argued, is heavy-handed and unable to respond sensitively to the subtleties of the human relationship between doctor and patient. Law is confrontational, they urge, dealing in certainties of right and wrong, while medicine is full of complexities which do not allow for certainty. Law is rigid, they continue, lacking the flexibility necessary for the dynamic nature of human relationships.

The difficulty with this approach is that what is said about medicine could just as well be said about any other profession. More importantly, the argument looks occasionally like special pleading. Doctors seem to be arguing that they, or their practice, should be outside or above the law, that simply by virtue of the fact that theirs is a caring and helping profession, the law should not turn its attention to what they do. A moment's reflection will make it clear that this is an impossible position. Medicine allows doctors privileges not granted to others. They can touch, cut, undress, give drugs and do a host of things not open to others. Such privileges carry responsibilities. Means must exist to hold doctors to account to ensure that these responsibilities are not ignored. Trust, although it exists in large quantity, is not enough. The seriousness which society attaches to the preservation of life and the avoidance of physical harm shows itself in its recourse to law. The law is the most solemn and significant means by which society holds its citizens to account. And the nature of medical care and treatment makes it inevitable that doctors must be subject to the law in the practice of medicine. The law may not be the first or most important mechanism controlling and regulating what they do. For the most part their training and their ethics are enough. But the law is always there as society's backstop. It shows the limits of the permissible to doctors. It reassures patients that there are objective and known standards against which to measure the conduct of the doctor.

The law, consent and the capable person

With this lengthy introduction behind us, let us examine what the law has to say about consent and the capable person. It may be helpful to do so in stages.

What is consent concerned with?

As we have seen, the law's insistence on the need for consent is so as to preserve and protect our freedom. But which particular freedom is being protected? In the context of medical care it is the freedom from bodily intrusion. The law's concern is with each person's bodily integrity. This is what is preserved and protected by the law of consent. Thus, the merest touching by one person of another is unlawful if done without consent (there are exceptions to this, such as treatment of the unconscious – see chapter 4 – but none applies as regards the capable person). And for the sake of completeness it must be noted that such a touching is unlawful not only if done without consent but also *ex hypothesi* if it is done in the face of refusal of consent. Consent and refusal are two sides of the same coin. Cardozo, the great American jurist, summed up the position in what has become a classic statement of civil liberties:

> 'Every human being of adult years and sound mind has a right to determine what shall be done with his own body; and a surgeon who performs an operation without his patient's consent commits an assault [sc. battery] for which he is liable in damages.'[1]

Thus, any medical treatment which requires that the doctor lay hands on or touch his patient, and this means all medical treatment other than counselling since a doctor will ordinarily examine his patient prior to treatment, may lawfully be done only with consent.

Treatment without consent

A doctor who treats a patient who is capable of giving consent without such consent (or in the face of a refusal) is liable in law. The patient may bring an action in battery. This action lies whenever one person touches another in a harmful or offensive manner without consent and without lawful justification. The patient does not need to prove that he was harmed by the touching. The tort of battery is as much concerned to preserve and protect the *principle* of bodily integrity as it is to protect from harm. It is, therefore, enough to show in the case of the capable person that the touching was without consent for it to be reckoned harmful or offensive. In the case of *Wilson v Pringle* Lord Justice Croom-Johnson held that 'harmful and offensive' meant that the touching had to be 'hostile'.[2] This view, however, which arguably would take medical touchings outside the scope of battery since they are not hostile touchings, was rejected subsequently by Mr Justice Wood in *T v T*. He stated:

> 'The incision made by the surgeon's scalpel need not be and probably is most unlikely to be hostile, but unless a defence or justification is established, it must in my judgment fall within the definition of a trespass to the person [battery].'[3]

This approach was affirmed by the House of Lords in *In Re F (Mental patient: Sterilisation)*.[4] To this extent battery serves a significant symbolic purpose, signalling the law's concern for freedom from all forms of bodily restraint or invasion. Furthermore, since battery is an intentional tort, any damages a court may award to a successful patient may include a punitive or exemplary element whereby the court can signal its disapproval. As we shall see later, the courts are reluctant to find a doctor liable in battery. The reasons are obvious. Doctors rarely act with other than the best of intentions. Theirs is a caring profession. To find a doctor liable in battery is, therefore, a very serious step. Although technically it does not mean that the doctor intended to harm the patient, it may appear to do so. A court would be reluctant to reach such a view. But, that said, if the treatment clearly is without consent, then a battery is committed.

We may notice in passing that in the same circumstances a doctor may technically also be guilty of a crime, at least the crime of battery, since the scope of the tort and crime would seem to be the same. A court is, however, unlikely to find a doctor guilty of a crime if he was acting in good faith.

As an alternative to an action in battery, a patient may have an action in negligence if touched without consent. Here the allegation, however, is different. It is not that the doctor ignored the patient's refusal or simply went ahead without consent. Instead, it is that the *quality* of the consent obtained was not good enough, that the patient, if he had really known what was being proposed would not in fact have consented. Since this is at the core of the vexed issue of 'informed consent', I will defer consideration of it until later.

Form

The doctor must obtain the patient's consent. That much has been demonstrated. But what form can this consent take? In law, there are two forms:

(i) Express

This simply means that consent is valid if it is expressly – explicitly – given. When a patient is admitted to hospital for surgery, he gives his express consent by signing a consent form authorising the surgery. The form indicates the basis on which the surgery will be carried out and when he signs it the patient will be assumed to have read and consented to what it says.

The existence of written consent forms has exercised some sort of mesmerising influence on doctors and dentists. They have come to believe that consent is valid only if it is written down, preferably in some consent form. This is a triumph of myth over reality, for at least two reasons. First, the law does not require consent to be in a written form. The only purpose of writing it down is so as to have a record subsequently. Express consent may just as validly be given orally or even by a nod of the head in response to a question. Writing is *evidence* of what was agreed. But notice a secondary myth: that all you need for valid consent is to get something in writing. This is equally wrong. A written 'consent' form will be legally valueless if in fact there was no agreement by the patient. Mr Justice Bristow put the point forcibly in *Chatterton v Gerson*:

'I should add that getting the patient to sign a *pro forma* expressing consent to undergo the operation "the effect and nature of which have been explained to me" . . . should be a valuable reminder to everyone of the need for explanation and consent. But it would be no defence to an action based on trespass to the person if no explanation had in fact been given. The consent would have been expressed in form only, not in reality.'[5]

The second reason for exposing the myth of written consent is so obvious that it goes entirely unnoticed. Even surgeons, while relying with elaborate ceremony on written forms before carrying out their operations, think nothing of examining their patients as outpatients or in hospital on the basis only of the oral permission of the patient. There is nothing in writing. But, nonetheless, if the consent given by the patient is genuine and real, it is entirely valid, regardless of the absence of writing.

(ii) Implied

This means that even though a patient has not expressly (or explicitly) given consent, it may in appropriate circumstances be implied. What are those circumstances? It would be wrong to think that there is some definitive list. Instead, the law takes the view that wherever a reasonable person could infer from a patient's conduct that he agreed to or acquiesced in some form of intervention or touching, this constitutes implied consent. As Fleming puts it: 'Actions often speak louder than words. Holding up one's bare arm to a doctor at a vaccination point is as clear an assent as if it were expressed in words'.[6] He refers here to the famous case of *O'Brien v Cunard SS Co.*[7] in which a woman did precisely that. The court decided that she could not later complain that she had been vaccinated against her will since her conduct implied her consent.

Implied consent should not be too widely construed. It is not a *carte blanche* for doctors or dentists to do whatever they wish on the grounds that they interpreted the patients' silence or acquiescence as consent. It will depend on the circumstances and an objective assessment of what a reasonable person would infer from the patient's behaviour. Take, for instance, the argument of some doctors that because a patient is admitted to a teaching hospital, he can be assumed to consent (his consent can be implied) to being used as a means of teaching students. No such inference can fairly be made. Leaving aside the fact that patients rarely have a choice as to the hospital they find themselves in and that some do not know what a teaching hospital is, it by no means follows that because someone is a patient in such a hospital he agrees to being used for teaching. In such a circumstance explicit consent would be necessary.

The notion of implied consent has taken on great contemporary significance in the context of testing for HIV. The view is advanced that people have their blood tested for a whole host of factors without explicit consent to each test. From that argument it is advanced that, therefore, consent to test blood for HIV can equally be implied. In response it can be said that quite apart from the lawfulness of carrying out other tests without explicit consent, to test for HIV is so significantly different that it may only be carried out with explicit consent. This is the position of the General Medical Council and the British Medical Association as regards medical ethics, and in my view properly reflects the law. The reason is obvious. Testing for HIV carries enormous personal and social consequences. A positive result means that a patient thereafter must live with the real prospect of succumbing to a fatal illness for which there is no treatment. The mere fact of testing, *whatever the result*, may thereafter affect the patient's ability to secure insurance and, as a consequence, a mortgage. And, again, if the test is positive, the patient may be the victim of a whole range of discriminatory practices. In such circumstances, it is clear that consent can never be implied. Testing for HIV can be performed only with explicit consent, save in the most exceptional circumstances – for example, a real, immediate and demonstrable risk of harm to another that cannot otherwise be avoided.

Exceeding consent

Consent will justify only that form of intervention or touching for which it is specifically given. Thus, ordinarily, a doctor will be liable in law if he chooses to go beyond that which expressly or by implication was consented to. Fleming puts it as follows:

> 'Consent is no defence, unless it is given to the precise conduct in question, or at least to acts of a substantially similar nature . . . [A] surgeon, charged with a particular operation is [not] justified to depart from instructions and perform a different one; the only occasion which would justify his proceeding without prior authority is "when it is necessary to save the life or preserve the health of the patient" (*Marshall v Curry* [1933] 3 DLR 260). In other words, here the balance between preservation of life and self-determination is found in authorising medical procedure only when it would be unreasonable, not just inconvenient, to postpone until consent could be sought.'[8]

We have to be a little careful with the exception mentioned by Fleming. The principle of necessity, or of acting in the public interest, recognises that the law must provide for some circumstance where it is justified to proceed without consent. But notice that we are concerned here with *exceeding* consent. What Fleming identifies is that there is a legal justification for proceeding in an emergency *without prior approval*. This is in essence an example of implied consent (based, some would say, on the 'thank you theory' of medical ethics: that the patient, once recovered, will thank the doctor for taking action). Fleming is not, however, suggesting that the law in any way offers a justification for proceeding *contrary to prior instructions* – in the face, that is, of a prior refusal. A doctor who did so would be exceeding consent and would as a consequence be liable in battery. This is so even if the intervention which had been refused was judged necessary to save the life of the patient.

In the Canadian case of *Mulloy v Hop Sang*,[9] for example, a doctor was instructed by his patient who had been injured in a car accident not to amputate his hand under any circumstances. The patient wanted to get home to see his own specialist. Once the patient was anaesthetised, the doctor was able to examine the hand which the patient had kept wrapped up. He formed the view that amputation was necessary. The amputation was performed. The court, when the patient sued in battery, held that the doctor's conduct was not justified in the face of the patient's prior instructions. And there are other cases such as *R v Blaue* [10] and *Malette v Shulman* [11] which confirm this view.

Content

We have seen the need for consent, the form it may take and its extent. Now, we have to identify its content or substance. In essence a consent is legally valid only if certain conditions are satisfied. This means that in any particular case a doctor or dentist must satisfy himself that any consent obtained from his patient meets these conditions. At their most general, they are:

(i)   the patient must be legally competent (i.e. capable of consenting);
(ii)   the consent must be freely given;
(iii) the person consenting must be suitably informed.

Of course, in saying that a doctor must be satisfied that these conditions are met, the law does not leave him entirely without guidance. There now exists a relatively detailed exegesis of each of them. Of course, this is good and bad news. If legal analysis exists, the doctor must be aware of it so as to ensure that he does not stray beyond the four corners of what the law allows. In making himself aware, the doctor will become aware of the central dilemma of law, familiar to all lawyers but all too often disconcerting to others. Where, as here, there is no statute to help us, the law emerges from a series of disparate cases. From these, we seek to develop or distil a body of principles. These principles are necessarily general. And, because they are expressed in words, they are inevitably open to interpretation. It is often a tall order to state exactly what they mean – in other words, what *precisely* the doctor has to do. Indeed the pursuit of certainty may be an illusion.

Every doctor is familiar with the lawyer who says 'it all depends'. This may be fine for the lawyer (and, of course, it is true). It is less reassuring to the doctor who just wants to know what he can and cannot do. After all, it will be the doctor who is sued and not the lawyer. There is, however, another side to the coin. While uncertainty may bring doubt, general principles permit, indeed invite, the exercise of discretion. And if the ability to exercise discretion (or judgment) is central to being a professional, then the more the law is expressed in general rather than specific terms, the more room it leaves for discretion and thereby serves to validate the professional in his own and his patient's eyes. Certainly, as we shall see, the judges seem entirely happy to go along with this to protect their 'brother' professionals from any over-detailed regulation. They are more than happy to state the law in terms which leave its application in particular cases to the judgment of the doctor. With these thoughts in mind, let us now examine the content of consent in detail.

(i) The patient must be legally competent

This chapter is concerned with consent to treatment and the capable patient. It should come as no surprise, therefore that we need to examine what the law has to say about capacity. What test does the law lay down to determine whether a particular patient's decision, whether consent or refusal, must be respected or can, indeed should, be disregarded? (I pause to draw your attention to the latter, thought it may be obvious. If a patient is legally incompetent, then his consent (or refusal) is the product of incompetence. He cannot by definition know his own mind so as to decide what is in his interests. Consequently, any expression of view has no force in law and may not be relied on by a doctor as justifying any action taken (see chapter 4)).

What is the meaning of competence (capacity)? Remarkably, given the central importance of consent in medical law and given that capacity is the key to consent, it was not until the mid-80s that the meaning of capacity in the context of consent to treatment came before the courts. The case, *Gillick v West Norfolk and Wisbech Area Health Authority* [12] was a *cause célèbre*. It had all the right ingredients to attract attention, including a campaigning, media-conscious plaintiff, Victoria Gillick, contraception, girls below the age of 16, and an ideological dispute about the proper relation between a parent and child. Interesting as these all are, what concerns us is what their Lordships in the House of Lords said about capacity. The question is easier to pose than to answer. As is common in cases which raise profound social questions and on which there is no previous law in point to guide them, the House of Lords did not speak with one voice.

Before the House was the question whether a girl under the age of 16 could in law give valid consent to contraceptive treatment without the involvement of her parents, or whether, by reason of the fact that she was under 16, her purported consent was invalid. In effect, the courts were being asked by Mrs Gillick to decide that capacity as a matter of law was determined solely by reference to the age of the person the doctor was confronted with. Parliament had previously decided by section 8(1),

Family Law Reform Act 1969, that a person over the age of 16 is deemed capable of consenting to medical treatment. Mrs Gillick argued that if a girl was under 16 she was *incapable* of consenting. The House of Lords were in a fix. They were being asked to decide a particular case concerning girls consenting to contraceptive treatment. Yet, as they well knew, their decision would have general application as establishing the meaning of capacity. It is a crime to have sexual intercourse with girls under the age of 16. Their Lordships did not want to appear to connive at this (why else did the girls want contraceptives?) but they recognised the need to make a decision which would apply generally. They did not want to let this highly-charged and politically sensitive issue dictate the basis for formulating a general meaning of capacity.

In the event, a majority of their Lordships rejected the notion that capacity to consent to medical treatment was linked to any specific age or status. They regarded it as self-evident that whether someone could consent to any particular procedure depended on the procedure and the person. It would be less than sensible for the law to state that a 12-year-old, by reason only that he was under 16 (or some other threshold), could *never*, as a matter of law, consent to having a plaster put on a grazed knee. At the same time, the law would pause long and hard before saying that the same 12-year-old had the capacity, on his own, to decline life-saving treatment. The key, the House of Lords decided, is *understanding*. As Lord Fraser put it,

'provided the patient, whether a boy or a girl, is capable of understanding what is proposed . . . I see no good reason for holding that he or she lacks the capacity to express [his or her wishes] validly and effectively and to authorise the medical man . . . to give the treatment'.

A person is capable of giving a legally valid consent if he understands what is being proposed. The person's age or his status – for example, the fact that he is a minor or a patient detained under the Mental Health Act – is irrelevant save to the extent that it offers some clue to his ability to understand. Moreover, the House of Lords' decision, though specifically addressing the question of a child's capacity to consent, quite clearly defines capacity generally. Thus, a doctor or dentist faced with a patient who is elderly and appears confused or who is mentally disordered must apply this same test of understanding as was applied by the House of Lords to the child patient.[13]

Of course, the law, like life, is not as simple as that. It is all very well to say capacity means understanding, but what does that mean? Let me raise three particular questions:

(a) What is the meaning of understanding?
(b) What are the criteria for establishing understanding?
(c) Who applies these criteria?

(a) The meaning of understanding

In concentrating on understanding, what in law does the doctor have to be satisfied about: that the patient does understand, that the patient has the ability to understand, or that any reasonable patient would have been able to understand? The difference between these interpretations is significant in terms of the burden the law casts on the doctor. If the doctor or dentist must be sure that the patient *does* understand before regarding any consent as valid, he would be in an impossible position. How could he be sure that the patient understands? The patient may give the impression that he does, but claim later that he really did not. Furthermore, it is not clear what the law would expect the doctor to do to make sure that the patient understands. The idea of setting his patient a little examination would meet the point but may not go down too well in the average out-patients' department.

So understanding cannot have this first meaning. As between the other two offered above, the clear favourite is that understanding means the *ability* to understand. The other meaning, referring to the reasonable patient, cannot be right. It would not seem to make sense to require that a patient should understand and then give a meaning to understanding which does not require this particular patient to understand, but only some notional reasonable patient to do so. And because it does not make sense, it is not the law.

Instead, in answer to our first question, the doctor, in determining whether a patient understands what is being proposed so as to be capable of consenting, must satisfy himself that his patient is capable of understanding. The doctor can never be sure that the patient does understand but at least the patient before him (and not some fictional patient) must be able to understand.

(b) Establishing understanding: the criteria

If the doctor must satisfy himself that the patient is able to understand, does the law offer some formula or guidelines which the doctor can apply to determine this? It will not come as a surprise that the answer is no. The law's approach is that a doctor knows a comprehending patient when he sees one. This robust, commonsensical approach, typical of the way English law proceeds, is all very well as far as it goes but it does leave some questions unanswered. Every doctor has met a patient who listens to what is said, appears to understand and then expresses a view which seems at least perverse if not plain silly. Then there is the patient who appears to understand but then, operating under some kind of delusion, reaches a conclusion which flies in the face of the evidence. And doctors will recognise a host of other variations on the same themes.

The following analysis may be of assistance. It has to be said that it is my view of the law since currently we have no specific case law on the subject. First, a doctor must not, sorely as he may be tempted to do so, conclude that a patient does not understand what is being proposed just because the patient reaches a view which the doctor does not agree with or judges to be silly. Otherwise the law would be that, to qualify as legally competent to consent, a patient must agree with his doctor. Mr Justice Gresson put it well in *Smith v Auckland Hospital Board* [14]: 'an individual patient must, in my view, always retain the right to decline . . . treatment however unreasonable or foolish this may appear in the eyes of his medical advisers'.

Secondly, a doctor may be faced with a view which appears to be irrational because it seems to fly in the face of reason and the facts. In such a case a doctor should be careful to draw the following distinction. On the one hand the view may be based on a temporary delusion born of some current illness. On the other hand it may derive from a set of beliefs and values which a patient has long held and led his life by, even if to others they appear to be irrational. An example may be a patient in a mental institution who refuses necessary treatment because it will prevent her from becoming a film star. In fact, she is elderly and has been in an institution since she was a child, but she seems to sustain herself by her belief that one day she will be a star.

What criteria should a doctor use in deciding whether a patient understands? Take the temporary delusion first. The assumption must be that it will pass, after which the patient will cease to be irrational. In such a case, the patient would not thank his doctor for regarding such a delusion as making an understanding and considered choice. The doctor would, therefore, be entitled to regard the patient as lacking understanding and thus incapable in law of giving a valid consent. By contrast, if the beliefs and values of the patient, though incomprehensible to others, are of long standing and have formed the basis for all the patient's decisions about his life, there is a strong argument to suggest that the doctor should respect and give effect to a patient's decision based on them. That is to say that the doctor should regard such a patient as capable of consenting (or refusing). To argue otherwise would effectively be to rob the patient of his right to his own personality which may be far more serious and destructive than anything that could follow from the patient's decision as regards a particular proposed treatment.

It may not be easy for a doctor to accept that this is how understanding should be interpreted. It seems literally unreasonable. Moreover, since a doctor tends to see himself as doing good, he may find it hard to stay his hand in the face of irrational decisions. But the phrase 'doing good' is eminently question begging. The argument of this chapter is that where the patient is capable, it is he who determines what is good. Here I am suggesting that a patient whose views appear irrational should nonetheless, in the circumstances proposed, be regarded in law as capable of consenting. His views of what is good for him are the product of a settled set of values and beliefs and a doctor should respect them and not seek to bring them crashing down.

Finally, a patient whose decision is based simply on a misapprehension of relevant facts cannot be regarded as having the necessary understanding to be legally capable of consenting. In such a case, however, assuming he has the capacity to appreciate the true facts if presented with them, it would be the doctor's duty to state these facts and then solicit the patient's view again, rather than regard the first decision as uncomprehending and therefore conclude that the patient is legally incompetent.[15]

In summary, a patient may be deemed to understand if he has made a considered choice in the light of the facts, and these are not the product of some temporary delusion but are based on beliefs and values which are either generally accepted or which, though odd to others, are long standing and form the basis of his approach to life.

(c) Who applies the criteria?

It must be clear by now that there is no simple test of understanding. As a consequence, the doctor has considerable discretion in making any judgment. We have already seen that this is both inevitable given the nature of the exercise and desirable in that discretion is the very *raison d'être* of any professional. The sceptical patient may well respond, however, that this leaves him somewhat naked. To have his consent (or refusal) accepted he has to persuade the doctor that he understands. He has to persuade the doctor that he is reasonable and rational (in other words, agree with the doctor) or risk the consequences. Although this may overstate the case, it reflects a real concern. The answer is that the law can only set out in general terms the basis for determining capacity. It must leave the doctor to stay within the four corners of the legal framework. He must make particular decisions on the facts before him. Since it is the doctor who must decide how to proceed, the law must trust the doctor to determine the capacity of the patient. The doctor, as a consequence, in the fulfilment of his legal duty, must pay due regard to the ethical obligation to behave with integrity. What this means here is that the doctor must keep uppermost the premise with which we began, that a patient has the right to determine what shall be done to him. This must be the presumption made as regards *each* patient. It should only be set aside on the grounds of lack of capacity after the most careful thought and on the basis of compelling evidence. To do otherwise is to abandon our starting premise.

I would like to say that this concludes my examination of capacity: that in law a patient is capable of consenting (or refusing) if he understands the procedure proposed, in terms of both short term and longer term consequences. Unfortunately, in 1991 a dark cloud appeared on the horizon which threatened to cast gloom on one important aspect of the law which I have just discussed. In *Re R (a minor)* [16] the Master of the Rolls, Lord Donaldson, chose to deliver a judgment which at best can be described as surprising.

The case posed the nightmare question for anyone interested in consent and capacity. What do you do with the patient whose mental state fluctuates between normal and disordered, and who while normal refuses to take the medicine necessary to prevent a further recurrence of the disorder? Nothing can be more frustrating for those caring for a person than to watch him slide into mania or depression, refusing help and even denying that the inevitable will happen. A strict application of law, as we have seen, would suggest that the doctor may not treat the patient as long as he is capable of understanding what is proposed and refuses treatment. The consequence is that the doctor must wait until the patient is ill – mentally disordered – before he may intervene (relying on the legal justification that it is in the now incompetent patient's best interests to do so). But, short of holding the patient down by force while he is still capable of refusing, the doctor appears to have no alternative and if he were to do this a battery action would probably succeed. The only other suggestion offered by commentators has been to view the patient's cyclic mental condition as a whole, to categorise the patient with such cyclic phases as mentally disordered despite the periods of normality and to detain him for treatment under the Mental Health Act 1983. This, it could be said, is a permissible bending of the rules if it gets the job done: if it prevents the mental and social anguish which follows manic or depressive attacks. The difficulty, of course, is that a hospital would be unwilling to detain such a patient indefinitely. Indeed, once the illness was controlled there would be no reason to do so. But, once released, the saga could repeat itself. The patient could simply refuse further treatment while normal and everyone would be back at square one.

It will come as no surprise that the law has no solution to this problem. In a sense it is the exception which demonstrates the general value of the rules which have been set out. But it also demonstrates that life is untidy and however hard you try to construct rational frameworks something is not going to fit.

Re R involved just such a problem. A girl of 15 suffered from interludes of psychotic illness of increasing severity. In between, she was lucid and rational. She refused medical treatment in the form of tranquilisers while apparently in a lucid state. She was made a ward of court. The court was then invited to consent to treatment on her behalf despite her refusal. On one reading of the facts the court could merely have decided that the girl was legally incapable of consenting (or refusing) when her mental capacity was taken as a whole. This may have required a little fudging of the law or the facts but may well have been the best way of dealing with a case which might otherwise distort or undermine the relatively settled law since *Gillick*. In fact, this is what the Court of Appeal did. Unfortunately, however, Lord Donaldson chose to go further. If ever one needed proof that 'hard cases make bad law', you have it here.

The Court of Appeal could have stopped at the point of finding that the girl was incompetent. But they chose to go on to consider what powers the court in wardship has when a ward is *competent*. The court began its analysis with the assumption that the girl, at the time of her refusal, was capable of understanding what was proposed. *Gillick* would suggest that this is the end off the matter. The fact that she was 15 (or 55) would be irrelevant since capacity turns on understanding, not age or status. The Court of Appeal saw it otherwise. The fact that the girl was a ward of court changed things. Once a child is a ward (and anyone up to the age of 18 can be made a ward of court), the Court of Appeal held that the court in wardship has the authority to consent to treatment (or refuse it) regardless of the fact that the child understands what is proposed and is therefore legally capable of reaching a decision. This is because, the court reasoned, the powers of the court in wardship are greater than those of a parent. *Gillick*, the court held (quite rightly) had concerned itself only with the relative rights of parents and children and had held that a child, on acquiring the ability to understand, could make his own decisions so displacing the authority of a parent. *Gillick* did not, they reasoned, determine the relative rights of the court and the ward. So, deciding the matter for the first time, the Court of Appeal held that a court in wardship has greater authority than a natural parent. In the exercise of its jurisdiction it may override either the consent or the refusal of treatment by a ward who is legally competent to decide.

This, you may think, is not a particularly grave exception to the principle that the competent are entitled to make their own decisions. Children who are made wards are likely to be at serious risk and perhaps need to be protected against themselves, at least until they reach maturity. Furthermore, the court's decision making will not be invoked save in circumstances of grave concern.

The arguments are fairly evenly balanced. The court threw its weight behind protecting the ward even though the principle of the law is that once competent a person should be entitled to make his own mistakes. But recourse to wardship will not be common (particularly in the light of section 8 of the Children Act 1989). By and large, therefore, the *Gillick* doctrine survives: that capacity means understanding whether the patient is a minor or an adult.

But enter now Lord Donaldson. He had clearly taken against *Gillick* and decided that he was going to provide a gloss to it. The gloss he provided is such that if it were accepted as law, the House of Lords would have been overruled by a lower court – a rare legal phenomenon indeed. Lord Donaldson took it upon himself to interpret *Gillick* in such a way that he arrived at the following conclusions. A child over the age of 16 or one under that age who understands what is proposed has the legal capacity to consent. But that capacity is also retained by a parent. Thus, if a child over 16 or under 16 but legally competent consents to treatment, the doctor may go ahead. The parents have no right of veto, since it is the consent of any of the parties which enables treatment to be carried out. If, however, the child *refuses* treatment, the parent, retaining the authority to consent, may consent on the child's behalf. The treatment may then lawfully be carried out despite the child's refusal. The significance of this view cannot be overstated. A patient under the age of 18, even though legally competent, would lose the most critical element of the right to self determination, the right to refuse.

Make of this what you will. If Lord Donaldson is right, it drives a coach and horses through *Gillick* and, if it were law, would amount to a significant amendment to the law relating to capacity in the case of young people. Neither of the other two judges in the Court of Appeal joined Lord Donaldson on this particular flight, reasoning quite rightly that it was unnecessary for the decision they had to reach. In my respectful view, Lord Donaldson is wrong. His interpretation of *Gillick* is unique, which is an achievement given the buckets of ink spilt in analysing that case. His failure to accept that the power to refuse is no more than the obverse of the power to consent and that they are simply twin aspects of the single right to self-determination borders on the perverse.

(ii) Consent must be freely given

It is trite to observe that someone cannot be said to have consented to something if his agreement or acquiescence was gained through duress or coercion. The law reflects this by demanding that consent to be valid must be freely given. In the context of medical law little more apparently needs to be said. The general proposition is obvious, but it need not detain us. Doctors do not go about coercing their patients into submission.

Notwithstanding the truth of this general response, there are at least two particular points which ought to be made. First, the notion of freely given consent is more subtle or complex than it may at first appear. Although twisting arms or making threats is not part of medical practice, it may be that patients are exposed to other more complicated forms of pressure or duress. Patients are ever anxious to please their doctor and doctors are aware of this. Honesty would compel us to recognise that, in many exchanges, a patient's compliance or consent is gained through the careful application of some sort of pressure. There is no question of a bad motive. All is done with the best of intentions: to care for the patient. But, if the patient is reluctant to go along with what is planned, or will not take his medicine, the doctor has a battery of techniques available to get his way.

This may well be desirable on occasions. It is certainly understandable. What is important is that we recognise that it happens and then analyse it. I would suggest there are three levels of pressure of the type we are discussing. The first may be the sort of pressure we think is permissible as part of the medical exchange. In no way does it undermine the patient's freedom to consent. The second may raise ethical concerns, but would not be such as to make any consent legally invalid. An example may be a doctor's use of a nurse to talk a patient into accepting treatment or drugs which he has previously refused, on the grounds that the nurse will otherwise get into trouble. Another example may be where a patient is cajoled or embarrassed into allowing a medical student to carry out an examination when he would prefer not to. The third type of pressure may well vitiate any consent the patient may have apparently given, so that any medical intervention relying on it would be unlawful. Examples of such pressure may from time to time come to light but mercifully they are rare. They would have the common feature that the patient was substantially deprived of his freedom to choose whether to consent to or refuse treatment because of the doctor's conduct. The old law was that only violence or the fear of violence would suffice (*Latter v Braddell* [17]). It is doubtful now that the law would be so restricted.

Secondly, I would draw your attention to the case of *Freeman v Home Office (No 2)* [18]. In that case Freeman argued that he had not consented to the treatment he received in prison. On the facts the court rejected his claim. More significantly for us, he also argued that because he was treated by a prison doctor, who was also as a matter of law a prison officer, any apparent consent was legally invalid because he had no choice but to agree. Freeman argued that the prison doctor's authority was such that he could, for example, be punished if he did not consent. From this he argued that *no* prisoner could ever legally be said to consent to treatment by a prison doctor because no prisoner was free from the duress associated with the very status of the doctor as a prison officer. The relationship was, he argued, inherently tainted. It could not be called a true doctor-patient relationship. The upshot of this argument would be, of course, that a prisoner could lawfully be treated only by a doctor outside the prison service. And it could have implications in other contexts where the doctor might find himself in a position of authority with conflicting loyalties to his patient and his employer.

The Court of Appeal rejected Freeman's argument. They refused to hold that as a matter of principle the status of the doctor as also a prison officer alone prevented the patient from giving a free consent. They conceded that certain situations such as the one in which Freeman found himself could give rise to problems. But they decided that in each case it was a matter of fact whether or not the patient had consented to the treatment complained of.

(iii) The patient's consent must be suitably informed

Here we meet, as the third element of consent, the issue of information. Put simply, the question is how much information must a doctor supply to his patient so as to enable the patient to give a consent which the law will regard as valid? This has come to be known by the shorthand phrase 'informed consent', which is unfortunate since information is, as we have seen, an aspect, but only one aspect, of consent.

Just as with the meaning of capacity, it was only in the mid-1980s that English law got around to providing an answer to the question posed. The case which provided the answer was *Sidaway v Governors of Bethlem Royal Hospital* [19]. This is not the place to rehearse all the arguments about the supply of information to patients. At bottom, they are ethical and political arguments which, unhappily, occupy polar positions. Patients' rights and self-determination are set against paternalism and the beneficence of doctors. Patient power (information being rightly seen as power) is set against doctor power. In the sound and fury of this debate the notion that the doctor-patient relationship is best seen as a partnership in which information is given willingly to patients so as to enable them better to play their role in the partnership is somehow lost.

But what does the law say? Let us proceed in stages.

(a) Battery or negligence?

We must notice first the respective roles of the tort of negligence. In two cases in the early 1980s (*Chatterton v Gerson* [20] and *Hills v Potter* [21]) the courts made it clear that an action in battery would not normally lie against a doctor who failed properly to inform his patient. The courts expressed a certain repugnance at holding a doctor liable for a tort which connotes intentional and harmful wrongdoing, when he has carried out a form of treatment perfectly adequately but has failed to inform a patient of some particular matter. The courts stated that the issue was to be dealt with through the tort of negligence. As Mr Justice Bristow put it in *Chatterton v Gerson*, once a patient has been informed 'in broad terms of the nature of the procedure which is intended', the consent is real and no action for battery will lie. Of course, this leaves open what Mr Justice Bristow meant when he spoke of being informed 'in broad terms'. In large part he himself provided the answer. An action in battery would lie, he stated, only if a wholly different procedure from the one agreed to was carried out or if the patient's agreement was obtained through fraud.

Thus in virtually every case we must look to the tort of negligence to determine the scope and nature of the doctor's duty to inform his patient.

(b) A duty to inform?

Our second question is somewhat technical. How does any duty to inform fit into the structure of the tort of negligence? Ordinarily, the law does not impose duties of affirmative action on people, requiring them to do things for others, except if a special relationship already exists between the parties. This led the US courts in developing their law of informed consent to decide that a doctor owed his patient a fiduciary duty, a duty based on trust. In this way they could justify finding that a doctor had a duty actively to inform his patient.[22] The English courts do not regard the doctor-patient relationship as a fiduciary one. So how did the House of Lords in *Sidaway* justify their decision that a doctor had a duty to inform? They simply regarded it as part of the doctor's general duty of care owed to each patient. In other words, it was part of the mainstream of the tort of negligence requiring no sleight of hand to get it past the purists.

(c) Inform about what?

Thirdly, what does this duty to inform involve? We are concerned in this chapter with consent. What we see emerging is a distinction between two types of consent. The first we can call 'threshold consent'. If a patient has not given this form of consent, an action in battery may lie against the doctor. The second, and the one we are discussing here, is 'informed consent'. This means that, besides any threshold consent, there is some element of information which a doctor must impart before a patient can be said fully to have consented. Failure to obtain this second-order consent does not invalidate the consent as a whole but may give rise to an action in negligence.

This distinction allows us to understand what information we are talking about here. We are not talking about information 'in broad terms about the nature of the procedure', as Mr Justice Bristow put it. Rather, we are talking about more detailed matters which a patient may wish to know because they may well affect his final decision whether to go ahead with treatment or not. Specifically, we are talking about any risks involved in the treatment and what alternatives to it there may be. So, our question becomes: to what extent, if at all, is a doctor under a duty in law to pass on to his patient information concerning risks associated with any proposed treatment and alternatives to it?

(d) Sidaway: the doctor's duty

We can now move nicely into the fourth stage of our enquiry, the *Sidaway* case itself. In a nutshell, Mrs Sidaway complained that she had undergone elective surgery to relieve pain in her neck, shoulder and arms. After the surgery, which was carried out with all due care, she was left in a worse state, with intractable pain. She had not been warned of a known, though small, risk that this might happen. Had she been so informed, she said, she would not have had the surgery. Thus, she alleged, her doctor was in breach of his duty to inform her of these risks so as to enable her to make an informed choice, she had suffered harm as a consequence and was entitled to damages.

The House of Lords unanimously dismissed her claim. It is important to notice that they did so on the basis that it was impossible to establish with any degree of certainty what in fact Mrs Sidaway's doctor had said to her. Many years had passed and the surgeon was dead. At best, as Lord

Scarman put it, her case was 'not proven'. This could have been the end of the matter. But the House of Lords, recognising the importance of the question and the desirability of offering clear legal guidance to doctors and patients, chose to explore at length the doctor's duty to inform.

Here is not the place to indulge in a detailed and lengthy analysis of the speeches of their Lordships.[23] It is a fair summary to say that the House was divided three ways. Lord Scarman opted for a radical shift. Lord Diplock adopted a decidedly conservative view of the law. Lord Bridge, with whom Lord Keith concurred, and Lord Templeman chose what may be described as a middle way, in what may be said to be the true tradition of the pragmatism of English law.

The fact that the House of Lords produced three strands of opinion, though perhaps inevitable in such a difficult area, is less than ideal. Far from clarifying the law, the case was initially seized on by various interested factions as justifying their particular (and quite opposite) points of view. Equally, it left the lower courts a range of options to choose from, which as we shall see was later to produce odd consequences.

It may be helpful before going any further to identify what I have described as the three strands of opinion. The first is that a doctor's duty as regards informing his patient is significantly different from the duties he owes as regards treatment and diagnosis. These latter duties are matters of technical expertise. By contrast, deciding what a patient may wish to know does not call for or depend upon any medical knowledge. Rather it merely depends on listening and responding to a patient's needs as expressed by the patient. It is an aspect of the patient's right to self-determination and should be analysed as such. Thus the doctor's duty must be to give the patient at the very least all the information which a reasonable patient would consider necessary or material. The second strand takes quite the opposite view. The duty to inform the patient is no different from the duty to carry out diagnosis and treatment. *All* of these duties are matters best decided by doctors since only they have the necessary skill and judgment. Patients do not necessarily know their own interests in this regard and, indeed, informing them of risks and alternatives could well frighten them or put them off having necessary treatment. Furthermore, in any event, the notion of informing patients is a nonsense since it would involve giving every patient a crash course in medicine. The third strand of opinion steers a course between these two opposites. It recognises that imparting information is a delicate task which should ordinarily be left to a doctor's judgment. At the same time it recognises that patients do have a right to make their own decisions about what medical treatment they wish to undergo. In doing so, it is important to point out the red herring that patients must be told everything. Adequate information is all that is called for – adequate for the choice to be made. As a consequence, the scope of the doctor's duty to inform should not be left entirely to doctors. The law, through the courts, should retain some residual power to indicate on suitable occasions that whatever doctors may say on a particular matter, a patient should be entitled to be informed.

In the House of Lords Lord Scarman opted for the first line of reasoning and Lord Diplock opted for the second. A majority, Lord Bridge, Lord Keith and Lord Templeman, opted for the third or middle course. So it is the third course which we must consider now more closely. In doing so it is perhaps easier to concentrate on Lord Bridge's speech. Certainly, once the dust had settled after the case, it was generally accepted that his speech was the heart of *Sidaway* and the key to the future direction of the law.

Lord Bridge rejected the approach of Lord Scarman, which would have imported into English law the Canadian, if not the American, notion of informed consent. Lord Scarman argued that the doctor's duty was to give his patient all material facts pertaining to his proposed treatment. Material facts were those which a reasonable patient in the particular patient's position would wish to know. Lord Bridge thought that this test for determining a doctor's duty to inform would be unworkable, although the reasons given for this conclusion are less than persuasive. Instead, he took as his starting point the law as stated in the famous *Bolam* case (*Bolam v Friern Hospital Management Committee*) [24]. In this case Mr Justice McNair stated that 'a doctor is not guilty of negligence if he has acted in accordance with a practice accepted as proper by a responsible body of medical men skilled in that particular art'. Lord Bridge took the view that this applied, *prima facie*, as much to the duty to inform as to any other duty a doctor may have. The consequence was that, at least *prima facie*, the question what information a doctor was in law under a duty to give to his patient was to be answered by saying that he must give, but need only give, that amount of information which other doctors ordinarily give. Lord Bridge then provided an interesting gloss on this by saying that where there is a division of opinion among doctors, the court could decide which opinion as to proper practice was to be preferred as representing the legal duty. This gloss is interesting because the ordinary law of medical negligence as expressed by the House of Lords in *Maynard v West Midlands Regional Health Authority* [25] specifically states that when there are various schools of thought about what is proper medical practice, a court may not choose between them so as to prefer one above the others.

Once he had stated the general principle that the duty was that set out in *Bolam*, Lord Bridge immediately moved to qualify it. He did so because he was acutely conscious of the fact that if he did not, he could be accused of abandoning the rights of patients in favour of a doctrine of 'doctor knows best'. Lord Bridge was most anxious to reiterate that he recognised that a 'conscious adult patient of sound mind is entitled to decide for himself whether or not he will submit to a particular course of treatment proposed by the doctor'. He was equally anxious to explain that his approach did not involve 'the necessity "to hand over to the medical profession the entire question of the scope of the duty of disclosure, including the question whether there has been a breach of that duty"'. So what qualifications did he propose? 'The issue whether non-disclosure (of information) in a particular case', he stated, 'should be condemned as a breach of the doctor's duty of care is an issue to be decided *primarily* (my emphasis) on the basis of the . . . *Bolam* test.' *Bolam* therefore is the beginning but not necessarily the end of the enquiry. In certain circumstances the law, that is the court, would insist that a doctor was under a duty to disclose information whatever the collective view of doctors may be. The circumstances Lord Bridge referred to were where there was a 'substantial risk of grave adverse consequences'. In such circumstances the patient had a right to be informed.

It is not immediately clear what the expression 'substantial risk of grave adverse consequences' means. Lord Bridge purported to offer some assistance by referring to the percentage risk that some adverse consequence may transpire. Resorting to percentages is not perhaps entirely helpful, not only because different experts will apply different numbers to the risk but also because it is not just the likelihood that a risk will eventuate that is important but also what it would do to that particular patient if it did.

That said, we can draw some conclusions from *Sidaway*. First, to establish a doctor's duty to inform his patient of the risk of adverse consequences associated with any proposed treatment, the law will primarily look to the practice commonly accepted by doctors. If the practice is to inform patients then ordinarily the doctor should do so unless he has good reason to do otherwise. If it is not to inform, the doctor will not be in breach of any duty to his patient if he chooses not to do so. Secondly, notwithstanding this general proposition, the law retains the right in any particular case to decide that a doctor should have informed his patient of certain risks if, in all the circumstances, the risks were sufficiently serious to persuade a court that a doctor should not properly keep them from the patient.

Admittedly, this is not a particularly specific set of guidelines but the House of Lords did not see it as their role to provide one, Their task was to set the general conditions under which consent was to be obtained by doctors in the future. In doing so they attempted to steer a middle path, although clearly closer to the medical profession's side of the river than the patient's. The House of Lords customarily take the view that it is for those advising doctors and patients and for the lower courts to do the navigation from now on, making sure that they keep more or less in the middle. Imagine everyone's surprise, therefore, when the first time the Court of Appeal was asked to interpret and apply *Sidaway* it ran straight into the river bank. In *Gold v Haringey Health Authority* [26] the court resolved the question of the doctor's duty to disclose information to his patient in that case solely by reference to the speech of Lord Diplock. No other speech was referred to. It is as if Lords Bridge and Templeman, not to mention Lord Scarman, had not been there. The Court of Appeal in *Gold* held, following Lord Diplock, that *Sidaway* had decided that *Bolam* was decisive in determining the doctor's duty to inform. *Sidaway* had done no such thing and it is difficult to understand how the Court of Appeal could be so perverse.

An attempt was made to persuade the House of Lords to hear an appeal from *Gold* but they refused. As has been said, they prefer to allow the detailed implications of their major decisions to be worked out gradually by the lower courts. No doubt they reasoned, somewhat loftily, that *Gold* was so much loose change in the commerce of the law and that things would settle down. Those advising doctors and patients are less sanguine. In my view *Gold* is to be regretted and the Court of Appeal (differently constituted) or the House of Lords should take the first opportunity to say so.

(e) Answering questions

Mention of *Gold* allows us to notice another quirk in the law after *Sidaway*. In *Sidaway* their Lordships speculated on a matter not before them, though relevant for our enquiry. What if a patient asks a direct question of his doctor? What does the duty to inform say about this? The view had been expressed by Lord Denning in *Hatcher v Black* [27] that doctors were permitted by law even to lie to their patients if in the doctor's opinion it was right to do so. More recently this view had attracted increasing criticism as representing the high water mark of medical paternalism. It was no surprise, therefore, that the unanimous view was expressed by the House of Lords in *Sidaway* that, whatever the doctor's duty may be as regards volunteering information, he undoubtedly has a legal duty to answer truthfully questions which the patient may put to him. Now for the quirk. Soon after *Sidaway* was decided there came before the Court of Appeal the case of *Blyth v Bloomsbury Health*

Authority.[28] Just as *Gold* had appeared to thumb its nose at the House of Lords, so too did *Blyth*. For despite the apparently clear affirmation in *Sidaway* of the doctor's duty to respond truthfully to questions, Lord Justice Kerr was able to hold that in response to general and even specific enquiries, the doctor's duty was that laid down in *Bolam*. 'The *Bolam* test is all pervasive', he stated. In other words, the doctor's duty is to be determined by reference to what other doctors would have replied to Mrs Blyth's enquiries. Lord Justice Neill expressly agreed.

Again, this leaves the law at best uncertain. It certainly makes the task of those who advise doctors and dentists no easier. In my view *Blyth* is out of step with the trend of the law as exemplified in *Sidaway* and should not be regarded as the last word on the subject.

(f) Enter causation

Let me now make a final point about the duty to inform. What we have reviewed so far is the precise nature of the doctor's duty. It should not be thought that this is necessarily the end of the story, so that if the patient shows that the doctor was in breach of duty, he will automatically recover damages if he has suffered any harm – if, for example, he has suffered unsightly scarring after an operation, which was a real risk of which he was not informed. In actual fact, the converse will often be true – even though he can establish a breach of duty he may still not recover damages. This is because in traditional negligence analysis the patient must show that the doctor's breach of duty *caused* the harm he complains of. For us, this means that the patient must show that, had he been informed of the risk associated with the treatment (or the alternatives to it), he would not have decided to have it. In many cases, the patient's case will fall at this hurdle. For, while it may sometimes be true in certain kinds of elective surgery, it usually will not be true otherwise. This is because the patient will ordinarily have to concede that if viewed objectively the benefits represented by receiving the treatment outweighed the burden of continuing with the condition or illness complained of. Much depends, of course, on whether things have to be viewed objectively – whether in other words, the test of causation is objective or not. If it is, the patient faces considerable difficulties in succeeding in any action despite a breach of the duty to inform by the doctor. If on the other hand the test is subjective, the patient's task is easier. He can say after the event that of course had he known he would never have consented. But it is this priority given to hindsight which makes it unlikely that the law would adopt a subjective test, given the courts' general reluctance to encourage recovery in actions in medical negligence. Mr Justice Bristow in *Chatterton v Gerson* seemed to hint that the test is subjective but it is not clear that he intended his view of the particular facts of the case to be elevated into a general test. In the absence of any clear guidance it may be speculated that a court would adopt the following approach. Following *Chatterton* the court could state that the test of causation is subjective: that the particular patient would not have consented had he been properly informed. The court could then stipulate that in seeking to prove this the patient must show that he would have acted reasonably, measured by reference to an objective standard.

Limits of consent

No consideration of the law relating to consent to treatment is complete without noticing that there are, of course, limits to what may be consented to. Conduct, for example, which is otherwise criminal cannot be made lawful simply because the patient requests it. This provides the basis for asserting that a doctor may not bring a patient's life to an end by active means even though the patient may wish him to do so. Equally, the doctor may not commit an act which would constitute the old crime of maim, a prohibition that persuaded a number of US centres not to carry out sex conversion operations on transsexuals.

This may of course be self-evident, but a reminder that there are limits to consent is not without importance. There are a number of medical interventions which hover at the edge of acceptability and permissibility. Examples are non-therapeutic sterilisation, certain forms of cosmetic surgery, and the use of experimental or unorthodox procedures. One view is that the key to the legality of any intervention lies in whether it can be categorised as *treatment* or not. This is of course to ignore the fact that treatment is at least in part a judgmental term. Merely choosing to call something treatment does not make it so. It will only become so when it is accepted by the medical profession and society generally. For this reason, among others, careful procedures should exist before any new forms of medical intervention are introduced into practice. Not only do they have to be shown to work, they must also be shown to be within the limits of that which is permitted and may be consented to.

Notes

1   *Schloendorf v Society of New York Hospital* (1914) 105 NE 92.
2   [1987] QB 237.
3   [1988] Fam. 52.
4   [1990] 2 AC 1.
5   [1981] 1 All ER 257.

6   J.G. Fleming *The Law of Torts* (7th edn, 1987) p. 72.
7   28 NE 266 (Mass 1891).
8   Fleming *op. cit.*, p. 73.
9   [1935] 1 WWR 714.
10 [1975] 3 All ER 446.
11 (1990) 67 DLR (4th) 321.
12 [1985] 3 All ER 402.
13 For a detailed discussion of *Gillick*, see I. Kennedy *Treat Me Right* (1991) chapter 5.
14 [1965] NZLR 191.
15 See *State of Tennessee v Northern* 563 SW 2d 197 (1978).
16 [1991] 4 All ER 177.
17 [1881] 50 LJQB 488.
18 [1984] QB 524.
19 [1985] 1 All ER 643.
20 [1981] 1 All ER 257.
21 [1984] 1 WLR 641.
22 See, e.g., *Canterbury v Spence* 464 F 2d 772 (1972).
23 For a detailed examination of *Sidaway*, see I. Kennedy *Treat Me Right* (1991) chapter 9.
24 [1957] 1 WLR 582.
25 [1985] 1 All ER 635.
26 [1986] FLR 125.
27 (1954) The Times, 2 July.
28 (1987) The Times, 11 February.

Chapter 4

Consent to Treatment: The Incapable Person

Treatment provided to, or withheld from, a patient who is unable to give legally effective consent is fraught with complexity and risk. Treatment decisions for incompetent patients pose a risk of legal liability for doctors and a risk of substandard care for patients. The law must have as its primary concern the rights, dignity, and welfare of the patient. By laying down a clear and consistent standard, the law can also guide the doctor on a legally safe and ethically sound course for treating patients who are incompetent.

The issue puts Parliament and the courts on the horns of a dilemma. If they allow doctors to treat incompetent patients in accordance with what the doctors believe is their best interests and with minimal formality and delay, patients are more likely to receive the everyday treatment and care they need. But this approach, which is essentially the one adopted in English law, has the distinct disadvantage that it may not ensure that patients receive treatment that is truly in their best interests and in accordance with *their* value system. In short, allowing doctors to provide the treatment they think best without the safeguard of patient consent or the substituted consent of a guardian or court leaves incompetent patients vulnerable and stripped of dignity.

However, the more safeguards the law introduces by way of formal review of the decision to treat an incompetent patient, the greater the obstacles and delay in providing the patient with beneficial treatment. If doctors must seek approval of a court or guardian every time they treat incompetent patients, it becomes less likely that patients will receive the treatment they need.

The problem is, in fact, even more complicated. A legal and ethical standard for the treatment of incompetent patients must take into account an array of factors. The uniqueness of every human being presents society with the awesome responsibility of ensuring that each patient receives the treatment that is most beneficial and, if possible, in accordance with his value system. A decision to provide or stop treatment may be viewed quite differently depending on the following circumstances:

(1) *Age* Compare a decision to stop treating a neonate, a five-year-old child, a 17-year-old 'mature minor' and an elderly person. The maturity of the patients' views, their settled beliefs, their quality of life, and their longevity may lead to different conclusions in each case.

(2) *The degree of incapacity* Competence is not an 'all or nothing' concept. Some people may have sufficient understanding to take some treatment decisions but not others. Other patients, such as those with severe mental illness, profound mental handicap or dementia, may have no capacity to take decisions.

(3) *Views and value systems* Incompetent individuals may express a wish to be treated, or may not express a preference one way or the other. It would be unjust to compel a protesting patient to be treated using the same legal standard as for those who agree or express no wish at all. A related problem concerns the distinction between a person who is currently incompetent and one who has never been competent. Patients who were once competent may have expressed views about their treatment. These views may be in the form of an advance directive (a 'living will' or durable power of attorney) or casual remarks, for example, 'I never want to live like a vegetable'. Alternatively, a person's views may be inferred from his value system. A Jehovah's Witness may have a known aversion to blood transfusions and a Christian Scientist a known preference for faith healing over traditional medicine.

(4) *The prognosis* The law is less rigorous in demanding medical intervention if the person is in a persistent vegetative state or terminally ill than if he has many years of good life ahead. How should the law guide decisions in less clear cases, such as an elderly patient in a nursing home or mental hospital who cannot sit up, or communicate, and who is in great pain?

(5) *The treatment* Many believe that there should be few obstacles to providing incompetent patients with beneficial, everyday treatment and care such as antibiotics, pain relievers, and decongestants. The provision of more serious treatment is also supported where it is clearly necessary, such as removal of cataracts or minor oral or orthopaedic surgery. Certain treatments, however, require more careful thought because they are more invasive (for example, coronary by-pass), irreversible (psychosurgery), life-sustaining (ventilation, artificial hydration and nutrition) or controversial (sterili-

sation or abortion). A distinction can also be drawn between emergencies which require minimal formality or delay and non-emergencies.

(6) *Vulnerability*   Treatment for incompetent patients in the community who have caring and informed family and friends may not require such careful supervision as treatment for the more vulnerable who may need greater safeguards. These might include those in nursing homes, residential care homes, mental hospitals, prisons and other institutions.

The law in England and Wales still has some way to go in taking into account the unique circumstances presented by patients who are legally incompetent. In order to understand the law relating to treatment of mentally incompetent patients, a number of questions need to be put: What is the test of competence? Who can provide substituted or proxy consent on behalf of an incompetent person? What standard should be used for making treatment decisions for an incompetent person? What procedures or safeguards against abuse are required?

The test of competence

Recognition of the patient's rights to dignity, autonomy and self-determination, as well as his health and welfare, is the primary goal of health law and ethics. Self-determination is best achieved by setting a low threshold of competence, thereby giving the individual the greatest opportunity to have control over his own body.

The entire foundation of the law of consent is based upon the competence of the patient. Yet the English courts have not explicitly and authoritatively set forth a standard of competence for medical treatment decisions. The courts have held that the consent must be 'real' in the sense that the patient must know what he is consenting to. Once the patient understands in broad terms the nature and purpose of the procedure, and gives consent, that consent is legally effective.[1]

The test of competence, then, is based upon a determination of what the patient *understands* (see Chapter 3). Other tests of capacity based upon *status* or *outcome* undermine patients' rights to make their own decisions about the health care they are to receive. A 'status' approach holds a person incompetent based upon a fixed rule such as age, diagnosis or residence in a psychiatric institution. No fixed status rule for consent to medical treatment has been adopted by the courts, but the special circumstances of children and mentally disordered persons warrants separate discussion (see below).

An 'outcome' approach bases the competence assessment not on what the individual understands but on whether the decision he has taken is wise and, in the assessor's view, in his best interests. Under an 'outcome' approach the person who makes the competence assessment makes his own judgment about what the individual needs using the assessor's greater skills, knowledge and experience in clinical medicine. The true test of competence depends not on outcome but on an objective assessment of whether the patient understands the treatment proposed. The doctor should not hold the patient to a professional standard of understanding nor should the doctor substitute his judgment for the patient's.

Children and consent

The right of a minor to consent to treatment depends not upon reaching a fixed age, but on the young person's maturity, degree of intelligence and understanding. Where children are too young or immature to give a valid consent, a parent or legal guardian can consent on the child's behalf. If such a child is in the care of a local authority, consent can be given by the authority. Competence requires 'a full understanding and appreciation of the consequences both of the treatment in terms of intended and possible side-effects and, equally important, the anticipated consequences of a failure to treat' (Lord Donaldson, Master of the Rolls, in *Re R (a minor)*.[2]

The Family Law Reform Act 1969 provides that the consent of a minor who has reached sixteen to medical treatment is as effective as if the child were of full age. Thus a minor of 16 years or older can provide legally effective consent as if he were an adult. The Act, however, preserves the common law right of a competent child below the age of 16 to consent on his own behalf. The House of Lords in *Gillick v West Norfolk and Wisbech Area Health Authority* [3] held that minors under the age of 16 have the legal capacity to consent to medical treatment, including contraceptive treatment, if they have sufficient maturity and intelligence to understand the nature and implications of the proposed treatment. The parental right to control a minor is a dwindling right as the minor matures in his ability to determine himself what treatment is appropriate for his benefit.

In *Gillick* the House of Lords upheld advice from the then Department of Health and Social Security that doctors could provide contraception for children under 16 without parental knowledge or consent. *Gillick* was concerned with the right of a competent child to consent to medical treatment provided in accordance with a respectable body of medical opinion. Technically, then, *Gillick* did not address the right of such a child to *refuse* treatment to which a parent or guardian consents. Yet Lord Scarman in the leading judgment made it clear that a parent could not overrule the decision of a competent child to refuse treatment: the 'parental right yields to the child's right to make his own decision when he reaches a sufficient understanding and intelligence to be capable of making up his own mind on the matter requiring decision'.

In *Re R* Lord Donaldson rejected this view, concluding that the parent or guardian and a competent minor have concurrent powers to consent. If *either* the parent or the child agrees, the consent is legally effective. Lord Donaldson supported his position by referring to the difficulties doctors would face if, relying on either the parent or the minor, they could be sued for failure of the other to consent. His *dicta* were *obiter* – not central to the judgment – and therefore not binding in law, but they might be persuasive in a later case.

His view was neither supported nor rejected by Lord Justice Staughton and Lord Justice Farquharson, the other two judges in the case. The Court of Appeal rested its decision to allow a 15-year-old girl to be given anti-psychotic medication against her will on its judgment that she was not competent to consent even in lucid intervals. In any event, Lord Donaldson and Lord Justice Staughton took the view that the court could consent to treatment over the objection of a ward of court who was fully competent.

The case has thrown the law on minors and consent to treatment into confusion. Lord Donaldson's reasoning runs counter to the philosophy of the Children Act 1989. Provisions in that Act, which came into force shortly after the decision in *Re R*, respect a competent child's right to self-determination. For example, where a child subject to a supervision order has sufficient understanding to make an informed decision on proposed treatment, the court cannot order him to undergo it unless he consents.

Parliament or the Law Lords need to clarify the right of a competent minor to reject unwanted treatment. Nothing degrades a human being more than to have intrusive treatment thrust upon him despite his full understanding of its nature and purpose and his clear will to say 'no'. It is unimaginable, for example, that a young, competent woman could have an abortion performed against her will based upon her parent's consent.[4] Medical treatment is so personal and fundamental to an individual's sense of self-identity and dignity that it should not be imposed against his will because others disagree with his judgment. Lord Donaldson's approach would place a competent minor in the invidious position of having his parents' values imposed upon him without the need to show that this was in his best interests.

Competence of mentally disordered persons

Part IV of the Mental Health Act 1983 regulates the circumstances under which certain patients *detained* under the Act can be treated without their consent. Part IV is applicable only to treatment for mental disorder, not general medical treatments or restraint, and (with the exception of treatments giving rise to special concern) does not apply to patients detained under the Act's short-term detention orders. For treatments which give rise to special concern – psychosurgery and sex hormone implants – the doctor must get the patient's consent *and* this must be verified and certified by a doctor and two non-medical persons appointed by the Mental Health Act Commission. For medication (after three months have elapsed) and electroconvulsive therapy the doctor must obtain the patient's consent *or* a second opinion from a doctor appointed by the Commission.

The overwhelming majority of mentally disordered persons are *not* subject to Part IV of the 1983 Act – for example, all informal patients in mental illness or mental handicap hospitals, patients detained for shorter emergency stays in hospital, and all other mentally disordered persons not subject to detention under the Act.

In any case where Part IV of the Mental Health Act 1983 does not apply, the question of whether a patient is competent to consent to treatment is a matter for the common law. Under the common law there are no fixed rules, based upon medical diagnosis or legal status, as to whether a mentally disordered person is competent to consent to medical treatment. In each case the question must be put whether the person understands the inherent implications of the treatment. Furthermore, a patient's competence may vary over time or depending on the particular treatment proposed.

As the Court of Appeal's decision in *Re R* indicates, particular problems arise in the case of mentally disordered patients with fluctuating competence. Even if a patient has lucid moments in which he fully understands a treatment decision, he may not be competent if, foreseeably, he will relapse and lose his capacity to understand. While this decision was specifically concerned with a minor who intermittently refused to take medication, it may also apply to adults consenting to long-term plans of treatment.

Substituted or proxy consent: who decides for the incompetent person and under what standard?

If a patient is temporarily or permanently incompetent, his consent will not be regarded as a defence to an action in battery. In these circumstances the doctor must either obtain a substitute or proxy consent by a person or body legally empowered to provide that consent or the doctor must have a justification, such as a medical emergency or other condition of necessity, for treating in the absence of consent.

Substitute consent for a minor

Legally effective substitute consent can be provided for an incompetent minor by a parent, a legal guardian, the local authority if a child is in care, anyone else with parental responsibility under the Children Act, or a court. The court has jurisdiction to make a minor a ward of court if it is in his best interests, and can order any beneficial treatment to be provided to the ward. Once a minor is a ward of court, no major treatment should be given without permission of the court.[5]

Sterilisation of a minor

Even if a parent consents, there are certain procedures which are so serious and controversial that the courts require judicial approval before they are administered to a minor. In *Re B (a minor) (Wardship: Sterilisation)*,[6] the House of Lords held that because of the seriousness of performing a non-therapeutic sterilisation on a severely mentally handicapped minor, the High Court's Family Division must give prior approval. The Law Lords reiterated the principle that the best interests of the minor is the paramount consideration in wardship proceedings. The prescribed procedure is designed to bring all relevant expert and other evidence before the court.[7]

In *Re B* the House of Lords said that sterilisation was the only reasonable course to prevent pregnancy in the ward's best interests. B was 17 years of age with limited intellectual development. She was found incapable of a long-term relationship or of rearing a child; of understanding the association between sexual intercourse and pregnancy; of understanding the need for contraception; and of making an informed choice about contraception and pregnancy. Paradoxically, she was found capable of reasonable hygiene in relation to menstruation and of understanding the link between pregnancy and a baby. It was unclear why she could not have received training and support to increase her understanding, enable her to take oral contraceptives, and enhance her ability to cope.

Reproduction is a fundamental human right which can be overridden only by an overwhelming case establishing that sterilisation is in the ward's best interests. Society, eugenics, public policy, and the convenience or anxiety of those who care for the ward are irrelevant considerations. Sterilisation, moreover, can be performed on a ward only as a last resort. Thus, if there are methods of contraception which can be achieved with less intrusion or permanency, they are preferable.[8]

Substitute consent for an incompetent adult

In England and Wales, neither statute nor common law provides a procedure for proxy consent to medical treatment on behalf of an incompetent adult. A large gap has been exposed in the law, as the two most likely alternatives – guardians under the Mental Health Act and the High Court – have both been found not to have the power to provide substitute consent.

Mental Health Act guardians

Two types of guardianship exist under the Mental Health Act 1983 – guardianship of the estate under Part VII (the Court of Protection) and guardianship of the person under section 8. The Court of Protection can make a broad range of financial decisions on behalf of those who are incapable of handling their property and affairs, including will-making and other disposals of property. The Court of Protection, however, has no power to consent to medical treatment on behalf of a patient under its jurisdiction. In *Re F (Mental patient: Sterilisation)* [9] Lord Brandon found that the expression 'property and affairs of patients' in Part VII of the 1983 Act does not include medical treatment. That expression should be construed as including only business, financial and legal matters.

Similarly, a personal guardian under section 8 of the Mental Health Act cannot compel a patient to receive treatment without his consent. A guardian can require the patient to live in a specified place; to attend a place for treatment, occupation, education or training; and to allow access by doctors or social workers. Although patients can be required to attend a place for the purpose of receiving medical treatment, they cannot actually be compelled to receive treatment without their consent. Guardianship patients have the same right to refuse treatment as any other patient. In Scotland, guardians appointed under the Mental Health (Scotland) Act 1984 have similarly restricted powers. But Scottish law does provide a mechanism for proxy treatment decisions which, although virtually obsolete, has been revived in recent years to plug the gap in the law. This is the power to petition the court for the appointment of a tutor-dative, who is entitled to manage both the personal welfare and the financial affairs of the incompetent adult.

Judicial approval

The House of Lords in *Re B* left open the question of whether the court has jurisdiction in the case of an incompetent *adult* to approve a medical procedure. The Law Lords returned to this subject in *Re F*, which concerned the sterilisation of a severely mentally handicapped 36-year-old woman. The House of Lords decided that there is no inherent jurisdiction to consent to a medical treatment for an incompetent adult. The court, however, could issue a declaration that the procedure, if carried out, would be lawful.

The House of Lords held that it was not strictly necessary (or even desirable) to obtain a court declaration before treating an incompetent patient. However, in a case involving a non-therapeutic operation, such as sterilisation, it was good practice to obtain a prior declaration that the operation would be lawful. Lord Brandon provided reasons why this was desirable for sterilisation: the procedure is irreversible, there is a risk of a wrong or improperly motivated decision, and a declaration protects the doctors from subsequent civil liability.

The United States,[10] Australia [11] and Canada have added stricter safeguards.[12] Courts in the United States and in Australia have held that sterilisation of a woman lacking the capacity to consent can be permitted only with the court's approval. The Canadian Supreme Court went further by ruling that non-therapeutic sterilisation without consent can never be lawful. In *Re Eve*,[13] Justice La Forest said:

'The grave intrusion on a person's rights and the certain physical damage that ensues from non-therapeutic sterilisation without consent, when compared with the highly questionable advantages that can result from it, have persuaded me that it can never safely be determined that such a procedure is for the benefit of that person. Accordingly, the procedure should never be authorised for non-therapeutic purposes under the *parens patriae* jurisdiction.'

Treatment in the absence of consent: standards for medical treatment under the doctrine of necessity

If no one is permitted to consent on behalf of incompetent adults, how is it possible to ensure that they receive beneficial treatment? In answering this question, it is helpful to distinguish between short-term and permanent incompetence. If the incompetence is transient – for example, from anaesthetic, sedation, intoxication or temporary unconsciousness – a doctor would not necessarily be justified in carrying out any procedure which he judged to be for the patient's benefit. The Canadian position would be likely to be adopted where necessary treatments are distinguished from those which are merely convenient; the former may be performed where the patient is temporarily unable to give consent, while the latter may not.[14] As a general principle, treatment which is given to a patient while temporarily incompetent should be the minimum amount necessary for health; any treatment which can reasonably be postponed until the patient regains competence should not be given.

A more troubling and important question arises as to how a patient can be treated (if at all) if he is permanently unable to understand the nature and purpose of the treatment. This is a major problem within the health services, for there are many patients in hospitals, nursing homes, residential care homes and the community who are incompetent and unable to give consent to medical treatment needed for their own well-bring – for example, patients who are severely mentally ill, severely mentally handicapped, or elderly and confused. Situations arise where highly vulnerable, isolated, and withdrawn patients require medical treatment to which they cannot give consent. Treatments needed may range from everyday care such as pain relief, antibiotics and dentistry to surgery for cataracts or cancers. The doctor's dilemma is that if he administers the treatment which he believes to be in the patient's best interests, he runs the risk of an action for trespass to the person; but if he withholds treatment he may be in breach of his duty of care to the patient.

A doctor will, in certain circumstances, be justified in providing treatment without consent. The legal ground upon which such a justification is normally based is the doctrine of necessity. Plainly, a life-saving medical procedure may be performed where a patient cannot consent – for instance where he is unconscious – and the treatment is necessary to sustain life or prevent a significant deterioration in health.

The House of Lords in *Re F* went considerably further in defining the range of circumstances in which doctors may treat adult patients without consent under the doctrine of necessity. Lord Bridge said it was 'axiomatic that treatment which is necessary to preserve the life, health or well-being of the patient may lawfully be given without consent'. A doctor in charge of the treatment of an incompetent patient may not only be authorised to administer treatment which is necessary, but may also be under a common law duty to do so.

If a rigid criterion of necessity were to be applied, patients might be deprived of beneficial treatment which was not strictly necessary. For this reason, the House of Lords adopted a 'best interests' test to determine the lawfulness of treating such patients. The Law Lords sought to place vulnerable incompetent patients in the same position as competent patients by ensuring that they receive all medical treatments deemed to be in their best interests. The treatment will be in the patient's best interests, said Lord Brandon, 'if, but only if, it is carried out in order to save their lives, or to ensure improvement or prevent deterioration in their physical or mental health'.

Lord Bridge stated that if doctors administered curative or preventive treatment which they believed appropriate for patients, the lawfulness of that treatment should be judged by a single standard. Under that standard (originally defined in the *Bolam* case [15] doctors would not be liable if they established that they acted in accordance with a practice accepted at the time by a responsible body of medical opinion skilled in the particular form of treatment.

The *Bolam* test was adopted by the House of Lords for the treatment of incompetent patients despite the fact that all three members of the Court of Appeal considered that it was insufficiently stringent for deciding whether medical treatment is in a patient's best interests. Lord Jauncey, while concurring with the use of the *Bolam* test, emphasised that the convenience of those caring for incompetent patients should never be a justification for treatment.

Critique of *Re F*

The House of Lords used loose and confusing terminology in setting a standard for deciding what medical treatment should be provided in the absence of consent. Throughout their opinions, several inconsistent standards were enunciated: necessity, absence of negligence (the *Bolam* test) and best interests. Although the Lords defined these terms almost interchangeably, they are, in plain English three quite different standards. Each standard would have very different results when applied to individual cases.

Necessity implies that the treatment is unavoidable, the doctor's actions being compelled by the patient's life-threatening or deteriorating condition and overriding need for medical intervention. Necessity suggests that the action must be taken urgently, immediately, and that there is insufficient time to go through a more careful process for discovering the patient's views or, at least, ensuring his best interests. Necessity, then, has traditionally been reserved for the most urgent or extreme cases.

The *absence of negligence* is almost the opposite of necessity, allowing treatment of any kind so long as the doctor follows a reasonable body of medical opinion. The absence of negligence represents the lowest standard of reasonable care, often far from the best. It is conduct which falls within the standards expected of a reasonably prudent doctor under the particular circumstances. A doctor is negligent not if he fails to provide the very best of care or even good care, but only if he provides such a low level of care that no reasonable doctor could be expected to act in such a way. 'Is it imaginable,' asks Carson, 'that any other group of people could have their *best* interests restated as simply the right not to have others make negligent decisions in relation to them?'[16]

The *best interests* rule truly searches for the optimal treatment and care of the incompetent person. 'Best' signifies the highest quality, of the greatest benefit to the person's health and well-being. The best interests rule is paternalistic in a positive sense, in that it ensures medical treatment and care which protects, nurtures, and improves the patient's physical and mental health.

The House of Lords, to be sure, was well intentioned in adopting the 'absence of negligence' standard. Concern that vulnerable incompetent patients should receive the same standard of medical care as any other patients led the Lords to make it as easy as possible for doctors to provide treatment for incompetent adults without fear of legal liability. This is a valid and humane concern. It helps to ensure that patients who are unable to request treatment to promote their own health and well being are not deprived of beneficial medical care.

'Best interests' *versus* 'substitute judgment'

Two traditional standards have been adopted for making decisions on behalf of incompetent patients – 'best interests' and 'substitute judgment'. The best interests standard, sometimes called the 'objective' test, asks the decision maker to choose the treatment that would be most beneficial to the patient. The substitute judgment standard, sometimes called the 'subjective' test, requires the decision maker to provide the treatment the *patient* would have chosen if competent.

The House of Lords in *Re F* purported to adopt the 'best interests' test for providing proxy consent. The best interests test remains the most appropriate standard for providing treatment for patients who are incompetent and have left no ascertainable views as to how they would wish to be treated. The classic application of the best interests test is on behalf of patients who have never been competent, such as those who have been severely mentally handicapped since birth. While some courts and commentators claim to use the 'substituted judgment' standard for the never competent, this is legal fiction. If the proxy decision maker has no basis upon which to determine the patient's real treatment preferences, the substitute judgment standard becomes impracticable. The substitute judgment standard, however, is preferable when applied to those who have expressed views about their treatment while competent. A decision to respect the views of a once competent patient is consistent with the ethical principle of autonomy and the legal principle of informed consent. A person, while competent, ought to be able to prescribe the limits of treatments he would, or would not, allow in the event that he becomes incompetent. Put another way, a person should not automatically lose the right to make judgments about his health and life once he becomes incompetent.

Treatment preferences can be expressed in several ways, ranging from more formal advance directives such as living wills or durable powers of attorney, to less formal expressions of wishes. The principle of controlling one's own destiny is so strong in the US that Congress enacted the Patients' Self-Determination Act in 1991. That Act requires most health care facilities to inform patients upon admission of their rights to make an advance directive and requires the facility to respect the patient's wishes. The substitute judgment standard forces the proxy decision maker to search for the patient's views, and to respect those views, before making tratment decisions.

Proposals for reform

The law needs urgent reform to meet the needs of mentally disabled patients. Both the Law Commission (for England and Wales) [17] and the Scottish Law Commission [18] produced discussion papers in 1991 canvassing options for change. The Law Commission's paper looks at the use of advance directives, extending enduring powers of attorney to cover treatment decisions, a statutory procedure for obtaining a substitute consent, reforming the existing guardianship framework to cover consent to medical treatment, and a more flexible guardianship scheme, based on a court or tribunal. The Scottish Law Commission suggests a new statutory personal guardianship, with the guardian's powers tailored to the mentally disabled adult's individual circumstances and capabilities. As an alternative, tutors-dative and guardians under the Mental Health Act could be retained, with the possibility for the guardian to apply for powers to take treatment and other welfare decisions.

The dilemma presented by incompetent patients is the need to protect them from treatment that is hazardous, controversial or unnecessasry, while ensuring that they receive the best possible treatment and care. This suggests two distinct roles for guardianship schemes – the protective role requiring safeguards and the enabling role requiring advocacy.

Protecting patients from unnecessary treatment: the need for safeguards

The standard of non-negligent treatment in *Re F* simply assumes that any treatment prescribed by a doctor, acting within the boundaries of his profession, is both needed and wanted by the patient. The *Bolam* test, moreover, effectively renders a single doctor the sole arbiter of the patient's interests. This leaves very little room for safeguards against treatment where the efficacy, safety, or morality is open to dispute. More important, it leaves incompetent patients without recourse if treatment is imposed over their expressed objections or their known preferences.

Many treatment decisions can safely and reliably be taken by doctors providing everyday care agreed upon by the multidisciplinary team, the family and, where possible, the patient. However, certain circumstances should call attention to the need for independent review or other safeguards: for example, if the patient, while competent, expressed views or had known value systems inconsistent with the proposed treatment; the patient, although currently incompetent, opposed the proposed treatment by words or behaviour, while competent; a close family member or other genuinely interested person opposes the proposed treatment; or the proposed treatment (or withdrawal of treatment) is unestablished, risky, invasive, irreversible, painful, life threatening, or controversial.

It may be that some procedures, such as sterilisation, are so controversial that they should require approval of the High Court before they are carried out. The Court of Appeal in *Re F* unanimously expressed the view that the court's review of sterilisation should not merely be a declaration of its lawfulness, but an approval of the operation. The court took this view because a declaration is not strong enough; it might be unopposed; and the public interest requires that the court give express approval to such a controversial procedure as sterilisation. While the House of Lords believed that a declaration had virtually the same effect as approval, it did emphasise the profound human rights implications of the procedure. If prior court sanction is, in practice, as important as the House of Lords properly believed, then the law should be altered to require this for sterilisation. This would put the mentally incompetent adult in the same position as a minor. There is, after all, little difference between sterilising a 17-year-old and sterilising a young adult.

Clearly, approval by the court is an inappropriate safeguard in all but the most serious cases. Court review is expensive, time-consuming and bueaucratic. Since *Re F* the High Court has held that court approval need not be sought for an abortion on a mentally handicapped adult, and that parental consent was sufficient for a therapeutic operation on a mentally handicapped minor which would incidentally render her sterile.[19] Enlightened safeguards of various descriptions could be adopted for most serious treatments. The structure of the safeguard provided is not important provided that it has certain hallmarks: the review body should be independent of the doctor or institution proposing the treatment; it should hear all sides of the issue including the medical, family and personal perspectives, if necessary through a patient advocate; it should respect the views and known preferences of patients; and it should observe a fair and open procedure while maintaining confidentiality. The review body should follow basic human rights principles ensuring respect for the patient.

Ensuring the best possible treatment for incompetent patients: advocacy

Currently, no affirmative duty is placed on doctors, social services departments or anyone else to ensure that incompetent patients receive the best possible treatment and care. To be sure, a doctor who fails to administer an effective antibiotic for pneumonia would be liable under the *Bolam* test. But the Law Lords' decision in *Re F* does little to ensure that the doctor positively reviews the needs of patients and provides a careful plan of treatment to improve their quality of life. Would a doctor be liable for failure to advocate a hip replacement, or an adequate diet, exercise, and nursing care for an incompetent patient? Doctors are so hard pressed that they are unlikely to have the time or inclination actively to seek out the best preventive measures and treatments for the wide range of their patients' health needs. Indeed, financial constraints may come into play – for example, a patient with schizophrenia or severe dementia may not be recommended for kidney dialysis. The standard of 'non-negligence' is hardly sufficient to ensure the patient's best interests in all these important respects.

The philosophy of the state as *parens patriae* signifies the importance of developing positive structures to ensure that the incompetent patient's needs are met. People who are incompetent cannot assess, plan and advocate for their medical and personal care. Accordingly, they require a positive guardian with a responsibility to ensure that there is a full and periodic assessment of their needs, that there is an individually tailored plan of treatment, as well as personal care and support, and that the necessary health and social services are provided for the patient. The guardian's role, then, should not be coercive or restrictive. Rather, it should be enabling, supportive and oriented toward vigorous advocacy for the patient's human rights and human needs. The advocate should work with health care, social services and other professionals to create an individual plan of treatment, care and support, and to ensure that the plan is carried out and continuously revised to meet the diverse needs of the vulnerable individual.

Conclusions

Decision making for incompetent patients is fraught with conflict and complexity. It is possible to err on the side of over-protection or under-protection. Any legal and ethical rules must apply to an enormous variety of circumstances posed by unique human beings. Ensuring the very best of health and well-being is a primary consideration. But nurturing the human spirit, and respecting the identity and dignity of the person, is equally important. Making decisions on behalf of incompetent patients, therefore, requires a deep respect for their human rights. Human rights principles include the duty to provide patients with the least intrusive and restrictive plan of treatment appropriate to their needs; to allow them to live as normal and integrated a life as possible; to allow them to make their own decisions with support and encouragement; and to allow them to take reasonable risks and to make reasonable mistakes in the same way as every other human being.

Notes

1 *Chatterton v Gerson* [1981] 1 All ER 257.
2 [1991] 4 All ER 177.
3 [1985] 3 All ER 402.
4 *Re B (Wardship: Abortion)* [1991] 2 FLR 426, *per* Hollis J (abortion is in ward's interests, despite objection of parent).
5 *Re G-U (a minor) (Wardship)* [1984] FLR 811.
6 [1988] AC 199, [1987] 2 All ER 206, [1987] 2 WLR 1213.
7 See *Re D (a minor)* [1976] 1 All ER 326, *per* Heilbron J.
8 Practice Note Concerning Applications to the High Court for Sterilisation [1990] 2 FLR 530.
9 [1990] 2 AC 1.
10 See *In Re Grady* (1981) 426 A2d 467.
11 See *In Re Jane* 85 ALR 409, 22 December 1988.
12 See L. Gostin 'Consent to Involuntary and Non-Medically Indicated Sterilisation of Mentally Retarded Adults and Children' (1979) 29 Mental Retardation 10.

13   (1987) 31 DLR (4th) 1.
14   Judicial authority is from a line of Canadian cases: *Marshall v Curry* [1933] 3 DLR
      260; *Murray v McMurchy* [1949] 2 DLR 442; *Parmley v Parmley and Yule* [1945]
      4 DLR 81; *Mulloy v Hop Sang* [1935] 1 WWR 714.
15   *Bolam v Friern Hospital Management Committee* [1957] 2 All ER 118, approved
      in *Sidaway v Governors of Bethlem Royal Hospital* [1985] 1 All ER 643.
16   D. Carson 'The Sexuality of People with Learning Difficulties' (1989) 355 JSWL
      372.
17   The Law Commission *Mentally Incapacitated Adults and Decision-Making: an
      Overview*, Consultation paper no.119 (1991).
18   Scottish Law Commission *Mentally Disabled Adults: Legal Arrangements for
      Managing their Welfare and Finances*, Discussion paper no.94 (1991).
19   *In Re G* (1991) The Times, 31 January; *In Re E (a minor)* (1991) The Times, 22
      February.

Chapter 5

Reproductive Medicine

For many years the law has played a part in regulating human reproduction. Over time that role has expanded considerably, particularly in recent years in response to technological change. This chapter will seek to explain and clarify the relationship between law and practice in this high-profile and sometimes contentious area. Human reproduction is, in part, regulated by law because it is seen as more than a merely private matter. Everyone is affected by population size, the moral tone of communities may be influenced by the law's response to abortion, and the capacity to circumvent infertility and the techniques available to do so raise profound ethical and legal questions not just for those seeking access to them, but for all of us.

Infertility

Introducing the Human Fertilisation and Embryology Bill in the House of Lords, Lord Houghton described it as 'a turning point in medical research and in the destiny of mankind'. This Bill, now the Human Fertilisation and Embryology Act 1990, seeks to control and regulate the so-called reproductive revolution. Of course this 'revolution' has been quietly going on for some time. Although it is probably true to say that the public's imagination was first captured by new techniques and technologies in 1978 with the birth of Louise Brown, the world's first 'test-tube baby', for many years leading up to that time doctors and scientists had been quietly making progress in the circumvention of infertility.

The background

It is widely said that infertility affects about 10–15 per cent of the population, and we are all aware of the distress that can be caused to individuals or couples who are incapable of procreation. Although a number of commentators have questioned the wisdom of investing so substantially in infertility treatments,[1] there can be no doubt that for many the incapacity to breed is a profoundly distressing condition. Whatever one's views on investment in reproductive technologies, there seems to be wide agreement that increased efforts should be made to trace and prevent the causes of infertility. What is interesting is that without the technologies themselves it is unlikely that the causes of infertility would be so clearly known. In other words, the techniques which are designed to circumvent infertility may also point in no small measure towards information which in the future could render these services obsolete for a number of people. For this reason, the technologies themselves cannot be entirely isolated from the concept of prevention, although, at the moment, their main aim is circumvention. This is also important, since unlike many medical treatments, these technologies are not designed to cure, or rather are not capable of curing, but are designed to palliate.

There is no doubt that the 1990 Act is a major and complex piece of legislation. In tackling the sensitive ethical, legal and social problems surrounding infertility and its treatment Parliament set itself an extremely difficult, time-consuming and occasionally highly charged task. The legislation, which was the culmination of many years of debate, followed on, but did not entirely follow, the recommendations of the Warnock Report on Human Fertilisation and Embryology.[2] Its most significant contribution is the creation of the Human Fertilisation and Embryology Authority which will regulate and license the provision of reproductive services throughout the UK. This authority will have power over private or public institutions which seek to offer such services, will have the authority to scrutinise and license, or remove licences, based, for example, on success rate or on the level of facilities available, and will issue clinicians and scientists with guidelines as to their professional conduct. One of the more interesting tasks for the future will be to follow the work of the authority and to assess its impact on access to, and provision of, services.

Artificial insemination

Artificial insemination was the first of the techniques developed to circumvent infertility. Whether artificial insemination is carried out using the semen of the husband (AIH) or the semen of a donor (AID), its value lies in raising the possibility of conception in situations where the woman is not infertile but her partner is either sub-fertile or infertile. Little controversy has ever surrounded the question of artificial insemination using a partner's semen. Although initially some did perceive moral problems in any intervention into the 'normal' methods of procreation, the fact that it represented no threat to the family meant that this concern has largely died away. However, considerable debate raged over the use of donor semen for artificial insemination.[3]

There were, and in some situations still are, three main strands of concern about AID. The first related to the question of whether or not the use of donor semen technically amounted to adultery. The question posed to the law was: does adultery require a physical act of intercourse, or is it sufficient that the reproductive organs of the woman are exposed to the semen of a man who is not her husband? Courts in a number of countries reached varying conclusions on this question, although in the British courts in the case of *MacLennan v MacLennan* [4] what seems to be the common sense approach prevailed. In this case it was held that adultery required the act of intercourse between two people one or both of whom were married to another person at the time that the intercourse took place. Given this approach, the transfer of semen could not amount to adultery, and indeed any other conclusion would have had some bizarre consequences. Since the person who actually introduces the semen to the woman's body would be a doctor rather than the donor, if this *was* to amount to adultery, then technically it might be the doctor who was guilty of adultery – a result which would have been manifest nonsense.

A much more complex question, however, and one which required to be addressed with care, related to the status of any child born as a result of artificial insemination using donor semen. According to the rules of marriage, any child born in this way, even to a couple who were married at the time of the insemination, would necessarily be illegitimate. Although the stigma attached to illegitimacy, at least in terms of succession rights, has been gradually eroded over the years, it remains the case that many families would find a situation in which a much wanted child was illegitimate for legal purposes unacceptable and distressing. It was therefore necessary for the law to address itself to this particular question, which it did in part before the 1990 Act, and much more comprehensively in the Act.

The question of the status of the child is, of course, of considerable interest to the 'parents' and to the child, but it must also be a matter of some concern for the donor of semen. If the child is illegitimate, then it is the illegitimate child of the mother and the donor. The mother, of course, both has – and in these circumstances clearly wants – obligations towards the child. The donor, on the other hand, might also have, but certainly does *not* want, such obligations. Were the law to insist on these legal obligations on the donor, it is more than likely that donors would be deterred from coming forward, thus jeopardising the entire programme.

Equally, from the point of view of the intending parents, it is more than likely that their intention, where the insemination was agreed to by both parties, was to raise the child as their own and to absorb all parental rights and duties. This would not be possible under the common law for the male partner, who would have no legal rights over the child that he was rearing and maintaining. The consequences of legal uncertainty probably included the false registration of the child's birth in an unknowable number of cases. In other words, the woman and her partner might have indicated to the Registrar of Births, Deaths and Marriages that the child was conceived in the usual manner, rather than admitting that the child was conceived by the donation of semen from a stranger. For many, putting families into a situation of feeling tempted to breach the law was an unacceptable aspect of the law's position on the status of AID children. Not only did it subject the family to additional stress, but where they were unwilling to break the law in this way their status as a family was compromised by the need to register the child as illegitimate. The Family Law Reform Act of 1987, which covers England and Wales but not Scotland, in section 27 directly dealt with the position of AID children. Any lingering doubts about status, however, have been clarified by the Human Fertilisation and Embryology Act 1990, predominantly in sections 27 to 30. The Warnock Committee recommended that, where the male partner of a couple had consented to AID the child should be treated as the legitimate child of the couple. Moreover, the committee wanted the law to create a presumption that consent had been given, which would be defeated only by evidence that it had not been given. Effectively, this is what section 28 of the legislation achieves. Where a woman is married, and a donation of egg or sperm is made, in all bar a few exceptions her husband is to be treated as the father of the child unless it can be shown that he did not consent to the insemination or other technique. This section also provides for the case where treatment services have been made available to an unmarried couple. In these circumstances, where the male partner is not the donor of the semen, with limited exceptions he will be treated as the father of the child.

A third problem which has dogged AID – and indeed all of the reproductive technologies which involve the use of donated gametes – has been the question of access to identifying information. This debate is going on worldwide, with countries adopting different rules about the identification of donors, and much concern expressed about the impact on donations of the availability of identifying information. Donation of semen has, particularly in countries where no payment is made, often been confined to certain groups – for example, medical students and the husbands of obstetric patients. For many men, the lingering fear was that they might be 'discovered' by children created by their donation. For this reason, it is traditional in the UK for absolute anonymity and secrecy to surround the identity of semen donors. This anonymity is said to be vital to the continued donation of semen. Remove it, and – some argue – no-one will volunteer to participate. The counter argument to this is that individuals have a right, and in some cases may have a need, to have access to information which identifies their genetic inheritance or their biological parentage. There are therefore two distinct interests at stake here.

First is the interest of donors in remaining anonymous, a concern which might be thought to continue even though the legislation is intended to absolve them of any legal responsibilities towards a child born as a result of their donation. It is argued by some that if donors could be identified this would lead to a serious reduction in numbers. Certainly in Sweden when anonymity was abolished there was an initial decline in the number of donors who came forward, and apparently also a decline in the number of couples who sought artificial insemination by donor. However, subsequently the numbers of donors have returned to pre-existing levels and the system seems to be working well.

The second concern relates to the 'need' of children to know their genetic or biological inheritance. While some may argue that this is merely a culturally determined need [5] and that we should not take it too seriously, there can be little doubt that for some people the desire to identify their genetic parentage can be strong. The UK appears to have conceded this point already by making available identifying information to adopted children who, on reaching the age of majority, wish to look for their natural parents. Arguably, children born as a result of donated gametes should not be treated any differently. Indeed, in some cases, it may be that a child or young adult has a genuine need to know his or her genetic inheritance in case of the transmission of any hereditary disease.

Section 31 of the 1990 Act provides that the Human Fertilisation and Embryology Authority must keep a record of information given to it by clinics which are offering treatment services within the Act. On reaching the age of 18, which is the same age as in adoption cases in England and Wales, an applicant can ask the authority to furnish certain information. After suitable counselling about the impact of receiving the information, the authority is required by law to provide it. However, for the moment, it is not intended that this information should be identifying – rather it should be information which provides the requisite details of genetic inheritance, without leading the young person towards a specific individual. At present, then, information which could lead to the identification of the donor will be maintained in secrecy, although the position is to be kept under review.

In vitro fertilisation

In vitro fertilisation (IVF) has proved to be one of the more controversial techniques of the reproductive revolution. There are a number of reasons for this, some of which have been directly addressed by the legislation and some of which have been left to practitioners and the regulatory authorities. One of the more immediate problems of IVF is that it involves the creation of an embryo *extra utero*. Given that doctors' practices had been to fertilise as many eggs as possible from any one cycle, this led to the inevitable consequence that a number of embryos would not be re-implanted. The question then arose as to what, if anything, was to be done with the 'spare' embryos? One obvious possibility was that they might be used in research, the possible benefits of which are said by many clinicians to outweigh any moral problems consequent on their use in this way. Against the background of a highly charged debate both in public and in Parliament, members of the House of Commons were allowed a free vote on the question of embryo research. The conclusion of that debate was that for certain agreed purposes, for example promoting advances in the treatment of infertility, research may be carried out on the human embryo up to a maximum of 14 days after fertilisation. Embryo research is supervised by the Human Fertilisation and Embryology Authority, whose guidelines must be followed by any centre seeking or holding a licence.

In addition, there were difficulties over storage of the human embryo. Those used as part of research projects are subsequently destroyed. Those which are not implanted in a woman and not the subject of research must obviously be dealt with in some way. The legislation provides that a storage licence can be granted for a period up to a maximum of five years and permits the freezing and storage of gametes for ten years and embryos for five years, after which they must be allowed to perish. However, storage requires the consent either of the person whose gametes they are, or of the people whose gametes were used to create the embryo or the woman from whom the embryo was obtained. While the straightforward question seems to have been resolved – what does one do with embryos which are not immediately implanted – there remain consequential problems which have taxed the minds of legislators throughout the world, for example the extent to which anyone has rights over the embryos, what may subsequently be done with them and what will happen to them should those whose gametes were used to create them predecease a decision about what happens next to the embryo.

It is widely accepted that the human body is not the subject of property rights, although in some countries it is possible, for example, to sell blood and payment may be made for the donation of semen. There is, however, for most people a significant difference between products such as blood and the embryo of the human species. Although the question of property rights remains to an extent unresolved, schedule 3 of the 1990 legislation does seem to indicate that those who provide gametes for the creation of an embryo *in vitro* have powers to refuse their consent to any proposed use of those gametes or the resulting embryo. In other words, although property rights may not exist, it is clear that some rights are extended to those who have contributed to the creation of the embryo. Moreover, again in schedule 3, any embryo which is obtained from a woman by lavage cannot be used for any purpose unless she has given her consent. Equally, the legislation provides that gametes must not be stored unless those who provided them consent to their storage and the embryo or gametes must be stored in accordance with the consent given. Decisions, therefore, about the disposal of embryos which are not to be used for implantation in the immediate future rest fundamentally with those who provided the genetic make-up of the embryo or who provided the unfertilised gametes. The Human Fertilisation and Embryology Authority will also control any financial arrangements which are to be made for the supply of gametes or embryos. Payment may be authorised where the authority thinks it appropriate that certain expenses are met, but it is thought that this will extend only to reimbursing donors for any necessary expenses incurred in making the donation.

Surrogacy

There can be few areas of assisted human reproduction which have generated so much concern, even condemnation, as surrogacy. It should be said at the outset that surrogacy is by no means necessarily a medical event. Since it entails the carrying to term of a child by one woman, with the intention of handing that child over to another woman, and perhaps her partner, then obviously surrogacy is something which may well have been going on over the years without any need for medical intervention. A woman may choose to become pregnant as a result of intercourse with the intention of handing over the child to someone else in what is a perfectly clear case of a surrogacy agreement. Indeed, the question of surrogacy was one which was relatively undiscussed until the media picked up the case of Kim Cotton.[6]

Mrs Cotton accepted payment from an American surrogacy agency to give birth on behalf of another couple to a child who was to be brought up by them as their own. The sperm donor was the husband of the commissioning couple. She fulfilled the terms of her agreement, was duly provided with the agreed fee and a court authorised the removal of the child from her to the 'parents' in the US. Nonetheless, the publicity surrounding the case led to an early, and some would say ill thought-out, piece of legislation to outlaw commercial surrogacy. The Surrogacy Arrangements Act of 1985, while stopping short of criminalising the parties to the surrogacy arrangement, nonetheless outlawed the intervention of commercial agencies in such arrangements. Commentators have noted the limitations of this particular piece of legislation and the initial confusion surrounding who might be lawfully held accountable where such agreements were entered into.[7] For example, the legislation did not preclude couples and surrogate mothers entering into agreements for a fee, although commentators suggested it might have made it difficult for them to obtain legal and medical advice.

Clearly, some of the problems stemming from surrogacy arrangements are shared with AID. The pregnancy may be brought about by artificial insemination with semen from the husband of the commissioning couple (partial surrogacy), or by using sperm and eggs from the commissioning couple or an embryo created from their gametes (full surrogacy). Inevitably, questions would be raised about who counts as the child's parents. These questions are resolved in the Human Fertilisation and Embryology Act. Under section 27, the surrogate mother will be the treated as the child's mother even in a case of full surrogacy or 'womb leasing', where both egg and sperm come from the commissioning couple. If she is married, section 28 provides that her husband will be treated as the child's father provided he consented to the surrogacy. To become the child's legal parents, the commissioning couple will have to adopt him or her or use the new procedure introduced by section 30 of the Act. This provides that a commissioning couple may petition the court to have a child born by surrogacy declared their child. They must apply for the order within six months of the birth or, where the child was born before the Act came into force, within six months of its coming into force. This provision, which was designed to secure the status of the child within the family, has led to some initial controversy. Since the legislation came into force in sections, not all of which become effective on the same date, there is some doubt about the date from which this six months will run. Unless this is resolved on a common sense basis, with the aims of the section very much in mind, some families may be unable to use the provision to have the child declared theirs. It is to be hoped that decisions will be taken on the basis of the underlying intention of the legislation.

Surrogacy raises an additional question: whether the agreement is enforceable. The Warnock Committee was extremely hostile to the entire notion of surrogacy, and its conclusion was that surrogacy should be outlawed, or at least that surrogacy arrangements should be declared not to be enforceable at law. Although the 1990 legislation clearly countenances the possibility of surrogacy arrangements, it provides in section 36, amending the Surrogacy Arrangements Act of 1985, that no surrogacy arrangement is to be enforceable by or against any of the persons making it. Surrogacy agreements will continue to require goodwill on both sides, and litigation is likely to arise should any party to such an agreement renege or seek to renege on the agreement. Such problems have already arisen in the US and in the UK.

If the surrogate mother decides against fulfilling her agreement with the commissioning couple, whether or not a fee is entailed, it is likely that the courts will become involved in the ultimate decision about who, if anyone, has rights. The provision in the 1990 Act that the woman giving birth is the mother for legal purposes will help to minimise the difficulties involved in deciding who has these rights. However, where challenge is made, the most important factor for the courts will be the best interests of the child. In the American case of Baby M, the court decided it was in the child's best interests to stay with the commissioning parents who had had custody of her for 18 months and who, the court felt, could provide her with a more secure home.[8] In an English case, *Re P (Minors)*, custody of five-month-old twins was given to their natural mother, with whom they had bonded.[9]

What is the legal liability of a doctor who participates in a surrogacy arrangement? The Act was designed to outlaw commercial agencies, but anyone who takes part in a surrogacy arrangement 'on a commercial basis' or who advertises with a view to making such an arrangement commits a criminal offence. This might cover a doctor who found a surrogate mother for a commissioning couple as part of an infertility service which charges its patients. But, arguably, helping to establish a pregnancy where the couple itself has found the surrogate would not be an offence.

Abortion

The question of whether or not a woman may choose to terminate a pregnancy is one which has provoked considerable controversy over many years. For some the fact that a potential life has been created by fertilisation and implantation is sufficient to require that that potential must be realised, at almost any cost to the woman. For others at the other end of the spectrum, a woman has an absolute right to control her own body and may choose to discontinue a pregnancy. This, of course, is an extremely simplistic statement of the extreme positions held on both sides of the abortion debate. The complexities and shades of grey in between are many and varied. However, not only has debate raged on the ethical aspects but the interpretation of the law on abortion has also generated considerable controversy.

It is worth noting that despite the existence of the 1967 Abortion Act, the law has not been the same in all UK jurisdictions and to a limited extent this remains the case. Neither the 1967 Act nor the amendments to it in the 1990 Human Fertilisation and Embryology Act apply to Northern Ireland. The 1967 Act, incorporating as it did previous English legislation, applies to England and Wales, but only in part to Scotland. The pattern, therefore, in the UK before the 1990 legislation can briefly be described as follows.

Abortion remained a criminal offence, but the 1967 legislation provided a limited number of defences to the doctor carrying out a pregnancy termination. In Northern Ireland, however, none of these defences was applicable, and abortion therefore remained a criminal offence in virtually all circumstances. In England and Wales, since the terms of the Infant Life (Preservation) Act of 1929 applied, there was a *prima facie* presumption that abortion could be legal, assuming that it was carried out within the terms of any of the specified defences, up to the point at which the child was 'capable of being born alive'. Considerable medical, legal and ethical debate has taken place as to the meaning of the phrase 'capable of being born alive'.

The Act laid down a presumption that a fetus of 28 weeks' gestation was capable of being born alive. This did not mean, however, that a fetus of shorter gestation – say, 24 weeks – was not considered viable, although 28 weeks was widely taken as a notional upper limit for abortions. In 1987 the courts were called on to define the phrase 'capable of being born alive'. In the Court of Appeal, Lord Donaldson, Master of the Rolls, defined viability as the point when a child could breathe either naturally or with the aid of a ventilator. This would put it at about 24 weeks.[10] In England and Wales, pregnancy terminations have been carried out beyond 24 weeks in only a handful of cases each year. In Scotland the 1929 legislation did not apply and, technically, therefore, there was no time limit on abortions carried out under the 1967 Act. However, for practical purposes, doctors in Scotland tended to operate on precisely the same criteria, and with the same time limits in mind, as their colleagues in England and Wales.

The fact that the 1990 Act gave the Human Fertilisation and Embryology Authority responsibility for the human embryo, both at the stage of its creation and throughout its development, permitted anti-abortion lobbyists to use the Bill as a vehicle for proposing amendments to the 1967 legislation. The aim of the amendments was quite clearly, and very directly, to reduce the time up to which a pregnancy could be terminated. Although some were prepared to concede that abortions might be lawfully carried out in some circumstances, and despite the evidence that very few pregnancies were terminated beyond 24 weeks,[11] the campaigners considered it desirable that abortions should be further restricted. Certainly, with advances in medical care the concept of viability is a changing one. If access to pregnancy termination were to hinge on whether or not a child could be mechanically sustained outside the mother's womb, clearly the time at which this was possible would reduce as medical science progressed. For some, of course, this remains a secondary rather than the primary question. In any event, the Bill was seen by the anti-abortion lobby as an ideal opportunity to test the mood of Parliament as to when, and in what circumstances, pregnancies could lawfully be terminated.

In a result which surprised many, the 1990 legislation, far from placing restrictions on the already limited availability of abortion in the UK, effectively created new grounds on which pregnancies may be terminated and in some situations extended rather than restricted the period of time within which abortions may be carried out. Pregnancies may now be terminated if this is necessary to prevent 'grave permanent injury' to a pregnant woman's physical or mental health. Additionally the pregnancy may be lawfully terminated where the continuance of the pregnancy would involve 'risk to the life of the pregnant woman, greater than if the pregnancy were terminated', and thirdly where there is a substantial risk that if the child were born it would suffer from 'such physical or mental abnormalities as to be seriously handicapped'. This last provision already existed under the 1967 legislation, but the crucial difference is that in each of these situations pregnancies may be terminated at *any* stage in the course of the pregnancy. A fourth ground, that the continuance of the pregnancy would involve a risk, greater than if the pregnancy were terminated, of injury to the physical or mental health of the pregnant woman or any existing children of her family has been carried over from the 1967 Act, but given a 24-week time limit. Section 1(4) of the 1967 Act, which provides that a pregnancy may be terminated where a single doctor decides it is immediately necessary to save the life or to prevent grave permanent injury to the physical or mental health of the pregnant woman, is unchanged. This would cover cases of immediate threat to life, such as eclampsia or placenta praevia.

The legislation for the first time also recognises a difficulty associated with reproductive technologies – the creation, by the re-implantation of a number of embryos or by the use of fertility drugs, of multiple pregnancies. The evidence is absolutely clear that multiple pregnancies carry more risks for the embryos or fetuses and also, of course, for the woman carrying them. Yet the creation of multiple pregnancies is one of the apparently inevitable consequences of the technologies as currently applied. The Interim Licensing Authority, now replaced by the Human Fertilisation and Embryology Authority, had, when it oversaw the provision of infertility services, issued guidelines as to the number of embryos which should be implanted at any one time, precisely because of the risks associated with the creation of a multiple pregnancy. At the same time, the practice developed of 'selective reduction of pregnancy'. This entails the destruction, whether or not including expulsion from the womb, of one or more of the implanted embryos. Leaving aside the legal debate over whether or not the consequence of this is a miscarriage or an abortion, the 1990 legislation, in recognition of the risks attached to multiple pregnancies, specifically permits the selective reduction of embryos where any of the grounds for pregnancy termination contained in the Act can be met.

In the UK, except in emergencies, the law still provides no rights to terminate a pregnancy beyond those which are given to two doctors acting in good faith certifying that the terms of the law are met. However often commentators may suggest that UK law is very liberal, it is notable for its failure to address the question of rights. Not only does a woman have no right to terminate a pregnancy – unlike the situation in the United States (although this is changing) [12] or in some European countries – but the way the legislation is formulated, coupled with the pragmatics of the situation, means that no one else has rights either. For those who oppose abortion, for example, there is an inherent paradox in the caution with which the law regulates the treatment of an embryo *extra utero* up to the stage of 14 days of development, while at the same time permitting the termination of embryos and fetuses which are *in utero* up to 24 weeks in some cases and up to term in others. For those who may be described as pro-choice, the need to obtain medical endorsement for a woman's decision to choose whether or not to continue with the pregnancy is in itself profoundly invasive of women's rights and for others the absence of any serious attempt to address any rights that the father of the embryo or fetus might have is seen as a failure of the legislation. There are, of course, reasons why fathers' rights may be difficult to assert, in particular that the woman has the right to consent to or refuse any invasion of her body under the general law independently of the question of pregnancy termination – but nonetheless cases have been raised in which fathers have attempted to assert rights in these circumstances. Most notably in the case of *Paton v Trustees of the British Pregnancy Advisory Service*, which ultimately reached the European Court of Human Rights, it was made clear that fathers have no right to a say in abortion decisions precisely on the grounds that it is for the woman to decide what can and cannot be done with her own body, subject of course to abortion legislation.[13] This was later reinforced in the case of *C v S*, in which the father of an illegitimate child failed to prevent his girlfriend from terminating her pregnancy, although, in the event, she ultimately chose not to and agreed that the child should be reared by its father.[14]

Maternal/fetal rights

Finally it is worth addressing the question of what impact reproductive technologies have on our attitude to the women who may bear children and to the embryos or fetuses which they may carry. Access to the technologies is by no means guaranteed, nor it would appear is it something which women can claim as a right. Thus, for example, controversy raged around the admission by the British Pregnancy Advisory Service that it had artificially inseminated a number of single women. In Western Australia, the Bill which will ultimately control the provision of reproductive services limits access to those who are married or who have been living together as a heterosexual couple for five years or more, thus not only overtly preferring married (or 'stable') relationships (thereby excluding single women) but also excluding gay men and lesbians. This sets assisted reproductive services apart from other medical services which are provided irrespective of marital status or sexual orientation. It is also worth noting that the trend in adoption services is away from such blanket presumptions about fitness for parenting. The UK legislation does not specifically outlaw access to single women or lesbian couples, although the 1990 Act states that account must be taken of the resulting child's welfare, including its need for a father. But given past practice it is unlikely that they will be considered by most clinics as suitable recipients of these services.[15]

Equally, and this has already arisen in the UK, other decisions about lifestyle may affect the availability of services. For example, in the case of *R v St Mary's Hospital Ethics Committee ex parte Harriott* [16] a woman was removed from an IVF programme because she was an ex-prostitute and had been turned down as a prospective parent. Her application for judicial review was unsuccessful on the grounds that such a decision would be quashed only if the ethics committee had acted unlawfully, and this was clearly not so. For some, however, it may be seen as an unhappy circumstance that 'fitness for parenting' decisions are being made in this way and are not subject to judicial review. For others, it may seem entirely right that such judgments are made. The question as to whether or not this approach is morally or ethically sound cannot be entertained in any great depth here, but it is worthy of note since it may be seen as a form of discrimination, counter to the recommendations of the European Office of the World Health Organisation in 1990 that IVF should not be refused on the basis of characteristics which have no relevance to the services sought. The counter argument would be that children have the right to be born into the best possible circumstances, and that these individuals would not provide the best possible circumstances. Leaving aside the fact that we do not test those who are capable of reproducing naturally for fitness for parenting, it also remains the case that we have no information which directly indicates that children would suffer were they born in these circumstances. What is crucial undoubtedly is that the welfare of any resulting child is borne firmly in mind when making decisions about the technologies themselves and that we, as in all areas of medicine, allocate resources on a compassionate, consistent and fair basis.

What is fascinating about the 1990 legislation is that (perhaps paradoxically) beyond the section dealing with pregnancy termination the interests of the child are well represented while the interests of women – or indeed men – are seldom addressed. Many women undergoing these new technologies will not themselves be infertile, and yet may be subjected to considerable risk, and certainly discomfort, when the technologies are applied. Since by and large the 'reproductive revolution' has concentrated on the female of the partnership, women who are capable of breeding, but whose partners are not, will still be the group who undergo the relevant treatment with all its attendant risks. Of course, this is a choice made by individuals themselves, but nonetheless the legislation could have addressed the question of the protection of women in more depth and with more commitment. This, for example, could have been done by broadening the scope of the legislation, through the powers of the Human Fertilisation and Embryology Authority to consider such tangential matters as, for example, the financial and other interests of commerce and industry in the provision of these services. The vast majority of those seeking infertility services are required to pay for them, and pharmaceutical companies are involved in the provision of the necessary drugs and in the financing of meetings and conferences which publicise the benefits of these technologies. The World Health Organisation's European Office 1990 report on the place of *in vitro* fertilization in infertility care states: 'The role of industry and commercial interests in IVF should be documented, including industry's role in funding IVF research and its involvement in service provision. This information should be available to the public.'

A shift in attitude in recent years towards the rights of the fetus may also directly and seriously affect women. The capacity, or the desire, to attribute rights or potential rights to embryos and fetuses has, particularly in the US, led to the creation of a direct conflict between a woman and her embryo or fetus. The prosecution of Pamela Rae Stewart, the incarceration of some pregnant young women to ensure proper antenatal care and the enforced Caesarean sections carried out on other women in the US were a result of giving embryonic or fetal 'life' priority over the wishes or rights of the mother.[17]

The case of Pamela Rae Stewart is of particular interest since it raised considerable public concern and debate. She was arrested in 1987 and charged with causing the death of her baby (who died at 6 weeks old) by drug abuse and failure to adhere to medical advice during pregnancy. She was subsequently acquitted on the ground that the law did not offer protection to unborn fetuses and that the state's interest in the matter did not outweigh the pregnant woman's right to privacy. Following her acquittal at least one California senator attempted to modify the state's child welfare legislation to deal with unborn children, an attempt which has not yet been successful.

In the UK, the parallel case was the failed attempt to make a fetus a ward of court in order to ensure that the pregnant woman's behaviour could be modified or predicted.[18] In this case, the woman was well known to the local social services department, had a history of severe mental disturbance and drug abuse and her first child was in care. The local authority sought to make the fetus a ward of court in order to force the woman to have her baby in hospital, but the Court of Appeal unanimously held that an unborn child could not be made a ward of court. Undoubtedly, the interests of women and the embryo or fetus which they are carrying have in some cases been in conflict since time immemorial, but it seems plausible to suggest that the publicity surrounding assisted reproduction coupled with the nature of some of the techniques have combined to push this conflict into the limelight. If this is so, we should take serious stock of the consequences which may follow. The fact that the pattern already emerging in the US is tangential, rather than central, to the practice of assisted reproduction, should not blind us to its potential as a weapon to be used against women nor to its consequences for human reproduction as a whole.

Conclusions

The UK response to the reproductive revolution is impressive in its scope, and on occasion detailed in its content, but it by no means answers or even addresses all the problems which might arise. Indeed, it may well be that no piece of legislation could do this, and for this reason the Human Fertilisation and Embryology Authority will over the years take on increasing importance, as medicine and science progress and as society becomes more aware of and involved in the moral and ethical problems which inevitably arise in the application of these technologies. As Morgan and Lee point out: 'That the Human Fertilisation and Embryology Act is incomplete does not mean that it is unwelcome. But it will not be the last word on the subject.'[19] Equally, the private behaviour of individuals in their reproductive practices, even if not covered by legislation, is under increasing scrutiny. Since no right of privacy exists *per se* in the UK, those who wish to resist such intrusion into personal decisions will have a hard furrow to plough. The medicalisation of pregnancy and childbirth, while undoubtedly offering benefits, may also have drawbacks in terms of individual liberty. The intervention of the law has concentrated on certain aspects of this and has not addressed others, leaving a somewhat piecemeal coverage of the issues raised by human reproduction. Whether this is a good or a bad thing remains to be seen.

Notes

1   G. Corea *The Mother Machine* (1988); R. Klein *Infertility* (1989); M.G. Wagner and P.A. St. Clair 'Are *In Vitro* Fertilisation and Embryo Transfer of Benefit to All?' (1989) Lancet, 1027.

2   M. Warnock (chairman) (1984) Report of the Committee of Inquiry into Human Fertilisation and Embryology (Cmnd. 9314).

3   For discussion see D. Cusine *New Reproductive Techniques: A Legal Perspective* (1988).

4   1958 SC 105.

5   See K. O'Donovan 'What Shall We Tell The Children?' in R. Lee and D. Morgan (eds), *Birthrights: Law and Ethics at the Beginnings of Life* (1989).

6   For her own description, see K. Cotton and D. Winn *Baby Cotton: for Love and Money* (1985).

7   See Cusine *op. cit.*; M.D.A. Freeman Commentary in *Current Law Statutes Annotated* (1986).

8   537 A 2d 1227 (1988).

9   *A v C* [1985] FLR 445.

10   *C v S* [1988] QB 135; [1987] 1 All ER 1230.

11   For discussion see D. Morgan and R. Lee *Human Fertilisation and Embryology Act 1990* (1991), chapter 2.

12   See *Webster v Reproductive Health Services* 109 S Ct 3040 (1989).

13 [1979] QB 276.
14 [1988] QB 135; [1987] 1 All ER 1230.
15 For discussion see Morgan and Lee *op.cit.*, especially chapter 5.
16 [1988] 1 FLR 512.
17 For discussion see S.A.M. McLean 'Women, Rights and Reproduction' in S.A.M. McLean (ed) *Legal Issues in Human Reproduction* (1989).
18 *Re F (in utero)* [1988] 2 All ER 193.
19 Morgan and Lee *op.cit.*, at p. 32.

Chapter 6

Ending Life

What is wrong with taking human life? The mere posing of this question can be calculated to draw a strong response. If killing is not wrong, then what is there left of morality? Very little, it would seem: to take the life of another is to deprive that person of everything, and killing therefore quite outshadows the other forms of wrong which can be perpetrated against others. Yet should the prohibition against the taking of life be an absolute one, or are there circumstances in which killing another person is morally and legally permissible?

Over the past few decades a number of philosophers concerned with medical ethics have found it increasingly difficult to justify the blanket exclusion of taking life. Harris, in his influential work on medical ethics, *The Value of Life*,[1] talks of killing as being a 'caring thing to do' (at least in some cases). Tooley, whose work on abortion and infanticide has caused considerable controversy, takes matters further and argues that a right of life is not inevitably a concomitant of being a human being, and that it does not necessarily extend to newly born infants.[2] Such a position is extreme, and distinctly a minority one, but it is significant nonetheless that influential voices in moral philosophy are questioning the ethic which strictly forbids any taking of human life. This has gone hand in hand with the increasingly important central role being given to the principle of autonomy. If respect for autonomy requires that we allow people as far as possible to make their own decisions, then why should people be denied the right to determine something as fundamentally private as the manner and time of their dying? Should not the person who says: 'I wish to die' be allowed to do just that? If he should not, then on what grounds, philosophical or legal, do we prevent him from pursuing his goal?

The philosophical debate over the permissibility in some cases of the taking of life has taken place against a backdrop of a firm legal exclusion of homicide. Whatever the moral claims of voluntary active euthanasia –

the consensual taking of the life of a suffering patient – the legal position is beyond doubt: deliberately to take the life of another is criminal homicide, irrespective of the motive of the perpetrator. Only in one European country, the Netherlands, has this principle been compromised, and even there the liberalisation of the law was initially achieved through the selective application of a criminal law defence.[3] The criminal code in the Netherlands still condemns all killing, although now under proposed legislation there will be no prosecutions for medically-performed euthanasia, provided that doctors meet certain conditions (including the requirement that a second opinion be obtained). It appears that doctors in the Netherlands are prepared to countenance euthanasia even where the patient has not been able to give a consent.

In the UK, and elsewhere in the common law world, the law's seemingly immovable legal objection to killing has meant that the focus of the discussion has shifted to the peripheral issues of how the objective of allowing for the 'caring' taking of life can be achieved without offending the legal prohibition of direct killing. The matter has become something of a game of cat and mouse: the intentional taking of life remains illegal, and will almost inevitably lead to criminal prosecution, but, short of that, legal possibilities for hastening death exist. Life may be shortened by certain forms of treatment or by the giving of no treatment at all, but to what extent do these steps approach the boundaries of legality?

Non-consensual non-treatment

The non-treatment of those who are incapable of expressing a view on the matter undoubtedly approaches active euthanasia in both the moral and legal sense. Such decisions are likely to arise most frequently at the extremes of life – in the case of the infant and in that of the elderly – although they may obviously occur in any case where disease prevents the patient from either understanding or communicating with others.

There is broad medical and lay consensus that, viewed objectively at least, certain lives are just not worth living in view of the suffering that they entail. A child born with severe spina bifida is an example of this. It may be possible in such cases to prolong life, perhaps even for a few years, but the life that is thereby ensured will be one of pain and distress, and many people would be inclined to say that in such circumstances the pursuit of treatment would be tantamount to cruelty. A similar view may well be taken in the case of a patient who, after a long life, is reduced to a condition of severe discomfort, with no prospect of improvement. If such a patient develops an infection which will result in death if untreated by antibiotics, then what is the point of treatment? Life may indeed be prolonged, but the patient is incapable of enjoying this prolongation and it is dubious then whether treatment could be considered a benefit.

The response of the medical profession in the UK to such cases by and large has been to allow death to ensue in a 'natural fashion' where this is thought to be in the best interest of the child. The practice of neonatal intensive care units has been well described by Laing,[4] who points out that the very term non-treatment is inaccurate, and that the philosophy of such units is to provide treatment to ensure as much comfort for the child as is possible in what remains of its life. The people who make such decisions are, of course, aware of the conflicting emotions involved, and reading Laing's moving account of his own practice leaves one with the impression that the intensive care unit is no place for the application of hard and fast rules. What call, then, is there for the law in this context? Should the courts stand back and allow these decisions to be taken by doctors, in consultation with families? The problem, of course, lies in deciding the parameters of the best interests test. Here it is difficult to see how this can be done without recourse to legal guidance, and indeed such guidance, in general terms, is now available in the form of a number of reported cases in which the courts have pronounced on treatment decisions involving seriously handicapped infants.

The first of these cases, *Re B (a minor)* [5] concerned a Down's syndrome child suffering from an intestinal obstruction. This obstruction was remediable by surgery but the child's parents refused this surgery. The local authority instituted wardship proceedings in order to obtain authorisation for the necessary operation, and in this it was successful. The court in this case took the view that the child should have the same chance in life as any other Down's syndrome child, and that it was not open to the parents to deny the child this chance. A similar parental view was also the issue in the controversial prosecution of Dr Leonard Arthur in the same year, a case which caused doctors to fear that they might face criminal proceedings for practices which a body of opinion within the profession apparently regarded as being perfectly ethical.

The infant in *R v Arthur* [6] also suffered from Down's syndrome but, significantly, did not have any overt complications. Dr Arthur, a paediatrician, wrote on the notes 'Parents do not wish it to survive: nursing care only', an instruction which in due course led to his appearance in court on a charge of murder, later reduced to attempted murder. He was acquitted, but the combined effect of his prosecution and the *Re B* case was to warn both doctors and parents of the fact that their views, although important, were not the sole determinants of which children should live and which should die, especially where the handicap did not preclude a life of at least some quality.

These two cases may have shown the outer limits of parental or medical discretion in this area but there were aspects of the legal position which remained more or less uncertain until the recent cases *Re J* [7] and *Re C* [8]. In *Re J* the court stressed that it would never sanction any step taken with a view to the termination of life, but identified certain factors to be taken into account in making decisions affecting handicapped children. As a starting point, in making treatment decisions, doctors must look at the matter from the patient's point of view. Viewed together with the requirement that choices must be made in the best interests of the child, this means that the convenience of doctors or parents is not to be taken into account. Life does not have to be protected at all costs, however; pain and suffering are factors which will have a bearing on the ultimate decision.

The child in *Re C* had no future but death, and the court was asked to pronounce on the issue of whether any life-prolonging treatment was required. The answer given accorded with what most people would surely regard as the only sympathetic view of such a matter – the aim of medical intervention in such a case can only be to ensure that the child is as comfortable as is possible in the circumstances. The use of antibiotics in such a case would not normally be appropriate, although one might imagine instances where antibiotics might be resorted to in order to make the child's death an easier one. The aim of treatment in such a case would not be the prolongation of life so much as the easing of death.

Does the law need to say more than this? The answer is surely no. What must be avoided is a situation in which doctors and parents are obliged to act against their humanitarian intuitions and to follow a course of action which is bureaucratically or legalistically prescribed. Humanitarian instincts will not, of course, always be legally acceptable – the parents in the Arthur case may well have been acting according to humanitarian intuitions – but there will be an area of choice in which such intuitions must be given room to be applied. To deny them this room is undoubtedly to intrude into an area which is quite properly private to the parents and medical staff caring for the patient.

Formulating a proper legal response to these requirements is not easy. The 'protect life at all costs' approach is too blunt, but the other extreme – which gives parents or doctors complete power to decide on life or death – is equally unacceptable. A 'best interests' test probably represents the most acceptable compromise. Under such a test, the life of the child is given value, but the possibility is recognised that in extreme circumstances it may not be in the best interests of the child to live. Determining when this will be so remains as difficult as ever, at least in some cases where there is a reasonable expectation of life, at any rate in terms of mere survival. Different cases may attract a different response, but this fact alone does not mean that the decision cannot be made. There may well be examples of children who have lived in spite of appalling handicaps, and who express pleasure at having been given the chance to live, but this does not mean that every person with such handicaps is benefited by life. Quite the opposite may be the case, and there is no philosophical absurdity involved in arguing that life has not been a benefit to one who has spent that life in pain.

The active/passive distinction

The fact that the law allows the doctor to abstain from treatment in certain cases where it is thought better that the life of the patient should not be prolonged may appear to be at odds with the legal policy of otherwise forbidding any act calculated to end life. It has been argued by some commentators that there is no moral distinction between allowing an outcome to occur through inaction and the pursuit of the result through positive steps.[9] The doctor who declines to administer antibiotics to a patient who he knows will die without such treatment causes the death of the patient as surely as if he administered a fatal injection, the only difference being the time taken in each case to achieve the desired objective.

There is considerable force in this argument. Omissions can be causes just as can positive acts, and insofar as causation forms a basis for the attribution of moral responsibility, omissions therefore become morally significant. (The law recognises this too, in that it will in certain circumstances attribute liability to those who cause harm to others through omissions.) Intuitively we feel that there is a difference between the person whose omission contributes to an occurrence and one whose act is the sole cause. This intuition has been rejected by some writers, and yet it reflects a significant difference in the actor's identification with an event. The person who stands by while something happens may be pleased that the event occurs but does not claim authorship of the event. This means that he distances himself in some way from the event; he makes no claims to be in a position to assume sole causal responsibility for it. It is here that the real distinction lies between the doctor who administers the fatal injection and the doctor who merely refrains from treating. The former claims the right to control the event (the death of the patient) as sole author; the other does not make such a claim.

Even if this distinction fails to satisfy the philosopher, it will certainly appeal to medical staff, most of whom intuitively feel that there is a major moral difference between the active administration of a drug designed to end life and abstaining from the vigorous pursuit of treatment. The implications of active euthanasia for whose who are obliged to carry out the task of ending life are considerable. Even if the philosopher can reassure the doctor that administering a fatal injection is morally indistinguishable from refraining from treatment, the actual step of injecting may be acutely distressing for the doctor. And if it is not distressing, or ceases to be distressing, then that too is worrying, as it may point to a blunting of sensibilities.

A difficult case

Legal and moral agreement as to the propriety in principle of non-treatment does not remove all the grey areas. In particular, we still have to consider whether there is a basic level of care which must be maintained even when the decision has been taken to exclude active treatment. It may be comparatively easy for doctors and relatives to decide not to treat a patient with antibiotics, or not to assist ventilation by artificial means, but the decision to withdraw naso-gastric nutrition or ventilation may not be taken quite so easily. This issue arises most starkly perhaps in the case of the patient in a persistent vegetative state. Such a person may be able to breathe without assistance, but is not going to recover consciousness and is therefore never again going to manifest those attributes which give real, human meaning to life. Indeed, there is a view that such a person is effectively dead, a breathing corpse.[10] This view, however, depends on an interpretation of brain death which is not legally accepted, and whatever the moral status of such patients may be, their legal status is that of a living human being. The law does not permit them to be treated as corpses, and the issue of whether or not to continue nutrition and hydration therefore remains.

The issue of nutrition and hydration takes us to the heart of the criminal law's recognition of the obligation to care for those who are unable to care for themselves. Anglo–American criminal law has traditionally been slow to impose liability for omissions, the theory being that such liability is vague and potentially open-ended. Criminal liability will be imposed, though, where a relationship or prior conduct on the part of an accused person has given rise to a legal obligation to prevent harm being suffered by another.[11] Textbook instances of such liability include that of the parent who neglects his child (pure relationship) or that of the person who has assumed responsibility for a sick or elderly person and who then fails to summon medical attention when required (prior conduct). In such cases, if death results from a failure to discharge duties of care, liability may be imposed for manslaughter. A classic instance is the late nineteenth century case of *R v Instan*,[12] where the defendant failed to feed or summon medical assistance for his dying 73-year-old aunt, but there are other, later cases of heartless relatives and malevolent keepers.

The gravely ill or unconscious patient falls clearly in this category of vulnerable persons who enjoy criminal law protection against neglect. In normal circumstances, criminal liability could be imposed on a doctor or nurse who failed to provide a patient with the essentials of life. Thus a nurse who failed to provide basic care for a patient who consequently dies would be liable for the death of that patient and, if the failure is sufficiently culpable, could expect to be charged with manslaughter. Yet this sort of case is obviously different from the case where a conscious decision is taken to refrain from the provision of care; in the latter case there is no negligence present, rather a decision is taken to refrain from care on the grounds that this is in the best interests of the patient.

Does this make a difference? There is undoubtedly a moral difference between wilfully neglecting to summon medical assistance for a frail relative whose presence in the house is a burden, and deciding no longer to feed a person who has no future and whose life has become meaningless to himself as much as to others. Yet can this moral difference be reflected in the law? There are grounds for saying that it cannot and indeed should not. The law of homicide does not distinguish between killing for a good motive and killing for a bad one, as has been evidenced in numerous judicial remarks on the unacceptability of 'mercy killing'. It is true that mercy killing may lead to a finding of diminished responsibility and a verdict of manslaughter rather than murder, but it is the sympathy of the court which produces this outcome, not the letter of the law.

In one view, the rigours of the criminal law inevitably lead to the conclusion that to deny food and water is to fail in a fundamental duty to care for the patient and must amount, then, to a crime of homicide. Such a conclusion will seem to many to be morally and practically counter-intuitive: what is the possible point of continuing to feed an unconscious patient who will never regain consciousness, or a patient whose life is clearly coming to an end and who will only have his suffering prolonged by the continued provision of food and water?[13]

The solution to the problem lies in the nature of the process of nutrition and hydration. The provision of fluids through a naso–gastric tube is an artificial process, akin, in a sense, to the use of a ventilator. Such techniques amount to treatment, rather than to the provision of care, and may be excluded on the same grounds as those upon which doctors abstain from other treatment. This can be done without abandoning the notion that there is still an obligation to provide basic care. There will remain an obligation to provide food and water if the patient is capable of taking it by natural means and can do so without being forced.

This analysis is likely to infuriate those who argue for the abandonment of such philosophical hair splitting in favour of what they see as a more honest and consistent approach to these ethically-charged issues. Such a critic might point out that if there is no obligation to provide fluid by means of a naso–gastric tube, there can be no obligation to provide it by spoon or beaker: the only difference between the two cases is the morally irrelevant one of the means employed. It is the same distinction as that between murder by poison and murder by shooting.

The defence of a morally significant distinction between artificial and natural feeding is not easy, but it can be made. A possible source of the obligation to feed is the natural sympathy we feel for those in need; the natural provision of the means of sustenance finds its roots in this sympathy. Such sympathy, however, is limited, and properly so. It does not extend to the taking of heroic measures, nor does it arise where no real point can be seen in feeding. Waking up a person on his death bed merely to give him a life-prolonging drink of water seems pointless, even cruel. There is also the question of dignity to be considered. The dignity of the patient is not compromised by the natural reception of food or water; it is compromised, however, by the insertion of tubes. A nasogastric tube need not compromise dignity when it sustains a person who can be expected to recover; in a hopeless case it merely emphasises the vulnerability and helplessness of the patient. A course of conduct which diminishes dignity can hardly be the basis of a moral obligation.[14]

The issue has yet to be decided in the UK, and any attempt to state the law would be largely surmise. Prosecution authorities in Scotland have stated that in their view it would be permissible to withdraw artificial feeding from a patient in a persistent vegetative state, but the correctness of this has not been considered in a Scottish court. In England, the position is just not clear, and doctors may well be advised to err on the side of caution and assume that artificial feeding must be maintained. In the US the matter came before the Supreme Court in the *Cruzan* [15] case, in which the court upheld a patient's right to refuse, in advance, artifical hydration and nutrition. As in many other American cases, however, the Supreme Court was concerned with the procedures whereby the patient's desires could be ascertained, and recognition was also given to the right of the state to protect human life and insist on adequate evidence of patient intention.

Much may depend on the state of the patient in question; the abandonment of artificial feeding in the case of an elderly patient whose condition is made all the more grave by serious complications may strike a court as more acceptable than the equivalent decision in relation to a young patient without complications. There is probably no real distinction between the two cases: the quality of life (or its virtual absence) is in each case the same, and a court may appreciate this fact. The cessation of natural feeding, though, is less likely to be accepted by a court, and it would be legally hazardous for a doctor to follow such a course of action as the law stands.

A right to die?

So far the discussion has focused on those who are incapable of expressing an opinion as to the continuation of treatment. There is another category of patients, of increasing importance: those who have asserted in advance their 'right to die'. Rights, and talk of rights, have proliferated in jurisprudence over the last two decades, and the alleged right to die has taken its place alongside the right to reproduce as one of the more controversial rights in the medico–legal context.

There can be little real objection to the principle of the right to die. If I am in the process of dying, and reconciled to, perhaps even enjoying the fact, and an officious bystander intervenes against my will to stop the process, a right of mine has undoubtedly been infringed. But which one? The answer is that it is probably my right of bodily integrity which is compromised; a right to die is merely a dependant of that right.

The right of bodily integrity is well-protected by the law, even when its exercise is likely to result in the death of the subject. This was made clear in the Canadian case of *Malette v Shulman* [16] in which an unconscious Jehovah's Witness was given a blood transfusion in spite of the fact that she bore a card which indicated her objection to such treatment. It was argued on behalf of the doctor that an advance refusal of this sort need not be observed on the grounds that the doctor could not be satisfied that the refusal was fully informed, but this reasoning was rejected. The prohibition of treatment stated on the card was held to be one which the doctor should have observed in the same way as a doctor should observe the stated wishes of a conscious patient. A similar view was taken in the Californian case of *Bouvia v Supreme Court of The State of California* [17] in which recognition was given to the right of a patient suffering from cerebral palsy to refuse artificial feeding and thereby to end her life. The legal battle of the plaintiff in this case had been a long one, and at earlier stages in the court proceedings the state interest in the protection of human life, even against the wishes of the individual, had proved a formidable obstacle. The matter has not been litigated upon in the same fashion in Britain, but there is little doubt as to the legal right to refuse treatment. This was recognised most recently in the case of *Re J (a minor)* [18] in which the Court of Appeal acknowledged that an adult patient in possession of his faculties has the right to refuse treatment even if this results in death. These cases will assert the right of the individual against unwanted bodily intervention, but they can also be read as asserting a right to die even when others take the view that one should continue to live.

The exercise of the right to die by those who are in a position to assert it may be widely accepted, but this is not necessarily so with those who are unable to express a view at the time at which medical intervention is proposed. One way of ensuring that wishes are respected is to state them in a 'living will' or advance declaration, a device which initially became popular in the US but which has now become the subject of discussion in the UK. An advance declaration states the maker's views on medical treatment in the event of his developing a grave condition which prevents him from consenting or refusing consent to treatment. The object of the declaration is to make it clear that were he in a position to express a view on certain treatments *at the time at which they become necessary*, then he would refuse them. These declarations may be specific or very general in their terms. They may, for example, list the medical conditions in which the patient would not wish any treatment to be pursued; they may exclude specific treatments (for example, artificial ventilation or artificial feeding) or they may merely reject all treatments which will have the effect of prolonging life in circumstances where it appears futile to do so.[19]

In some US states the legislature has enacted statutes to give effect to advance directives, and it is clear that even taking into account the restrictions surrounding the implementation of such documents they have had a substantial effect on medical practice. In the UK the effect of advance directives has not been legally tested, and no legislation has as yet been proposed. Their legal efficacy is likely to depend on the extent to which the courts would be prepared to recognise the previously expressed wish of the patient as representing his state of mind at the time when the medical decision has to be made. Various possibilities should be taken into account here. In some situations the patient may be capable of having a view on treatment, but may be unable to communicate it by virtue of physical impediment to speech or other movement. In such a case, it is possible to argue that the advance directive represents what the patient is likely to be currently thinking, and to give effect to it is merely to give effect to the patient's unexpressed thoughts. This will not be so where the patient is unconscious – the most likely situation in practice – and here one may say that the advance declaration expresses the views of the patient if he were able to form them at the time. Presumed consent is often used in a paternalistic way, but at least in this case presumed consent is based on evidence of the patient's views on the subject, which gives any decision a far greater degree of legitimacy.

A variety of arguments can be made out against giving effect to advance declarations. One refers to the possibility that the patient's mind has changed between the time of the expression of the wishes and the onset of the incapacitating condition. There is always a possibility that giving effect to an advance declaration may involve a misinterpretation of the current wishes of the patient, but this should be weighed against the likelihood that in many other cases, probably the vast majority of cases, the views of the patient will not have changed. To ignore such views in order to prevent the occasional misinterpretation of wishes is possibly to do a greater injustice than to give effect to the majority at the cost of the misinterpretation of a minority.

Another argument against the advance declaration focuses on the legal efficacy of advance directives in general. Consent, it is argued, must be reasonably current to be valid. Yet the law gives effect to many advance directives in other contexts. Wills do not cease to be effective merely by virtue of the fact that they were executed many years before the testator's death. Contractual rights survive the passage of time, as do waivers of rights. Powers of attorney may also now endure after the granter becomes legally incompetent. In all of these cases, the position of the individual is affected by legal acts performed well in advance, and the question may be asked why advance declarations about the way of one's dying should be treated any differently. If there is any answer to that, it must be that death is something in a category of its own. We can declare our future minds about most affairs, but it is impossible to say how we shall feel about death when it actually draws near. Death, perhaps, is too important, too awe-inspiring to be pronounced upon in advance.

Until the validity of advance declarations is settled in the UK by court decision or statute, doctors should treat such declarations with caution. They should certainly be taken into account in determining treatment, but the overriding consideration must still be what is in the best interests of the patient. It may be that a doctor will conclude that it is in the best interests of the patient that his wishes expressed in this way should be observed, but it may be that the opposite conclusion is reached. It is certainly important that the criminal law dimension be taken into account: the consent of the patient will in no way legitimise the taking of any steps which could amount to homicide. The criminal law accepts the right of the competent patient to refuse treatment, but it is not absolutely clear that it would in every case permit the non-treatment of the unconscious patient, even if there is evidence of a previously expressed desire not to be treated in certain circumstances. This area therefore remains legally grey, and unacceptably so. If advance declarations become popular, then doctors have a right to know where they stand legally, and there should be some legislative or judicial resolution of the uncertainty.

Some doubts

Proponents of voluntary euthanasia may look back over the last few decades and say that very little has changed. There is no legislation on active euthanasia, and the various bills proposed by the euthanasia legalisation societies have all come to naught. Euthanasia remains the crime of murder (or possibly manslaughter), and assisting another to take his life remains an offence under the Suicide Act 1961. Even the provision of advice, as opposed to material help, will in some circumstances be criminal, as was confirmed in the case of *Attorney General v Able*.[20]

Yet it would be misleading to paint a picture of stasis. There have been important changes in the legal landscape surrounding assisted death, and the cases discussed above at least establish a reasonably clear framework within which the doctor can work. In relation to incompetent patients, particularly in relation to handicapped infants, the legal picture is certainly clearer than it used to be, and a reasonable compromise has emerged. Heroic efforts to prolong the lives of gravely handicapped infants are not legally necessary, and doctors and parents need not fear that their humanitarian instincts will be thwarted by the law. At the same time, infants whose life presages awkwardness and inconvenience may not be disposed of at will, and such conduct remains, quite rightly, a serious criminal offence.

As far as adults are concerned, it is true that we still hold back from accepting radical measures, such as the withdrawal of fluids, but other forms of intrusive and pointless treatment do not have to be pursued. There is no real opposition to natural death in the UK amongst doctors, lawyers or the public, and we have been spared some of the litigation over moribund patients which has seriously disfigured the medico–legal scene in the US. Ultimately, the prospect of a death with dignity is more likely to be guaranteed not by the 'judge at the bedside' but by the continuation of humanitarian, principled medical practice, which thinks not in terms of profit, or survival statistics, or technical wizardry, but of kindness, sympathy and human dignity.

The above sentiments are predicated on an important assumption: that there are people who want to be left in peace to die a natural death. That they should be allowed to do so is surely beyond question, and certainly the law should prevent the frustration of their desires. It remains very important, though, that a desire to respect individual autonomy in this context should not obscure the fact that there are many, perhaps the majority, who do not want to die. A desire not to inflict a lingering end on those who do not wish to be detained should not be taken as a licence to hasten out of the way those who are frightened of dying, or reluctant to die for whatever reason. There is a real danger that an acceptance of non-intervention leads to an acceptance of premature death, *even for those who do not want it*. Indeed, it may be that we are witnessing the arrival of a generation of doctors who believe that inconvenient old people have no right to cling on to life, and that the treatment of such people is a waste of time and resources. Non-treatment tidies up hospitals; it empties much-needed beds; it can be altogether very convenient.

Perhaps any discussion of the issue should be preceded by the simple observation: in the last analysis, most people do not want to die. They hold on to life, to the very end, as many experienced doctors will tell one. So any assumption that they really do not want to live, or that they would, if they were able, ask to die, must be treated with the greatest caution. Criminal lawyers should be careful to remember this. If the law is tardy to endorse self-determination in dying, this is perhaps for the best. Legal rigidity in this area may seem conservative and unsympathetic, but to the vulnerable, the frightened, the unproductive and demanding elderly, it may be a very important and highly-prized lifeline.

Notes

1   J. Harris *The Value of Life* (1985).
2   M. Tooley *Abortion and Infanticide* (1983).
3   M.A.M. Wachter 'Euthanasia in the Netherlands' (1990) 300 Brit Med J 1093.
4   I. Laing 'Withdrawing from Invasive Neonatal Intensive Care' in J.K. Mason (ed) *Paediatric Forensic Medicine and Pathology* (1989).
5   [1981] 1 WLR 1421, CA.
6   (1981) The Times, 6 November. For discussion, see D. Brahams 'Putting Arthur's Case in Perspective' [1986] Crim L R 387.
7   [1990] 3 All ER 930.
8   [1989] 2 All ER 782, CA.
9   Most forcefully by H. Kuhse *The Sanctity of Life Doctrine in Medicine* (1987).
10 This is the position, for example, of K.G. Gervais *Redefining Death* (1986).
11 For valuable discussion see R.F. Goodin *Protecting the Vulnerable* (1985).
12 [1893] 1 QB 450. On this question, see P.R. Glazebrook 'Criminal Omissions: the Duty Requirement in Offences against the Person' (1960) 76 LQR 386; I. Dennis 'Manslaughter by Omission' [1980] Crim L R 255.
13 The issue is canvassed at length in J. Lynn (ed) *No Extraordinary Means* (1989).
14 For further discussion, see K.C. Micetich *et al* 'Are Intravenous Fluids Morally

Required for a Dying Patient?' (1983) 143 Arch Intern Med 975; R.S. Dresser and E.V. Boisaubin 'Ethics, Law and Nutritional Support' (1985) 145 Arch Intern Med 122.

15   *Cruzan v Director, Missouri Department of Health* 110 S.CT. 2841 (1990).
16   (1988) 63 OR (2d) 243 (Ont High Ct).
17   (1986) 225 Cal Reptr 297.
18   [1990] 3 All ER 930.
19   Advance declarations are fully discussed in Age Concern, Institute of Gerontology and the Centre of Medical Law and Ethics, King's College, London, *The Living Will* (1988).
20   (1984) 1 QB 795.

Chapter 7

Organ Donation and Transplantation

Death due to failure of a single vital organ must, in general, involve a relatively young person who would otherwise anticipate many more years of useful life. There is a particular sense of waste in such circumstances. There is an equal, if not greater, sense of unnecessary loss when an otherwise healthy person dies as a result of an accident. Most people would agree that fatal accidents should be prevented so far as is possible; almost as many would say that, given that accidental death cannot be wholly eliminated, such good as is available should be salvaged from the bad event. The case for transplant therapy is, therefore, valid from the point of view of both the recipient and the donor.

It is enhanced when more than one life is saved. Thus, technical considerations aside, the concept of kidney transplantation has always been attractive on the grounds that two lives can be saved from the one lost; today, as the movement towards the multi-organ donor gathers momentum, between four and seven recipients could in theory benefit from the kidneys, liver, heart, lungs and pancreas of a donor under 50 years old. This, however, depends upon a permutation of improved techniques, including advanced immunosuppression, maintenance of the cadaver in intensive care and sophisticated administrative arrangements between donor and recipient operating teams. Great strides are being made in all these directions but, ultimately, a limit is set by nature herself; quite apart from the effects of physiological and biochemical changes that occur in the body after death, the permissible times during which the isolated tissues can be deprived of oxygen differ from organ to organ, varying from more than 24 hours in the case of the kidneys, through eight to twelve hours for the liver, to only four hours for the heart and lungs.[1]

Even so, the potential is there and, at the very minimum, it can be said that transplant surgery has passed the boundaries of experimental therapy. According to the most recent figures from the Department of Health, 1730 renal transplants – including both live and cadaver donations – were performed in the UK in 1990; in the same year, 329 hearts and 359 livers were transplanted and there were 95 heart-lung operations. More than 8,000 people are alive today in Britain by virtue of donated kidneys. Perhaps more importantly, the Under-Secretary of State for Health, Stephen Dorrell, has agreed that kidney transplantation, at least, is not 'high-tech' medicine diverting resources from other patients in the National Health Service. 'No-one with any understanding of the economics,' he said in the House of Commons on 28 March 1991, 'can be under any doubt about the value attached to successful kidney transplantation and the benefits which that scientific advance has brought to patients through the NHS'.

Thus, there are also good practical reasons for legislation which will facilitate the transplant therapy programme but this must, at the same time, take into account a degree of public antipathy to interference with the dead human body and, even more importantly, a vague mistrust of those who seek to do so. Much of this probably derives from a misunderstanding of the concept of brain stem death – a problem to which we will return. First, however, consideration must be given to the alternative source of organs – the living donor.

The living donor

Until recently, there was no statute law relating to living donation of organs. In 1989, however, a public outcry over the sale of live kidneys led to hurried legislation to control living donation to unrelated recipients. Nonetheless, even within an established relationship (see below), living donation will be subject to the common law and it is convenient to address that aspect first.

Case law concerning consent to personal injury has now been consolidated in Attorney General's Reference (No 6 of 1980) [2] which was concerned with the general public policy considerations. The opinion of the Court of Appeal was that reasonable consent to some activities which cause actual bodily harm, among them surgical interference, can be given lawfully; this, admittedly, related to therapeutic surgery only but, even so, it is impossible to see anyone questioning the underlying legality of the donor operation. It is recognised inherently in the Human Organ Transplants Act 1989 and currently some four per cent of renal transplants in the UK come from the living.

Two provisos need mention. In the first place, there is no licence to consent to a practice in which the risk-benefit ratio would be manifestly to the consenter's disadvantage. Thus, although it scarcely needs emphasis, a living person cannot consent to donate his or her heart no matter how great may be the desire to do so. At present, for practical purposes, this limits living donation to a single kidney or portions of the pancreas. It may well be that living donation of a lobe or segment of the liver or lung will become the norm in paediatric, or even adult, practice. Those currently engaged in this line of research have laid down very strict criteria in order to limit the failure rate [3] but it is doubtful if the practice is, as yet, acceptable in the UK; it seems that the conditions would have to be very special before the morality and legality of such an experimental operation could be guaranteed. This leads to the second proviso: while a person cannot consent to a lethal donation, it is equally unlawful to consent to accept an organ in the certainty or near-certainty that it would be fatal to do so. Thus, given the present state of the art, it seems extremely unlikely that a human could lawfully consent to accept a heart from a non-human species even though he was prepared to sacrifice himself in the cause of experimentation or research. And if consent was unlawful, so too would it be to undertake the operation.

Common law considerations aside, living donation of human organs is now controlled to a large extent by the Human Organ Transplants Act 1989. Under section 2(1), a person is guilty of an offence in Great Britain if he removes from a living person an organ intended to be transplanted into another person or transplants an organ removed from a living person into another person unless the donor and recipient are genetically related. An order in council, made under the Northern Ireland Act 1984, extends the conditions to Northern Ireland. A genetic relationship is defined for the purposes of the Act in section 2(2) and goes so far as to include children by the half-blood of uncles and aunts by the half-blood. The Human Fertilisation and Embryology Act 1990 specifically excludes from the ambit of the 1989 Act those maternal and paternal relationships which derive from assisted reproduction and which are recognised only by virtue of statute. Moreover, the regulations stipulate the use of stringent and sophisticated tests by which to establish a relationship.[4]

No offence is committed under section 2 of the 1989 Act if a live, non-genetically related transplant operation is authorised by the Unrelated Live Transplant Regulatory Authority (ULTRA) which has been set up under the Human Organ Transplants (Unrelated Persons) Regulations 1989 (SI 1989/2480). Before authorising such an operation, ULTRA must be satisfied that no payment is involved, that the donor has been counselled and understands and consents to the nature and risks of the operation and that both the donor and the recipient have been interviewed in such a way as to enable the counsellor to identify any difficulties in communication.

Almost inevitably, advancing medical technology exposes difficulties in the interpretation of statute law. This is exemplified by what is referred to commonly as the 'domino' transplant. It is, for example, more satisfactory clinically to transplant a heart and lung into a cystic fibrotic patient rather than a lung alone; this operation, then, leaves the recipient's heart available for donation. Clearly, this second operation will be 'an unrelated live transplantation'. Equally clearly, the donation is not of the type which ULTRA was designed to control; the precise legal situation is, therefore, currently uncertain.

Donation by minors

Nowhere can the ULTRA regulations be more important than in relation to donation by children. Once again, however, the position at common law must be clarified before statute law can be applied.

The basic law concerning consent to surgical operation lies in the Family Law Reform Act 1969, section 8 which states, at section 8(1), that a person over the age of 16 years may validly consent to medical treatment without reference to a parent or guardian.[5] The Act says nothing about the child *under* 16, whose common law capacity to consent is probably stated in the important case of *Gillick*.[6] In essence, *Gillick* decided, in the words of Lord Scarman, that the parental right to determination of their child's medical treatment 'terminates if and when the child achieves a sufficient understanding and intelligence to enable him or her to understand fully what is proposed'. It is, however, to be noted that the 1969 Act also provides at section 8(3):

> 'Nothing in the section shall be construed as making ineffective any consent which would have been effective if this section had not been enacted.'

Most commentators consider that this merely confirms the common law right of the minor under 16 who understands the nature of the proposed treatment to give a valid consent. The alternative is that it preserves the right of the parents to consent to an operation in face of the child's refusal and this interpretation seems to have been supported in the 1991 case of *Re R*,[7] where Lord Donaldson, Master of the Rolls, said that parental consent would enable the operation to be undertaken lawfully.

There are serious doubts, however, as to whether either statute or common law empowers a parent to consent, say, to non-therapeutic research or experimentation on behalf of a child.[8] There have, accordingly, been attempts in the United States to categorise organ donation as therapeutic to the donor in helping a sibling or preventing the emotional disturbance which might follow the sibling's death.[9] Brazier regards such reasoning as highly artificial, although convenient, and doubts that it would be followed by an English court; she believes that the Council of Europe resolution on the harmonisation of transplantation legislation, which contemplates the removal of organs from minors or otherwise legally incapacitated persons, might be followed – but only as a last resort.[10]

There is, in fact, European precedent to look to, the most specific from France. There, living donation by a minor is limited to siblings; consent to organ removal must be given by the donor's legal representative; and the procedure must be authorised by a committee of at least three experts. Two of the experts must be doctors, one of whom must have practised for at least 20 years; and, if the minor is mature enough to be consulted, refusal on his part to donate an organ must be respected in all cases. This is a comparatively permissive attitude. In Germany, for example, living donation is frowned upon and, although there is no specific legislation and the opposition is based mainly on the possibility of commercialism, it seems unlikely that living donation from minors would be acceptable. Within the Commonwealth, legislation in Australia is now clear-cut. Recommendations from the Federal Law Reform Commission, similar to those adopted in France, were rejected by the individual states and it is not now lawful in Australia to remove non-regenerative tissue from a living child for the purpose of transplantation;[11] similar prohibitions exist in Canadian provinces. By contrast, the situation in the UK is undecided and one wonders whether the discussion, albeit of academic interest, has any practical significance. I have not discovered a currently practising British transplant surgeon who would accept a live child as an organ donor. Cystic fibrotic 'domino' transplants aside, information supplied by the European Dialysis and Transplant Association indicates that, in the last decade, only one such instance, involving identical twins aged 17, has arisen in the UK. Only five living child donors have been used in the Eurotransplant catchment area and none is recorded by Scandiatransplant; significantly, no cases have occurred in France despite the enabling legislation.

The search for compatibility does, however, raise the possibility of the deliberate production of siblings to act as tissue donors. At present, such activity as has been reported has been confined to regenerative tissue – in particular, bone marrow. At first glance, this does seem to be a classic case of using human beings as a means to an end. It is equally clear that, in practice, people can and do have families for disparate reasons including some which are thoroughly hedonistic; there is no way in which this can be prevented and many would hold that there should be no way.[12] Once born, the child is protected by the law, and it is very doubtful if a British court would prohibit the parents consenting to a potentially life-saving procedure provided that the donor was sufficiently mature to cope with the physiological effects of the operation. Yet it is only a short step to applying the same process to the donation of a kidney, and at this point one feels intuitively that the law should step in, possibly by applying an incontestable minimum age to the donation of non-regenerative tissue. Fortunately, it is only in the case of bone marrow that clinical requirements could be used to justify the intentional creation of a donor.

The donor as vendor

The most controversial issue arising from live organ donation is whether the sale of organs should be allowed. Effectively, the issue resolves into whether, on the one hand, the state has a duty to protect its more vulnerable citizens from exploitation or whether, on the other hand, an individual's right to autonomy extends to the disposal of body parts as and when the owner wishes.

There are several theoretical bases for justifying intervention by the state to prohibit the sale of body parts. None, however, can fully withstand critical analysis and it is doubtful if the current legislation derives from complex philosophical theory. Rather, it is likely that the Human Organ Transplants Act 1989 represents little more than a rather hurried and intuitive recoil from what appears to be a fundamentally degrading process which is likely to have adverse effects on society's values as a whole.[13]

The main thrust of the 1989 Act is to be found in section 1(1) which criminalises the making or receipt of any payment for the supply, or offer to supply, of any organ which has been or is to be removed from a dead or living person and is intended to be transplanted into another person. It is also an offence to seek to find a person willing to sell an organ, to initiate or negotiate any such arrangement or to take part in the management or control of corporate activities which include the initiation or negotiation of such arrangements. Section 1(2) also makes it an offence to advertise for donors willing to accept payment for their organs. 'Payment' does not include reimbursement of any reasonable expenses or loss of earnings incurred by a person supplying an organ from his body. An organ is defined for the purposes of the Act as any part of the human body consisting of a structured arrangement of tissues which, if wholly removed, cannot be replicated by the body (section 7(2)). Unlike, say, the Surrogacy Arrangements Act 1985, the 1989 Act contains no section specifically exonerating the principals – in this case, the donor and recipient – from its criminal provisions; clearly, however, the main concern is to eliminate commercial agencies from the transplantation programme and to prohibit hospitals and individual staff from indulging in a market for organs.

The 1989 Act was undoubtedly precipitated by the publicity surrounding the use of paid Turkish donors within the private sector of British medicine. All the criteria of exploitation were there – the donors were foreign and poor while the recipients were rich queue-jumpers; the public conscience was aroused and the Bill passed through the legislature virtually without debate. Nevertheless, even within such a setting, the seeds of concern could be seen to be germinating, for one of the donors said his motive was to raise money for his daughter's medical treatment. Where, it might be asked, is the difference between donating a kidney to one's daughter for treatment of her renal condition, which would be laudable, and donating a kidney elsewhere to facilitate treatment of her non-renal disease, which is condemned? If we accept that the risk from kidney donation is so slight as to make altruistic living donation legitimate, we cannot plead risk as a reason for prohibiting donation for money; and even if a risk exists, what is the moral difference between accepting that risk and accepting high wages for a risky job? Consent, it is said, cannot be voluntary and unfettered against a background of poverty and potential reward; but it is arguable that the moral coercion inherent in donation within the family is, if anything, greater than the financial pressure exerted in a commercial setting. It is also said that to allow payment would be to open up a traffic in organs; but this could be obviated, say, by legalising paid donations only by way of the Unrelated Live Transplant Regulatory Authority. Finally, it was the American jurist Cardozo, whose judgment forms the foundation stone of consent theories in medical practice, who said, in a slightly different context: 'Every human being of adult years and sound mind has the right to determine what shall be done with his own body'.[14]

Most, this author included, have a definite prejudice against payment for organs, but it is difficult to establish a precise moral basis for that stance.

The General Medical Council

The General Medical Council assured the government that it would deal 'strongly, toughly and promptly' with any doctor who transgressed the provisions of the 1989 Act. In the event, it went further and took retrospective action against those responsible for the Turkish affair; the name of one was erased from the register and two others' practices were severely limited. Even so, there is not a great deal of pre-existing guidance on the subject. The problem had surfaced in 1985 when the GMC advised:

> 'No surgeon should undertake the transplantation of a non-regenerative organ from a living donor without first making due inquiry to establish beyond reasonable doubt that the donor's consent has not been given as a result of any form of undue influence'.[15]

The British Transplant Society had been more precise in insisting that there must be clear evidence that the motivation of the donor was both altruistic and charitable and that the donor received no money over and above reasonable expenses, but this had no legal force. According to the society, in 1974 in the UK most kidneys from living donors were transplanted to patients from overseas who had come to the UK for treatment.[16] This may have been due to lack of a transplant service in some areas but one may, at least, wonder whether that was the whole reason. The action of the GMC in this instance may be seen as a good example of the rule that no boundaries are set to the definition of serious professional misconduct.

Cadaveric donation

The limited common law rights of the deceased as to the disposal of his remains have now been, to an extent, replaced by the Human Tissue Act 1961.[17] The meat of the Act lies in section 1 which covers the use of parts of the dead body for therapeutic use and for purposes of medical education and research. Section 1(1) deals with the situation where the deceased has expressed his wishes during life – which may be in writing at any time or orally before two or more witnesses during the terminal illness. On the assumption that these instructions have not been withdrawn, the person lawfully in possession of the body may act on them after death. Section 1(2) concerns the deceased who has made no provisions in life. In such circumstances, the person lawfully in possession of the body may authorise the removal of parts of the body if, having made such enquiry as may be practicable, he has no reason to believe that the deceased had expressed an objection to the use of parts of his body after death, or that the surviving spouse or any surviving relative objects.

The Act is disarmingly simplistic and the wording gives rise to a number of difficulties. The question as to who is in lawful possession of the body caused much difficulty in the past when it was suggested that the next-of-kin, who are undoubtedly entitled to possession, were in possession for the purposes of the Act. The point is of practical importance because that person may, not *must*, authorise disposal under section (1); effectively, therefore, the relative in possession would have the power of veto over the deceased's stated wishes. The generally accepted opinion now, however, is that the person in possession of the body is the hospital administrator. This is made clear by section 1(7), which empowers that official to delegate his authority.

In addition, the expression 'any surviving relative' is confusingly open-ended and must be interpreted so as not to defeat the objectives of the statute. The vast majority of cadaver donors will have been maintained for some time in intensive care; there will have been opportunity, therefore, to identify the nearest – or, at least, most concerned – relative who can canvas views within the family and, as a result, may be taken to speak for the rest. It is uncertain what the position would be if the nearest relative agreed to a donation under section 1(2) and a distant relative attempted to apply a veto; it seems likely that the obligation would be honoured on pragmatic, rather than legal, grounds. The situation is approached more explicitly in Australia where the next-of-kin are graded as to 'seniority'; authority to consent to donation is vested in the most senior next-of-kin who can be contacted.[18] This leads to the third difficulty – what constitutes 'such reasonable enquiry as may be practicable'? There is no ruling on this point but it seems safe to conclude that an enquiry which incurred such delay as to render the organs therapeutically useless would be considered unreasonable.

This, however, is now a relatively theoretical issue. The great majority of potential donors come from the intensive care unit; the availability of mechanical ventilation and the acceptance of the concept of 'brain stem death' combine to ensure that at least the majority of cadaver donations will be, in effect, of the 'beating heart' type.

Beating heart donation

A beating heart donation, which combines the efficiency of a living donation with the impersonal nature of the cadaver operation, is possible when the cardiorespiratory function is maintained artificially after death. This, in turn, depends upon the concept of 'brain stem death'.

Brain stem death

The rationale and use of brain stem death are now well established within good medical practice and the fact of brain stem death can be equated with the fact of death.[19] The medical Royal Colleges have laid down strict criteria for the diagnosis. Attention is often directed mainly to the tests of brain stem function that are to be carried out; it is, however, at least equally important to eliminate drug overdose, hypothermia, metabolic or endocrine disturbance and the use of neuromuscular blocking agents as causal factors of coma and to establish the existence of a disorder which can lead to brain death. A flat electroencephalogram is not essential to the diagnosis but could be of immense consolation to the relatives. Empathy with the next-of-kin may be improved if it is understood that the establishment of brain stem death is primarily a device for removing a corpse from intensive care, not for providing organs for transplantation. There is no legislation on how the diagnosis must be made but it is clearly advisable to adhere to the recognised code of practice. The doctor is exonerated from civil or criminal liability for the death of the patient when removal from intensive care can be seen as good medical practice.[20]

Perhaps the only outstanding matter for discussion concerns the distinction, if any, to be made between death of the whole brain and brain stem death. The subject is discussed in detail by Pallis.[21] For our purposes it is enough to note that, provided the other possible causes of coma are eliminated and a disorder which can lead to brain death is found, it is almost inconceivable that there can be brain stem death in the absence of cerebral death. Nevertheless, voices are still raised against the whole concept of brain death as a marker of somatic death. A somewhat surprising dissent by the Danish Council of Ethics was published as recently as 1989; it is, however, very unlikely that current thinking will be reversed on a major scale.

Medico-legal problems

Although there is a limit to how long a brain stem dead body can be maintained artificially, the time at which the diagnosis is made is obviously largely a matter of choice. That choice may have significant legal effects – for example, in relation to suicide clauses in life insurance policies – and the doctor may be under pressure, say, to forestall his decision. These eventualities are unlikely but one that cannot be avoided is the assessment of the order of death for succession purposes, for the standard legal presumptions which govern the simultaneous death of, say, husband and wife are rebuttable by way of available medical evidence.[22] There seems to be no way of solving this positively but it can be said that no inference as to survival can be taken from the fact that one person was declared brain stem dead before another, for no test will indicate how long each has been dead on the ventilator.

A more immediate problem lies in the Human Tissue Act 1961, section 1(4), which states that the doctor removing the organs 'must have satisfied himself by personal examination of the body that life is extinct'. This must be taken literally for, by contrast, section 1(4A)(b)(ii), inserted by the Corneal Tissue Act 1986, specifically validates a statement by another practitioner to that effect in the case of corneal grafting. Some surgeons insist on cessation of ventilation and a flat electrocardiogram before the donor operation but this, to an extent, removes the therapeutic advantages of a beating heart donation. It would, for example, almost certainly be detrimental to a neonatal cardiac transplantation. It seems however that, at the very least, the death certificate should be signed and presented to the surgeon before the donor operation – a routine which would certainly fortify the next-of-kin when making their final decision.

The role of the coroner and the procurator fiscal

The Human Tissue Act 1961, section 1(5) stipulates that no removal of organs from a body that may be the subject of an inquest or a medico-legal autopsy may be authorised except with the consent of the coroner. Section 1(9) amends this for Scotland, where no removal of parts of the body may be authorised when the procurator fiscal objects. These restrictions are important because, although the proportion is decreasing, a number of donor organs will derive from unnatural deaths, particularly from motor accidents.

The role of the coroner still gives rise to some ambiguity. It is important to note that the fact that a person is being declared brain stem dead and removed from intensive care is no reason, of itself, for involving the coroner; what matters is the reason for admission to the ventilator. Home Office guidance to coroners states that permission for donation should be refused only when the organ might be required in evidence or might be of value to any further inquiry.[23] Clearly, any opportunity for discussion with the coroner must be taken up before death is certified; the coroner then has the opportunity to register any objection to the removal of a particular organ. A useful variation on this theme has been developed in some areas of Scotland whereby the fiscal's pathologist attends the donor operation; this, in effect, becomes part of the medico-legal autopsy. Finally, it must be emphasised that the coroner or fiscal can only object or not object to donation. Authorisation or consent to the operation remains subject to sections 1(1) and 1(2) of the 1961 Act irrespective of the mode of death; moreover, it is no part of the coroner's or his officer's duty to supervise the consent procedure, which remains a matter between the physicians and the relatives.

Contravention of the 1961 Act

Somewhat unusually, the 1961 Act specifies no penalty for contravention. Whether sanctions exist and can be applied by any other route is, even now, uncertain.[24] This is no place to go over the arguments, which are fairly esoteric. Suffice it to say that it is difficult to imagine any criminal liability arising out of non-compliance with the Act in the ordinary case. However, when the death is subject to inquiry by the coroner or procurator fiscal, there is little doubt that a hospital or doctor removing organs contrary to section 1(5) could be accused of the common law offence of obstructing the coroner in the execution of his duties – but the action must actually cause an obstruction which would be unlikely if, say, the kidneys were removed.

Whether there would be any civil liability in tort to the next of kin who were not consulted under section 1(2) is equally uncertain. In my opinion, the only possible damages recoverable would be based on the infliction of 'nervous shock', though the chances of the courts extending this concept would seem to be slender. Perhaps, in the end, the most potent sanction lies with the General Medical Council.

The availability of organs

Whether there should be legislation aimed at increasing the number of organ donors can be decided only in the light of the probable reasons for the current deficit. Many surveys have been conducted in an effort to assess the problem but none has been conclusive. In general, it can be said that no link in the chain of provision is wholly sound. In the early days of transplantation, it was widely believed that the major responsible factor was apathy on the part of medical staff. Reluctance on the part of the donor's doctors is not hard to justify; in particular, the maintenance of the brain stem dead donor's condition pending the arrival of the transplant team may become as effort-intensive as was treatment during life. Even so, this is apparently now not a significant factor. The coroner and the procurator fiscal have been blamed but, for reasons already discussed, they are likely to be at worst a declining impediment to donation. The proportion of potential donors regarded as medically unsuitable is also being reduced as wider exceptions are admitted to the pool and fewer are lost due to deterioration of the tissues following brain stem death. On the whole, it seems that the most intractable factor lies in the relatives' consent rate. This may be a function mainly of the way in which requests are put but, overall, the general acceptance rate is in the region of 65 per cent.

This low response can only reflect a vague but persistent mistrust of beating heart donation which is not confined to the lay public but is shared by some highly respected doctors. In fact, it is not difficult to stoke the embers of doubt. Actively to seek an increased supply of organs must inevitably shift the balance between the acceptable use of the dead body and the manipulation of death, even if the shift is only incremental. The current movement in favour of elective ventilation for the purposes of donation, however carefully considered and controlled it may be, has to be seen as a step along a particularly dangerous path, and this is an ethical hazard acknowledged by all who are engaged in this form of treatment. It follows that any proposed legislation must take these misgivings into account and certainly must not exaggerate people's fears. The near certain way of doing this would be to change to a full-scale 'opting out' regime; the cry of 'grave-robbing' would rise loudly and clearly and, despite its evident acceptance at first instance in several EC countries, it is doubtful if any UK government would be prepared to undertake such a change of direction.

An alternative legal approach, initiated in the US,[25] is to place a positive obligation on the deceased's medical team to seek consent to donation from the relatives of every potential donor. Such a policy of 'required request' infringes the clinical freedom of the health carers – for the bereaved are as entitled to sympathetic treatment as any others involved in the process – and its efficacy is uncertain.

The present governmental policy was expressed by the Under-Secretary of State for Health, Stephen Dorrell:

'We must accept that nobody has a right to anybody else's organs. If something untoward happens, our organs may be of value to someone else but that should be the result of an altruistic decision about how we want our bodies to be used when we die. It should not be as a result of a right of the recipient. We must make that philosophic approach clear and accept it as the basis on which we encourage organ donorship. It is our responsibility to make such a decision and to ensure that our friends and relatives are aware of our views. It is the responsibility of the living whose organs may be of use to someone else; it is not anyone else's job to claim the organs.'[26]

Many would, however, contend that the law as it stands is unduly biased agains the recipient and there are some amendments to the Human

Tissue Act 1961 which might be made with advantage. First, it seems unnecessary that there should be any ambiguity as to who is empowered to act on behalf of the transplant team; if the person in lawful possession of the body is the hospital authority, then let the Act say so. Second, and more important, the confusion associated with the words 'any surviving relative' should be removed so as to simplify donation. The legislation in Australia seems to operate well and the concept of a 'senior relative' would almost certainly be acceptable in the UK. Finally, it is widely agreed that a major source of relatives' reluctance to consent is a confusion between death and dying. This would be alleviated if a death certificate had to be completed and handed over before any donor operation began. This should be made a legal obligation.

The final possibility for increasing the supply of cadaver organs might be their purchase, a process which can be more subtle than an uncomplicated exchange of money. The morality of payment for organs from the living has been discussed at length above and the argument has been crystalised by Davies: 'As long as there are adequate safeguards, any ethical or legal fastidiousness demanding that donation be only gratuitous could condemn the sick'.[27]

It is difficult, however, to devise a generally acceptable case for deriving profit from the sale of a dead relative's body. Most people would accept intuitively the provisions of the Human Organ Transplants Act 1989 which criminalise the sale of cadaver organs. Nonetheless, there are ways of compensating a donor family which fall short of direct payment and one wonders – at least on utilitarian grounds – if it is ethically correct to jeopardise a potential increase in the number of donations simply because of distrust of the donors' motives.[28]

If there is to be no radical legislation, the supply of organs must continue to depend upon the public's response to encouragement to donate. I believe this response faltered markedly at the time of introduction of the more exotic transplant techniques – perhaps, especially, heart transplantation. The public saw this as experimental surgery which had a uniformly poor result and that view has persisted. If this analysis is correct, the major need is for emphasis to be laid on the greatly improved success rate of modern therapy. The concept of the multi-organ donor must also be popularised. Fewer people are likely to be impressed by the one to one life benefit of, say, a cardiac transplant than by the salvage of four or more lives from one unfortunate death. However, this will call for continued monitoring and improvement of the logistics of transplantation therapy. There is little doubt that the UK government is aware of the need for continued encouragement and administrative assistance – the establishment of the United Kingdom Transplant Support

Service Authority,[29] backed by the obligation to contribute to a centralised data bank,[30] are, perhaps, significant straws in the wind.

The neonate as an organ donor

The demand for organs suitable for transplantation into infants is persistent – many of those in end stage liver failure will benefit from liver transplants and about 160 children are born each year in England and Wales suffering from death-dealing cardiac malformations that might be amenable to transplant therapy. Liver transplantation in infants is now accepted practice and raises few medico-legal hazards that have not been discussed already. Heart transplantation is, however, another matter; it is still regarded as an experimental procedure and is subject to two considerations. First, is it no more than exceptionally dangerous research and, therefore, outside reasonable parental consent, or is it acceptable innovative treatment? Secondly, if the latter, is the expectation of benefit sufficient to justify raising the hopes of parents and/or the expenditure of resources? The procedure has probably passed the non-therapeutic research stage and become an acceptable treatment option, enjoying much the same status as adult therapy did 25 years ago. Given that there is a need for such treatment, can it be satisfied? There is virtually no pool of accidental deaths on which to draw. The donor organs must not only be functionally 'viable' but they must also be viable at cellular level; therefore, death must result from a condition which does not compromise the health of the donated organs and which can properly be managed in the intensive care unit. It has been estimated that some 3000 infants in North America might benefit from treatment each year and that the supply of organs could meet the demand if all potential donors were used. In ordinary circumstances, the practical, legal and ethical problems associated with neonatal transplant therapy are essentially the same as those arising from adult treatment. The estimate of potential donors is, however, likely to be optimistic and the supply of organs would be enhanced were anencephalic neonates to be used also. Around 40 such infants are born alive annually in the UK. In practice, very few anencephalic donors are used but they pose special legal and ethical problems which merit specific discussion.

The anencephalic neonate

Legally, anencephalic donation in the UK has been greatly influenced by the provisions of the Infant Life (Preservation) Act 1929, which makes it an offence to destroy the life of a child capable of being born alive before it has an independent existence.

Now, however, the Abortion Act 1967, section 1(1)(d) removes any time barrier to termination on the grounds of fetal abnormality, while section 5(1) exonerates the doctor from criminal liability under the 1929 Act when performing an otherwise legal termination of pregnancy. The effect of these insertions, made by the Human Fertilisation and Embryology Act 1990, must be to limit still further the availability of relatively mature anencephalic organs.

Effectively, the only sources will now be neonates born to women who object to termination on any grounds or fetuses which are known to be anencephalic but which the mother wishes to mature in order to provide organs. There are many who would regard the latter as intrinsically immoral and some such attempts are possibly frustrated by the conscientious objection of the doctors. It could be said that the fetus is being used as a means to an end. Nonetheless, the anencephalic infant's death is inevitable and the benefits of altruistic gestation would seem to compensate for any infringement of moral philosophical principles.

Much the same arguments apply to the method used for a late termination of an anencephalic pregnancy. Should the obstetrician use one which is deliberately non-feticidal in order that the organs may be harvested? While most would agree that good should be salvaged from a bad situation whenever possible, this is clearly a matter that is subject to the consent of the woman concerned; not only has she the right to reject a form of treatment which could be to her disadvantage but also she must be given the opportunity to decide what should happen to the aborted fetus.[31]

The anencephalic donor is born alive; the conditions of the Human Tissue Act 1961, section 1(4) – under which the donor's surgeon must satisfy himself that the donor is dead – must, therefore, be met. Therein lies a major difficulty. Neonatal organs, especially the heart, are particularly susceptible to deprivation of oxygen when warm; it follows that any donation must be of the 'beating heart' type, the legality of which depends, as we have seen, on the acceptance of brain stem death. But how is it possible to establish the fact of brain death in an anencephalic? The difficulties are such that attempts have been made to alter the concept of death in order to meet the exceptional case. The anencephalic has been described as 'brain absent' and, therefore, not 'alive', philosophers contend that the anencephalic is not a 'person' and lawyers may argue that he is not a 'reasonable creature in being' – all trying to clear the way by conceptual or semantic juggling. In my opinion, such movements should be resisted; to be 'dead' is not to be 'as good as dead' or 'at death's door'.

The breathing anencephalic is in the same situation as the adult in the persistent vegetative state. The Royal Colleges have stated that 'organs for transplantation can be removed from anencephalic infants when two doctors who are not members of the transplant team agree that spontaneous respiration has ceased'[32] and this will almost certainly become the basis of accepted practice. Nevertheless, the need to maintain oxygenation of the tissues is such that there must be a temptation to limit the duration of the test; it would be stretching credulity too far to suppose that the certifiers did not know of the intention to transplant. This must raise doubts, expressed particularly by McLean,[33] as to whether one can, in practice, legally establish death by this means while simultaneously serving the needs of the recipient. The precise legality and morality of anencephalic donation are, indeed, matters for concern, but it seems probable that their eventual solution will be founded on pragmatism rather than on strict moral principle.

The fetus as a donor

The disposal of fetal remains following spontaneous or therapeutic abortion is subject only to the dictates of public health and decency. There is no statutory form of burial and, since the non-viable fetus has never been alive, the Human Tissue Act 1961 has no application. It follows that the only control of the use of fetal tissue in transplantation therapy lies in good medical practice. This has now been codified in the form of the Polkinghorne Report,[31] which recommends that any use of fetal tissues, whether in therapy or research, should be subject to the informed consent of the mother.

The therapeutic value of fetal tissues depends on the fact that fetal cells are proliferating actively, a property which contrasts with the adult cell most vividly in the case of neural tissue. Assuming that Parkinson's disease is, at least in part, due to dopamine deficiency, there is a reasonable scientific basis for implanting cells from the substantia nigra of the fetal brain into the patient's brain in the hope that they will provide a new reservoir for the hormone. Calls for a moratorium on the procedure may be unduly cautious but there can be no doubt as to the experimental nature of the treatment. It is rather more worrying that the procedure is being used in other degenerative neural diseases on very insecure scientific grounds; this is surely a trend to be discouraged.

We are concerned here with the ethical and legal issues, perhaps the most important of which relates to the difficult problem of fetal 'death' for, since live cells are to be used, this is one situation where the concept of 'brain death' is clearly incompatible with the proposed treatment. It might be possible to fall back on the argument that, since the aborted fetus has never been 'alive', it can only be dead, but the proposition has an unfortunate casuistic ring to it. The physiologists assure us that the 10-week fetus can feel no pain. Nevertheless, this is an aspect of fetal brain implant therapy that gives rise to serious and widespread disquiet.

An almost equal source of concern derives from the fact that the treatment is inevitably linked to abortion. Those who are opposed to abortion will, therefore, be equally opposed to fetal brain implant therapy. Once again, it seems right to extract some good from an arguably bad precondition but the objection underlines the need to separate the obstetricians from the experimental therapists. Indeed, the Polkinghorne Committee, in Chapter 5 of its report, recommended the creation of an intermediary post to ensure that the parties are distanced.

The fetal cells must be immature and are best harvested at 10–14 weeks' gestation. There is, therefore, a very real danger that pregnancy could be undertaken for the express purpose of providing fetal cells. In practice, the 170,000 or more therapeutic terminations undertaken annually in Britain provide such a pool of material that such action would be superfluous. Nevertheless, the danger is there; a young woman might perhaps be pressurised into providing therapeutic material for her grandfather. In my opinion, legislation would be justified prohibiting payment for fetal tissues and donation of such tissues within, at least, the direct line of family descent – unless, possibly, genetically compatible cells were found to produce markedly better results, which is unlikely. Control could well be placed in the hands of the existing Unrelated Live Transplant Regulatory Authority.

Finally, the existence of an inherent repugnance to the utilisation of other people's brains must be acknowledged. The science fiction concept of transference of the persona is too close to reality for comfort. On this ground alone, the recommendation of the British Medical Association that nervous tissue should be used for implantation only in the form of isolated neurones or tissue fragments is to be fully commended.

It is, perhaps, fitting to end this chapter with a plea for comprehensive and well considered legislation which covers the whole spectrum of transplantation therapy and which, especially, takes note of the changes, both good and bad, which have evolved since 1961.

Notes

1   J. Wallwork 'Organs for transplantation' (1989) 299 Brit Med J 1291.
2   [1981] 1 QB 715, [1981] 2 All ER 1057. For the less definitive Scottish authority, see *Smart v H M Advocate* (1975) SLT 65.

3   P.A. Singer, M. Siegler, P.F. Whitington, *et al* 'Ethics of liver transplantation with living donors' (1989) 321 New Engl J Med 620; L.R. Shaw, J.D. Miller, A.S. Slutsky, *et al* 'Ethics of lung transplantation with live donors' (1991) 338 Lancet 678.

4   Human Organ Transplants (Establishment of Relationship) Regulations 1989 (SI 1989/2107).

5   The common law in Scotland is now codified: Age of Legal Capacity (Scotland) Act 1991, ss. 1 and 2(4).

6   *Gillick v West Norfolk and Wisbech Area Health Authority* [1986] AC 112, [1985] 3 All ER 402, HL.

7   *Re R (a minor) (Wardship: Medical Treatment)* [1991] 4 All ER 177.

8   P.D.G. Skegg *Law, Ethics, and Medicine* (1984), pp 56 *et seq*; J.K. Mason and R.A. McCall Smith *Law and Medical Ethics* (3rd ed, 1991), pp 368 *et seq*.

9   See the widely quoted Massachusetts cases originally reported by W.J. Curran 'A problem of consent: Kidney transplantation in minors' (1959) 34 N Y Univ L R 891. Similar reasoning was applied in the case of a mentally incompetent donor: *Strunk v Strunk* 445 SW 2d 145 (Ky, 1969) but has also been rejected in the United States: *Lausier v Pescinski* 226 NW 2d 180 (Wis, 1975).

10   M. Brazier *Medicine, Patients and the Law* (1987), pp 275–6.

11   E.g. Human Tissue and Transplant Act 1982, ss. 12,13 (WA); Human Tissue Act 1983, s. 10 (NSW).

12   J. Rachels 'When philosophers shoot from the hip' (1991) 5 Bioethics 67.

13   R.G. Titmuss *The Gift Relationship: From Human Blood to Social Policy* (1970); R.F. Chadwick, 'The market for bodily parts: Kant and duties to oneself' (1989) 6 J Appl Philos 129.

14   In *Schloendorff v Society of New York Hospital* 105 NE 92 (NY, 1914).

15   General Medical Council Annual Report for 1985 (March 1986).

16   British Transplant Society 'The shortage of organs for clinical transplantation: Document for discussion' (1975) 1 Brit Med J 251.

17   The Anatomy Act 1984 is distinct and relates only to the donation of bodies to schools of anatomy; it is not considered further here. The Corneal Grafting Act 1952 was repealed by the 1961 Act; the Corneal Tissue Act 1986 is concerned mainly with technical considerations.

18   E.g. Human Tissue Act 1983, s. 4 (NSW).

19   Conference of Medical Royal Colleges and their Faculties 'Diagnosis of brain death' (1976) 2 Brit Med J 1187; 'Diagnosis of death' (1979) 1 Brit Med J 332.

20   *R v Malcherek, R v Steel* [1981] 2 All ER 422, [1981] 1 WLR 690; *Finlayson v H M Advocate* 1978 SLT (Notes) 60.

21   C. Pallis *ABC of Brain Stem Death* (1983).

22   Law of Property Act 1925, s. 184; Succession (Scotland) Act 1964, s. 31.

23   Home Office Circular no. 65/1977.

24   P.D.G. Skegg 'Liability for the unauthorized removal of cadaveric transplant material' (1974) 14 Med Sci Law 53; I.M. Kennedy 'Further thoughts on liability for non-observance of the provisions of the Human Tissue Act 1961' (1976) 16 Med Sci Law 49. And see now: I. Kennedy, and A. Grubb *Medical Law: Text and Materials* (1989) pp 1033–6.

25   US Public Law 99–509, para 9318.

26   Official Reports, H C, 28 March 1991, vol 188, col 1142.

27 I. Davies 'Live donation of human body parts: A case for negotiability?' (1991) 59 Med-leg J 100.

28 For discussion, see D.S. Kittur, M.M. Hogan, V.K. Thukral *et al* 'Incentives for organ donation?' (1991) 338 Lancet 1441.

29 United Kingdom Transplant Support Service Authority (Establishment and Constitution) Order 1991 (SI 1991/407); United Kingdom Transplant Support Service Authority Regulations 1991 (SI 1991/408).

30 Human Organ Transplants (Supply of Information) Regulations 1989 (SI 1989/2108).

31 G. Polkinghorne (Chairman) Review of the Guidance on the Research Use of Fetuses and Fetal Material (Cm 762).

32 Report of the Working Party of the Conference of Medical Royal Colleges and their Faculties in the United Kingdom on Organ Transplantation in Neonates (1988).

33 S. McLean 'Facing the dilemma of a life and death issue' (1991) The Scotsman, 26 August.

Chapter 8

Clinical Research

Introduction

A great deal has been written about the legal and ethical issues arising out of the conduct of clinical research in man. This is not surprising considering the wide range of activity which can fall within the term 'clinical research' and given the variety of approaches to the subject in different countries. In a chapter of this length it will not be possible to examine all or any of the issues in detail. It is intended, rather, to highlight the main areas of interest and concern and to describe how they are approached according to the law and principles applying in the UK with reference to developments in the European Community. The term 'clinical research' is used in this chapter in its widest sense to cover research projects involving both patient and non-patient ('healthy') volunteers.

The relationship between law and ethics

'It would not be correct to say that every moral obligation involves a legal duty but every legal duty is founded on a moral obligation,' said Lord Coleridge, Lord Chief Justice, in *R v Instan*.[1] It is this relationship between ethics and the law which may in part explain the dearth of legislation worldwide specifically designed to regulate the conduct of clinical trials.[2] Aspects of clinical research have always been and remain controversial. Public mores and therefore opinion of what is ethically acceptable vary over time and between cultures. While ethical parameters remain undefined, it is clearly difficult to draft any law which could be comprehensive or fulfil the function of representing the public consensus. The difficulty has been compounded by the rapid and significant developments in science and medical technology increasing both the scope for research and the means of performing it and, therefore, the range of ethical questions to be addressed. The situation is changing, however, with a few countries adopting legislative measures and a general awareness of the need for certainty and harmonisation within the EC. There is a fine balance to be preserved between removing some of the legal uncertainty which surrounds research and producing a suitably flexible and practical framework.

International guidelines

The Nuremberg Code

The disclosure of the unacceptable human experimentation carried out upon prisoners of war and civilians during the Second World War led to the Nuremberg Code of 1949. This reflected an understanding of the value of research in humans balanced against the need to establish legal and moral boundaries in order to protect the interests of the research subject. It stated:

> 'The great weight of the evidence before us is to the effect that certain types of medical experiments on human beings, when kept within reasonable, well defined bounds, conform to the ethics of the medical profession generally . . . such experiments yield results for the good of society that are unprocurable by other methods or means of study. All agree, however, that certain basic principles must be observed in order to satisfy moral, ethical and legal concepts.[3]

The Declaration of Helsinki

Fifteen years later in June 1964, building upon the ground work of the Nuremberg Code, the World Medical Assembly adopted the Declaration of Helsinki containing 'recommendations guiding physicians in bio-medical research involving human subjects'. The Declaration was kept under review and has been updated three times (in 1975 in Tokyo, in 1983 in Venice and most recently, in 1989 in Hong Kong). The Declaration provides a succinct description of the only justification for research in human subjects:

> 'The purpose of biological research involving human subjects must be to improve diagnostic, therapeutic and prophylactic procedures and the understanding of the aetiology and pathogeneses of disease'.

It also draws a distinction between 'medical research in which the aim is essentially diagnostic or therapeutic for a patient and medical research the essential object of which is purely scientific and does not imply direct diagnostic or therapeutic value to the person subjected to the research'.

The research protocol should always contain a statement of the ethical considerations and indicate compliance with the principles contained in the Declaration of Helsinki. The Declaration comprises a statement of twelve fundamental principles to which reference *must* be made in the planning and performance of all research in human beings.[4] The same basic elements of the Nuremberg Code are restated and extended. In particular, the Declaration provides for the submission of the research protocol to an independent specially appointed committee for advice, consideration and comment. It also deals in more detail than the Nuremberg Code with the overriding matter of obtaining subject consent by addressing the position of subjects in a dependent relationship with the investigating clinician and the position of those who may be legally incompetent to give consent, such as the mentally impaired and minors. In distinguishing between patient and non-patient research, the Declaration specifies additional considerations to be taken into account in each case. Where a trial involves patients to whose condition or ailment the experimental treatment and procedures are relevant, the following recommendations are made:

(1)   The physician must be free to use a new therapeutic measure if in his judgment it offers hope of saving a life, re-establishing health, or alleviating suffering.

(2)   Potential benefits, hazards and discomfort of a new method should be compared against the advantages of the best current method.

(3)   Every patient should be assured of the best proven diagnostic and therapeutic method.

(4)   Patient refusal to participate must never interfere with the physician/patient relationship.

(5)   If the physician considers it essential not to obtain a form of consent from a subject, the special reasons should be stated in the research protocol.

(6)   Physicians may combine medical research with professional care and thus acquire new knowledge to the extent that is justified by the potential value for the patient.

With regard to non-patient subjects, the following provisions are made:

(1)   The duty of the physician remains the protection of the life and health of the subject.

(2)   The subject must be a volunteer for whom the experiment is not related to any illness suffered by the subject.

(3)   The research should be discontinued if it may, if continued, be harmful.

(4)   The well-being of the subject overrides the interest of science and society.

The Declaration of Helsinki underpins the conduct of all clinical research and provided the foundations for the voluntary national guidelines which operate in the UK [5] and elsewhere. Compliance with the Declaration is referred to almost as a matter of rote in clinical research applications and protocols, yet in general it is questionable whether investigators have fully considered its content and its omissions. The Declaration is not comprehensive. There are several major issues which must be faced by any person initiating or conducting clinical trials on human beings upon which it offers no guidance. In such cases, national voluntary codes may fill the gaps and can be expected to do so in different ways. In addition, the Declaration by its nature does not, and was not intended to, offer detailed practical recommendations. The translation of its principles into national guidelines in the UK has therefore in any event involved a degree of supplementation.

Within the European context, an important recent development has been the issue by the European Commission of Guidelines for good clinical practice for trials on medicinal products in the European Community prepared by the Committee for Proprietary Medicinal Products (CPMP) working party on efficacy of medicinal products.[6] The guidelines, although they are subject to criticism for lack of detail in some areas, were drafted to deal specifically with the handling and recording of data generated by a trial, the design of the trial and its procedures, statistical analysis and quality assurance. The idea of inspection by 'competent authorities' of investigation sites is also introduced. Like all international and national guidelines, they do not have the force of law and indeed questions have been raised as to whether the Commission is competent under the Treaty of Rome to propose harmonisation of ethical issues of this type. A further debate has been prompted by the issue, in January 1991, by the European Commission of a discussion paper [7] regarding the need for a European directive dealing with clinical research incorporating the principles contained in the guidelines. Should this be agreed, member states will be required either to pass specific legislation for regulating the conduct of clinical trials or, insofar as legislation already exists, to ensure that it is consistent with the terms of the directive.

In the discussion below, reference will be made where appropriate to the applicable principles of the Declaration of Helsinki, to its shortcomings and to the way in which national or European codes of practice have dealt with the lacunae left by the Declaration. It is necessary first, however, to look briefly at the way in which certain regulatory provisions affect the initiation of clinical trials.

Regulatory approval

While there is no specific legislation regulating how a clinical trial in the UK must be conducted, there is provision for notification or approval by the licensing authority (the UK Health Ministers and Agriculture Ministers) of clinical trials prior to their commencement. This is done through the Medicines Control Agency.

Phase II and Phase III trials and pharmaceutical companies

Under the terms of the Medicines Act 1968 a supplier of an unlicensed medicinal product intended to be used in a trial in the UK involving *patients* [8] must (unless he is already the holder of a product licence which authorises the trial) first apply for a clinical trial certificate – a CTC. A CTC (effective for two years but renewable) may be granted only after detailed pharmaceutical and toxicological data regarding the drug in question have been provided and assessed by the licensing authority (often with advice from an expert advisory committee) as not likely to involve serious risk to trial subjects. This can be a rigorous and lengthy procedure. Fortunately since the passing of an order in 1981 [9] it has not been necessary in every case to apply for a CTC. The order introduced a scheme under which suppliers may be exempted from the need to hold a CTC for a new product for three years, provided certain undertakings are given and the licensing authority finds no objection. This is a form of negative clearance involving no assessment of the data and cannot be taken therefore as an indication of positive approval or that the licensing authority considers the proposed trial safe.

Doctors and dentists

Doctors and dentists conducting their own trials are exempt in some circumstances from the requirements to hold licences and certificates. Where a clinical trial in patients is to be initiated and conducted by a doctor or dentist *other than* under arrangements made by or with the manufacturer or supplier, there is no requirement for a CTC provided that certain conditions are met.[10] This exemption is generally referred to as the 'DDX' provision. In order to qualify the doctor or dentist must show:

(i)   that the seller or supplier of the product is selling or supplying it 'exclusively for the purposes of the trial', or if not, insofar as it is also sold or supplied for other purposes, these are covered by a product licence or certificate or under an exemption.
(ii)   that the clinical trial is 'not to be carried out under arrangements made by or on behalf of' the product's manufacturer, seller, supplier or the person responsible for its composition.
(iii)   that the doctor or dentist has notified the licensing authority of the trial, specifying the product, its use and the supplier's details.

In such cases the company supplier or seller is not required to have a product licence or a CTC.

The order means, for example, that if a doctor wishes to carry out trials on a drug which is licensed for certain indications but the trial is designed to investigate the use of the product in different indications, he would need to apply for a DDX. The manufacturer of the product would be supplying the doctor for the purposes of the trial. However, the manufacturer may also be supplying quantities of the drug to the same practitioner for use in its licensed indications, in which case those supplies must be covered by a product licence or an exemption provided by the Act.

To qualify for the DDX exemption, the trial must be the practitioner's responsibility and on his initiative. A DDX should not be sought where the trial is in reality to be carried out to the manufacturer's or supplier's design or at his desire, in which case a CTC or CTX should be obtained by the manufacturer or supplier.

It is not unusual for new drugs to be the subject of trials after licensing (Phase IV). A requirement for some form of subsequent monitoring of a newly licensed drug can often be made a term of the product licence. If a doctor is carrying out his own study with a licensed product and the study involves using the product for the indications for which it is licensed, the trial needs no regulatory approval provided that notification has been given to the licensing authority and proper arrangements made for reporting adverse reactions.[11] This provision would cover trials instigated by doctors whether within general practice or working within hospitals or clinics.

The application of general legal principles

In the UK, until the principles set out in the various codes of practice are enshrined in legislation, regard needs to be had to general principles of judge-made or 'common' law and general legislation [12] with a wider potential sphere of application than the conduct of clinical trials. In either case, the importance of compliance with the existing codes of practice cannot be overlooked. They represent in an authoritative form accepted standards of approach and method in relation to clinical research. A judge considering, for example, whether the common law duty to exercise reasonable care has been discharged in all the circumstances of a particular case will be likely to measure the conduct of the investigator, sponsor or other party involved in a trial according to the standards represented by such codes.

Legal obligations of the parties to clinical research

The sponsor's obligations to the investigator

The contract between the sponsor/manufacturer and the investigator will govern the legal relationship between them. Ideally, to avoid uncertainty and possible unnecessary dispute, the agreement should be in writing and clearly expressed.[13] There is no model format for such contracts [14] – they may be and often are contained in a letter. The overriding concern, however, is that they should be unambiguous and contain all the crucial details relating to the protocol to be adopted, information to be made available about the test product, reporting of adverse drug reactions, the duration of the study, the maintenance of patient confidentiality, the publication of results, liability for injury to subjects and the fee for the study. Under English law,[15] certain conditions are implied additionally into any contract for services. These include that the service will be performed with reasonable care and skill and in a reasonable period. There are also rules under statute [16] which may restrict the ability of the parties to exclude their liability for damages for personal injury caused by negligence.

The sponsor's obligations to the research subject

Contract

The Declaration of Helsinki does not address the matter of how the subject/sponsor relationship might be structured or recorded. In general, the sponsor and a patient subject do not enter into a direct contractual arrangement. However, where studies are to be conducted upon healthy volunteers a form of contract may and usually will exist. In 1970 the Association of the British Pharmaceutical Industry (ABPI) published a report [17] to which a simple form of written contract was appended. In 1986 the Royal College of Physicians [18] issued a report on healthy volunteer studies in which it advocated the use of a 'simple form of contract' mainly to ensure that the subject would be compensated for any injury occurring during a trial. In the appendix to the report the college provided a checklist of matters which should be considered when drawing up such a contract. In 1988, the ABPI published revised Guidelines for medical experiments in non-patient human volunteers which contained both a model patient information form and draft provisions for a volunteer agreement and consent form and stated that all volunteers 'must sign a simple form of agreement' (recording the basis upon which they agreed to participate and dealing with four other basic matters) with the sponsor or outside research establishment (depending upon who had the responsibility for recruitment and supervision).

Negligence

The tort (meaning a legal wrong) of negligence is based upon the principle that a person [19] owes to another a duty to exercise reasonable care and skill in order to avoid any act or omission which may injure that other person. A sponsor of a clinical trial has such a legal duty to the research subject and a negligent act or failure to act in relation to the design or conduct of a trial may expose the sponsor to liability for damages for any injury which arises as a result of that negligence. The yardstick against which the sponsor's actions and decisions will be judged is that of the state of scientific knowledge and standard medical practice at the relevant time.

The Declaration of Helsinki states that: 'Biomedical research involving human subjects must conform to generally accepted scientific principles and should be based on adequately performed laboratory and animal experimentation and on a thorough knowledge of the scientific literature'. Exposure to liability may arise in relation to the decision to proceed with a clinical trial. It is a significant event and the sponsor must have undertaken sufficient pre-clinical testing and have reviewed thoroughly the results of both those pre-clinical experiments and all relevant literature. On the basis of this examination, the sponsor must have reached a scientifically justifiable decision that it is sufficiently safe to proceed with the introduction of the research substance to humans.

The Declaration of Helsinki requires that 'the design ... of each experimental procedure involving human subjects should be clearly formulated in an experimental protocol . . .' and that a research project should proceed only if the hazards are believed to be 'predictable'. A sponsor must take care to design a protocol which, in accordance with ethical principles, has the potential to produce meaningful results and which does not expose the research subject to unnecessary hazard. As Mason and McCall Smith have commented:[20] 'Badly planned research loses all ethical justification if, as a result, the findings are scientifically useless'. It is probably fair to state that an unethical trial is likely to prove an unlawful one.

Similarly, care must be exercised in the manufacture of the compound to avoid any defect in the quality, such as contamination, arising. In practice, this should be a rare occurrence given the application of strict quality control systems.

Not only must the sponsor, having weighed all the information and collected data in relation to the research compound, have satisfied himself that it was reasonable to proceed with the trial, he must also ensure that reasonable care is exercised in the selection of a suitably qualified, experienced and competent investigator. Making appropriate enquiries to ascertain the potential investigator's credentials will generally discharge that burden. The Declaration of Helsinki specifically states that research should be conducted 'only by scientifically qualified persons . . . under the supervision of a clinically competent medical person'. It is left to the sponsor to judge correctly the level of qualification and experience which a particular trial merits.

The sponsor must also ensure that adequate information regarding the drug substance and its use is passed to the investigator at the outset and that new information arising during the currency of the trial is also passed over so that the investigator may himself judge the safety of the drug and the adequacy of the protocol design and make a proper selection of suitable trial subjects. However, it should be noted that the onus is also upon the investigator to ensure that he has all the information he needs to make an assessment of the drug and proposed protocol.

Strict liability

The impact of the 1985 EC Product Liability Directive [21] upon the sponsor's position in cases of injury suffered by research subjects has been minimal. Far from increasing the sponsor's exposure to damages, it probably excludes most cases involving research products. The directive provides that a 'producer' of a product (it is generally accepted that this *does* include research products) is strictly liable – in other words, liable even where there has been no negligence – for injury arising as a result of a defect in that product. A product may be judged defective not only on the basis of its physical make-up and properties but also on the basis of its presentation. In either case, a product will be defective only if its safety is 'not such as persons generally would be entitled to expect' having regard to all the circumstances. Since in making this assessment, the manner and purpose for which a product is supplied are relevant circumstances and since, in the field of research, the nature of a product is, by definition, experimental, it would seem difficult for a fully informed research subject to demonstrate that he was entitled to expect the product to be totally safe.

Obviously, where there was a simple failure in the production process leading to a defect in the quality of the substance itself, a volunteer would have a cause of action; but where the defect proved to be in the innate design of the product, the manufacturer would be liable only if the 'state of scientific knowledge at the time . . . was not such as to enable the existence of a defect to be discovered'. This is what is referred to as the 'development risk defence'. The inclusion in national law of such a defence was left optional under the terms of the product liability directive. Only Luxembourg chose not to incorporate it and has a true strict liability regime. The directive was implemented in the UK by the Consumer Protection Act 1987. The development risk defence as introduced into that Act has given rise to a great deal of controversy culminating in a formal letter to the UK government from the Commission in April 1989, and subsequently a 'reasoned opinion' from the Commission that the UK version offers a wider-based defence to producers than was intended or is in fact permitted under the terms of the directive. The Consumer Protection Act provides a defence where 'the state of scientific and technical knowledge at the relevant time was not such that a producer of products of the same description as the product in question might be expected to have discovered the defect if it had existed in his products while they were under his control'.[22] The argument is that the Act wrongly allows, at least indirectly, factors other than the theoretical ability to discover a defect to be taken into consideration – for example, practical and economic feasibility. The outcome of this dispute [23] could prove significant for sponsor/manufacturers in relation to the extent of pre-clinical experimentation undertaken before the decision to conduct clinical trials. If certain testing is theoretically possible, even though not generally or not extensively undertaken – for example, primate experiments – and if carried out would have permitted the discovery of certain hazards associated with the research substance, a sponsor would be in difficulties in asserting that the development risk defence, as interpreted by the European Commission, was applicable. It should also be borne in mind that the UK approach does not necessarily apply in other member states, where the most restrictive interpretation of the directive will be a feature of the national law.

Criminal liability

Currently there are two areas in which criminal sanctions will apply to the sponsor of a clinical trial:

(a) Medicines Act 1968. Failure by the manufacturer to obtain a clinical trial certificate (CTC), or an exemption from the need to hold a full certificate (CTX), or where the sponsor is a doctor or dentist, a DDX for the supply of medicinal products in a clinical trial involving patient subjects may lead to sanctions.

(b) Consumer Protection Act 1987. Section 10 of the Act requires that products supplied for private use or consumption must meet a general safety requirement. Again, all circumstances are taken into account in determining whether a product is 'reasonably safe'. Given the nature of the product, where regulatory requirements have been complied with and all other precautions to limit risk have been put into effect, it would appear that this general requirement would be satisfied.

The investigator's obligations to the sponsor

Contract

As discussed above, the agreement reached between a sponsor and investigator should specify their obligations towards one another. Investigators are normally expressly obliged to carry out the trial in accordance with the protocol with reasonable care and skill. Failure by the investigator to perform in accordance with the contract would be a breach of contract remediable in damages.

Negligence

In theory, an investigator who is negligent in performing a trial and has therefore rendered the results worthless to the sponsor could be said to have caused 'injury' to the sponsor in terms of lost time, waste of product and resources. However, there has been a legal debate as to the extent to which pure economic loss, not allied to damage to property or person, is recoverable in tort. A distinction is drawn between situations where the parties involved are in a special relationship, akin to a contractual one, and where the relationship is more distant. In the former case it is arguable on the basis of recent decisions that pure economic loss would be compensatable. There should be no difficulty in establishing such a relationship between the sponsor and investigator. However, given the existence of the contract between the two, there would be no apparent need in any event to pursue a claim in tort. Moreover, the actual loss suffered by the sponsor could be extremely difficult to quantify where it related to an *assumed* loss of marketing time on the basis that the research would have led to a successful product licence application. Since, during clinical trials, there is no guarantee that such an application can be made at all on the basis of the results this would prove a difficult area. In practice legal proceedings on any basis against the investigator would be unlikely.

The investigator's obligations to the research subject

Contract

The Declaration of Helsinki gives no guidance on how the subject/ investigator relationship should be structured or recorded. In general, there will not be a contractual relationship between the investigator and a trial subject. However, where the trial subject is a patient being treated in a private hospital or clinic or a healthy volunteer a contract may exist which will govern the relationship. It is not unusual to see consent forms used which are extensive and are, in effect, contracts between the parties, setting out obligations on both sides. For example, the investigator undertakes to maintain patient confidentiality and the volunteer agrees to disclose full medical information. In theory, a breach of such a contract could give rise to a claim for damages but in practice legal actions would be unlikely, certainly against the volunteer. However, a volunteer who failed to comply fully with the subject's obligations under the trial could, if injury occurred, find his damages reduced for contributory negligence.

Strict liability and negligence

The provisions of the Consumer Protection Act are unlikely to be of significance for the investigator in most cases. Strict liability applies only to the 'producer' of the product, so unless the investigator is preparing his own research product the Act will generally not apply. A mere supplier of product will be deemed to be a producer only in limited circumstances –

where, for example, the investigator is the first importer of a product into the European Community and/or cannot identify the person who supplied the product to him in the first instance. In the case of trials sponsored by the manufacturer, this situation is unlikely to arise.

In the majority of cases the investigator's liability to the research subject arises only in tort. The investigator must exercise reasonable care for the subject's welfare during the conduct of the trial and this conduct will be judged according to the standards of a recognised body of opinion skilled in science and medicine. In effect, if the investigator's actions (or non-actions) would be considered reasonable by a body of respected opinion in the field, he will be found to have exercised reasonable care.[24]

Most likely points of exposure to liability

The most likely points at which exposure to liability may arise are:

(1)   Upon receipt of the protocol and in the assessment of the pre-clinical data and information supplied by the intending sponsor of the trial.

   As has already been indicated, the investigator cannot simply rely upon the judgment of the sponsor. In accordance with the provisions of the Declaration of Helsinki, the investigator must, in order to discharge the responsibility to act with reasonable care, make a proper assessment of the trial project as a whole and satisfy himself that it is properly designed and scientifically justified and that the balance between the potential benefit and the anticipated risk inherent in the trial product is acceptable, taking into account whether the volunteer is a patient or 'healthy'.

(2)   When applying the selection criteria to possible volunteers.

   The investigator must do this conscientiously to ensure that unsuitable volunteers (those suffering from a condition or taking medication which is contraindicated) are excluded from the trial.

(3)   When supervising or conducting the trial, carrying out procedures and monitoring the subjects' response and condition.

   This involves the continuous re-assessment of the product over time both generally and as regards particular patient needs. Under the terms of the Declaration of Helsinki, physicians must cease any investigation where the hazards are discovered to outweigh the potential benefits generally and must place concern for the interests of the subject above those of science and society. The Declaration emphasises the doctor's ultimate responsibility for the well-being of all subjects whether patients or healthy volunteers.

(4)   On giving information and advice to a volunteer, both to obtain consent to participation in the trial and to ensure that the volunteer is kept informed thereafter so that subjects can, at any time, exercise their right to withdraw.

Central to the Declaration of Helsinki is the subject's right to 'safeguard his or her integrity', and the respect which must be accorded to that right by the investigator.

Obligations of others

Hospitals/medical establishments

The hospital or establishment in which a trial is to be conducted has a legal duty to ensure that the facilities and equipment available for a trial carried out on a site under its control are in proper order and safe in normal conditions of use.

Ethics committees

The need for independent review of proposed research protocols was firmly established by the Declaration of Helsinki. In practice, approval by an ethics committee is now essential for most research throughout Europe, although in most countries there is still no legal requirement to refer a proposal to an ethics committee. Unfortunately the Declaration gives no detailed guidance on the constitution or practice of such committees.

In the UK the Royal College of Physicians recommended in 1967 that all research projects carried out in medical institutions should be approved by an independent group of doctors and in 1973 made further recommendations concerning the composition and function of such committees. Two years later the Department of Health endorsed the college's proposals and issued a circular requiring health authorities to implement them, but it was only in 1984 that the college issued more detailed guidelines relating to the constitution and functions of the committees. Even now, the practice of committees is far from standardised.[25] In October 1989 the Department of Health began consultation on guidelines which, when introduced, would supersede the circular sent out in 1975. It relates to all research, whether in patients or healthy volunteers, and provides some guidance on the constitution of ethics committees, their functions and procedures. After some lengthy period, during which, in particular, the question of indemnities for individual ethics committee members from claims for damages was long debated, a final version was circulated within the NHS in August 1991. The issue of the potential liability of committee members remains unsettled. In theory, each individual member of a committee could be a defendant to an action alleging that the committee had been negligent in approving a trial in which the plaintiff took part. There is a strong argument that public bodies cannot be liable in negligence for the way they carry out their public functions because they owe no duty of care to individuals. However, the possibility remains. The Department of Health guidelines state that committee members employed by an NHS body are covered by NHS indemnity arrangements and that other members should be covered by the district health authority appointing the committee 'unless the member concerned is guilty of misconduct or gross lack of care', provided he notifies the health authority of any claim and cooperates fully. District health authorities may give undertakings to this effect to members who are not NHS employees.

Regulatory authorities

Claims have in the past been made against the licensing authority and its advisory committee (the Committee on Safety of Medicines) for damages for negligence in approving a drug for marketing. Similarly, in principle the licensing authority and its advisory committees could find themselves facing an action over the approval of a research proposal submitted in support of a CTC application. Actions over drug approvals have been started but have never gone to trial; in these cases the defendants have argued that public bodies owe no obligations under private law to individuals who may be affected by their decisions and actions. In addition, it may be difficult to show that the licensing authority or its committee acted unreasonably when they have acted in line with the opinion of a recognised body of medical and scientific experts (the committee members).

The trial monitor

The CPMP Guidelines make specific reference to the concept of the trial monitor, 'a person appointed by the sponsor . . . to be responsible to the sponsor . . . for monitoring and reporting on the progress of the trial and for verification of data', whose role is that of 'principal communication link between sponsor and investigator'. Where the monitor is an employee of the sponsor, the sponsor will be vicariously liable for injury resulting from any failures to perform the monitoring obligations. Where this is not the case, the monitor may be directly liable for his own negligence to an injured party. However, since the responsibility to appoint a properly qualified monitor is the sponsor's, any failures arising from lack of experience could become the responsibility of the sponsor alone unless the monitor also knew he was unfitted for the job.

Consent

Validity

It is in the area of consent that some of the greatest difficulties can arise. The issue of consent to treatment has been the subject of several court decisions in recent years and some of the general principles which apply to consent to treatment can equally be applied in the sphere of clinical research. The consent of a research subject (as with a patient undergoing orthodox treatment) to undergoing any procedure or exposure to a drug substance will render lawful what may otherwise amount to 'trespass to the person' (or even a criminal assault). Consent will also prevent a claim for damages if a trial subject has been warned of a particular risk and the risk materialises, because he will be taken to have assumed the risk.

In the absence of consent, any deliberate act which leads to physical contact (outside what may normally occur in daily living) is technically a 'battery'. There is some doubt about the extent to which a claim for trespass might properly be brought by a research subject following a court decision in 1987 [26] which suggested that the act in question would need to be not only deliberate but also involve a hostile element. No clear definition of what was meant by this was given and it is certainly arguable that an act by a physician in the course of his profession could never be so characterised. In any event, subsequent cases have not pursued this approach, holding only that express consent is required to conduct outside what normally occurs during everyday life. It should also be noted that an omission on the part of a physician to disclose all or any of the risks which a procedure may involve will not necessarily render the subject's consent void – and therefore make the act a trespass to the person – if in all other respects it was genuine. (By contrast, a failure to warn may be sufficient to found a claim for damages in negligence.)

Consent may be express or implied, but it must also be demonstrated to be genuine in the sense that the volunteer must have been adequately informed of the nature and general purpose of the study and have given consent freely without being placed under duress or pressure of any kind.[27] Consent, however, also presupposes a degree of understanding and the ability on the subject's part to appreciate what is being explained and to weigh up the position before reaching a decision. Obvious difficulties arise in relation to those who are legally incompetent (lacking legal capacity to consent on their own behalf) – children and the mentally impaired. Neither are specifically mentioned in the Nuremberg Code, and the Declaration of Helsinki provides only that 'in the case of legal incompetence, informed consent should be obtained from a legal guardian in accordance with national legislation. Where physical or mental incapacity makes it impossible to obtain a form of consent, or where the subject is a minor, permission from the responsible relative replaces that of the subject in accordance with national legislation'. There is, of course, no such legislation in the UK and again those involved in the sponsoring and conduct of research have to fall back upon common law and ethical principles.

Children

Department of Health guidelines [28] state that investigations using child subjects should be carried out only if 'absolutely essential' and raise the thorny issue of consent by or on behalf of a minor.

The validity of consent given by a legal guardian (usually a parent) on behalf of a child may depend on the type of research involved. Where the research is therapeutic in nature so that the child has potential to benefit from participation, it is easier to apply the principles derived from court decisions on consent to treatment to the research. Under English law:

(a)   a child under 18 but over 16 can properly consent to treatment without regard to the wishes of his or her parents (Family Law Reform Act 1969);
(b)   a child under 16 will have the capacity to consent if he has the maturity and understanding to make an informed decision;[29]
(c)   a child under 16 who does not have the capacity to understand as described above may have consent given on his or her behalf by the legal guardian.

There was an interesting development of this approach in a Court of Appeal decision in July 1991.[30] The case involved the *refusal* of treatment by a 15-year-old mentally unstable girl. In the course of his judgment Lord Donaldson, Master of the Rolls, said that a child mature enough to make an informed decision 'could consent but if he or she declined to do so, consent could be given by someone else who had parental rights or responsibilities'. This would mean that if such a child refused treatment but parental consent was obtained, treatment could lawfully be given. However, the Department of Health guidelines for ethics committees issued in August 1991 state: 'The giving of consent by a parent or guardian cannot override a refusal of consent by a child who is competent to make that decision'.

The analysis is more difficult where the research is non-therapeutic in nature and thus does not carry the potential to benefit the child subject at all. In theory there seems to be no reason why the child's capacity to understand and to make an informed choice regarding participation should not apply equally here, but there is no direct legal authority. The matter which raises the greatest difficulty is whether a legal guardian can ever consent on behalf of a child to medical procedures which carry even a minimal risk which is not balanced by the potential to produce individual benefit. If the parental duty can be defined as an obligation not to do anything clearly against the child's best interests, it would seem arguable that a parent may take into consideration issues other than direct individual benefits such as the contribution to the general welfare and scientific progress in coming to a proper decision. If this view is correct and a study has otherwise been found acceptable by an ethics committee, consent by a parent to such research *may* be valid and effective. Until the issue has been fully argued before a UK court, however, legal uncertainty will persist and this has led to a reluctance to carry out research on children which may well carry long-term implications. Early statements issued by the Medical Research Council [31] and the Department of Health [32] expressed the view that there could be no effective proxy consent in cases of non-therapeutic research. 'In the strict view of the law, parents and guardians of minors cannot give consent on their behalf to any procedures which are of no particular benefit to them and which may carry some risk of harm.' Most bodies, in particular the Medicines Commission, advise that efforts should not be made to include child participants in healthy volunteer studies of medicinal products. In its 1991 guidelines to ethics committees the Department of Health has barely altered its position. While appearing to acknowledge that in cases involving virtually no risk, parents may give consent without any adverse consequences, the circular points out that in permitting a child to be subjected to non-therapeutic research parents may be acting 'illegally'.

The mentally impaired

Here also there is a lack of clear and specific legal authority. Starting from the principle that the law is intended to safeguard the personal physical integrity of all individuals, the standard approach has been that no measures should be taken unless a mentally impaired subject is in a position to consent on his own behalf. Where this is not possible it has been stated that proxy consent cannot authorise research procedures.[32]

In a case involving a non-therapeutic operation – sterilisation to prevent pregnancy – a 17-year-old mentally handicapped girl was made a ward of court so that the court could decide whether she should undergo the procedure.[33] The Court's decision was reached by applying the approach adopted in all wardship proceedings; that of determining what is in the child's best interests. It is difficult to see how, in cases of pure research, a court could find the 'best interests test' satisfied.

Reference to the court for a declaration of legality was also made in the case of a mentally impaired adult where her doctors and family considered that a termination of a pregnancy and subsequent sterilisation were in the mentally handicapped woman's best interests.[34] The court was asked to declare that the procedures would not amount to trespass to the person and did so on the basis that two matters had to be taken into account: the patient's best interests and what would amount to good medical practice. The case indicates that a doctor may *treat* an adult who is legally incapable of giving consent, provided it is in that patient's best interests, but the Law Lords indicated that cases involving non-therapeutic procedures, such as sterilisation to prevent pregnancy, should be referred to the court as a matter of good practice. This is hardly likely to be practical in cases of research.

In cases of therapeutic research, therefore, where a patient could be anticipated to derive some benefit from participation in the trial, it would seem logical to apply the principles which appear to emerge from the cases discussed above, but these could not provide any firm assurances for investigators.

Information, consent and negligence

In discharging the duty of care towards trial subjects, the investigator must disclose to the volunteer, and offer advice with regard to, any 'material risks' to the subject's health (both physical and mental) which may arise out of participation in the research.[35] The subject can exercise the right to self determination only if the investigator has supplied sufficient information in all the circumstances. If, having been given that information, the subject nevertheless chooses to participate in a study and risk injury and that injury occurs, the subject will have no legal claim for damages. His consent, in effect, provides a defence to a claim in negligence which is based upon the existence of the risk. This does not mean that the investigator would be absolved from responsibility for any separate negligent act or omission which occurs during supervision of research or during treatment of the subject. An investigator cannot 'contract out' of exposure to liability for death or bodily injury which arises out of his own negligence.

The issue which arises is the degree of information which must be given in a particular case to discharge the burden of responsibility. It might be assumed that the general principle that a subject must be able to give 'informed consent' means that in every case nothing less than a *full* explanation of *all* the possible risks would suffice.[36] However, again drawing on common law made by cases involving treatment, this is not in fact the law.

In the UK, recent cases suggest that the doctor's obligation to disclose information regarding risks is limited to such disclosure as is reasonable in the light of all the circumstances. A doctor, therefore, who acts in accordance with accepted medical practice is unlikely to be found negligent.[37] However, it is unlikely that a failure to disclose any material risk would be acceptable.[38] The Nuremberg Code states that 'risks reasonably to be expected in relation to a trial should be disclosed to the subject'. The Declaration of Helsinki says subjects should be 'adequately informed of the aims, methods, anticipated benefits and potential hazards of the study and the discomfort it may entail'. Neither affords much assistance in drawing the practical line. What is 'reasonably to be expected' is clearly something less than what in theory may occur and the phrase 'adequate information' begs the question. There is no doubt that too much information can lead to confusion and may be counter-productive, yet individuals in recent times have become better informed and less likely to accept without question the judgment of professionals in health matters. Where the subject asks for information it ought to be provided subject, arguably in the case of patients only, to the doctor's duty to have regard to the best interests of the patient.[38]

Certainly in the case of healthy volunteers, who can hope to have no direct benefit from participation in the study, most risks involved in *any* procedures to which they will be subjected will be 'material' because they cannot be offset against potential personal benefit. Confusion is not likely to arise which could lead to the rejection of potentially beneficial treatment and so it would be an unusual case where disclosure to a volunteer could be less than complete. UK ethical guidelines certainly seem to take a tough line consistent with that applied in many US states. The CPMP guidelines of 1990 and the legislation of 1988 (amended in 1990) in the Republic of Ireland both endorse the full disclosure approach. Moreover the duty to inform is a continuing obligation.

In advising a *patient* to participate in and continue to participate in a controlled trial, the doctor's overriding duty is to act in the best interests of the patient. It is difficult therefore, for a doctor to advise a patient to enter a study unless it appears that, at the very least, the patient's health will not be prejudiced by taking part. The Declaration of Helsinki puts the matter more positively than this when it says that there must be a chance, through participation, of saving life, re-establishing health or alleviating suffering and that every patient should be assured of the 'best proven diagnostic and therapeutic method'. Where a trial has been designed to compare two therapeutic groups, the fact that the doctor genuinely does not know whether the established treatment or the product under investigation will prove the better treatment is unlikely to pose a problem. Since most of these trials are randomised and conducted under blind conditions, it is advisable that the patient should be made aware of this, bearing in mind that the patient assumes that the physician will choose what he genuinely considers to be the best treatment for the patient and consent is generally given on that basis. As the Medical Research Council has pointed out: 'The progress of medical knowledge has depended and will continue to depend in no small measure upon the confidence which the public has in those who carry out research.'[31]

Problems may occur where the intention is that the research treatment should be tested against a placebo. The Declaration of Helsinki seems to allow for 'control groups' but does not address how the investigator reconciles the obligation to assure the best proven therapeutic or diagnostic method with this type of trial design. Where there is, in fact, no alternative to the treatment under trial, or where the study is to establish the effect of adding the new treatment to a course of therapy under an existing treatment, it is easier to argue that the use of the group is acceptable since it does not involve a withholding of treatment. Commentators appear to agree that the central issue in such cases is one of consent: that if the patient is made aware of the possibility of being switched to a placebo in the course of a study, if the risks are minimal and if the patient agrees, there should be no question of negligence arising. This appears to be borne out by the Irish legislation which states that a patient should be made aware of the possibility of receiving a placebo and therefore appears to accept that this is legitimate practice. The CPMP guidelines make a similar recommendation.

Form of consent

A matter which has often been discussed is whether the consent of the subject should be oral or written. The Declaration of Helsinki refers to 'preferably written' consent. German law requires that the consent of the patient must either be in writing or be witnessed independently. In the Republic of Ireland, written consent (subject to certain exceptions) is also required. So far as the UK is concerned, there are no particular legal requirements although ethical guidelines endorse the view that consent in writing is preferable. Genuine and effective consent can be given orally, although from a practical point of view it is more difficult to prove. If given orally, consent should therefore preferably be witnessed. Department of Health guidelines advise NHS bodies to obtain written consent to all research and to record this in a patient's case notes.[39] Most of the codes of practice and guidelines advise that consent and a note of the information which has been disclosed in order to obtain it should be recorded in writing. The CPMP guidelines agree. In many cases researchers use standard printed consent forms which may refer the patient to a standard information sheet which should be read before signing. This type of documentation assists in providing evidence of a subject's agreement; however, it cannot be decisive. Analysis of the volunteer's state of mind and the nature of the information and advice received is fundamental. Moreover, since an underlying principle of all research is that the subject must be free to withdraw from the trial at any time, the issue of consent remains a live one throughout the currency of any trial.

Compensation and indemnities

The issue of compensation is not dealt with at all by the Declaration of Helsinki. Injury does not automatically lead to compensation. In the UK and most EC member states a patient injured as a result of participation in a clinical trial will be entitled to compensation only if his injury results from negligence or his case falls within the provisions of the strict liability legislation. If neither of those conditions is fulfilled, he must rely upon the possibility of an *ex gratia* payment from the trial sponsor or investigator. In view of what has been said above, it will be clear that it can be very difficult in research to show that negligence has occurred. By definition, injury can arise irrespective of the degree of care which is shown. Moreover, the burden of proving negligence rests with the claimant, who will not have the same degree of specialism or knowledge as the sponsor or investigator.

The general issue of compensation for personal injury has become controversial in recent years, set against the background of an increasingly litigious public. The fact that a volunteer, whose participation is necessary for the advancement of medical and scientific knowledge which could benefit society, can be left without financial help has been the subject of criticism, particularly since the volunteer is least able financially to bear the burden of the risk of research study.

Compensation arrangements vary according to the type of body sponsoring research. The Medical Research Council in the UK has said that it will consider making *ex gratia* payments in 'appropriate' cases but makes no commitment. The Department of Health draft guidelines contained a similar statement. However, the published guidelines significantly omit any reference to NHS bodies' readiness to consider *ex gratia* payments. The recommendation of the Royal Commission on Civil Liability and Compensation for Personal Injury [40] that volunteers who suffer severe damage should have a right to claim compensation on a strict liability basis has never been pursued. Other proposals have included a no-fault compensation scheme financed on an insurance basis by those promoting and involved in research.[41]

The issue is, however, addressed in the industry association codes of practice. The ABPI codes differentiate between research involving healthy volunteers and research using patient volunteers. For the former, the ABPI recommends [42] a specific and contractually binding undertaking to compensate them or their dependents in the event of 'any significant deterioration in health or well-being caused directly by participation in a study'. The code recommends compensation calculated by reference to the level of damages which would be obtained from an English court for similar injuries had liability and negligence been established. The undertaking should also make provision for arbitration in the case of dispute. The principle is that a volunteer should be provided for with as little bureaucracy and delay as possible. Where there may be an issue as to whether the investigator's negligence caused the injury, this should not hinder payment by the sponsor to the subject. The sponsor may still take action against the investigator for an indemnity or contribution towards compensation paid. The guidelines very clearly do not seek to prevent a volunteer from pursuing a claim in negligence or strict liability if he wishes. Both the Medicines Commission and the Department of Health have recommended that the undertaking to provide compensation should be accompanied by evidence of the sponsor's ability to honour the undertaking.

So far as patient volunteers are concerned, a discussion of the arrangements for compensation may not always be appropriate, depending upon the state of health of the intended volunteer.[43] The physician may not wish to hand the patient a consent form or contractually binding undertaking to compensate. The ABPI considers that 'the imposition of a contractual relationship between individual patient and pharmaceutical company against a background of treatment normally being given outside a contractual setting is fraught with problems'. The association believes any attempt would be 'unworkable' in practice.[44] The ABPI guidelines advise member companies initiating or sponsoring research to give an 'assurance' to the investigator, and thus ethics committees, that the guidelines will be adhered to in the event of injury attributable to participation in the trial. While this is not legally binding, as a matter of practice, one could not imagine a situation where a company sponsor would be prepared to break faith with the assurance and expose itself to criticism and damage to reputation which may render it difficult to arrange a trial in the future.

It should be noted that the assurance that compensation will be paid ceases upon expiry of the trial. Patients whose doctors choose to continue to use the treatment after that date would not be covered, and the ABPI advises members to continue supplying the product only if the physician agrees to assume responsibility for its administration. Also it should be emphasised that these guidelines do not apply to Phase IV (post marketing) trials nor to trials initiated by doctors or dentists who obtain a DDX.

There is also still a difference between what is required of a company sponsor and what arrangements can be expected from government and academic bodies involved in initiating research. In the latter case, research subjects still depend upon the mere possibility of receiving an *ex gratia* payment in cases of injury. This has been criticised by the Royal College of Physicians in its 1990 report on research in patients. The guidelines from the Department of Health do provide that an ethics committee should ensure that research volunteers are made aware of the compensation arrangements which exist. It is arguable, therefore, that where there are no arrangements, this should be brought to the attention of the volunteer, who may as a result decline to participate.

Both investigators and the health authorities in whose hospitals research takes place will want to ensure that they are protected against claims for damages arising out of the conduct of clinical trials. Where research activities fall outside the normal course of the physician's employment, he will need to rely on his defence organisation for protection against claims. However, it is not unusual for an investigator to ask a sponsor to indemnify him against any liability and expenses he may incur as a result of a successful claim by a volunteer. Generally, this indemnity would not extend to cases where the injury was caused by the investigator's negligence. The sponsor quite rightly often makes the indemnity conditional upon being kept fully informed and being given notice of any claim or circumstances likely to give rise to a claim, and will occasionally reserve the right to take over the conduct of the defence.

Some health authorities have sought to establish a standard form of indemnity for studies which cover not only the investigators individually but also the authority against *all* losses, except those which arise as a result of the negligence of the authority or its staff. In negotiating such indemnity arrangements, some authorities will also seek proof of the indemnifying company's ability to pay out under the indemnity. While these are commercial issues between the authority and the sponsor, it has been a question of concern that in some cases local research ethics committees have been asked to make protocol approval *conditional* upon an indemnity of this nature. To do so would take the ethics committee outside its remit, which is purely the ethical vetting of the study.

Against this complex and often uncertain background, the parties to research projects might hope for more helpful and legally authoritative guidance emerging eventually from Europe.

Notes

1   [1893] 1 QB 450 at 453.
2   There is no legislation in the UK governing the actual performance of clinical research. Trials involving healthy volunteers are completely unregulated. In Europe, only France, Spain, Eire and Germany have enacted any legislation. (See Protection of Persons undergoing Biomedical Research, Law no 88–1138–1988 as amended in 1990 and 1991 (France); Control of Clinical Trials Act 1987 as amended by Control of Clinical Trials and Drugs Act 1990 (Eire); German Drug Law 1976 BG Ble.1.1976 p 2445 Sections 40–42; Law on Medicines no 25/1990 (Spain).
3   The Code includes the following summarised 'basic principles':

   (a)   the voluntary consent of the subject is absolutely essential;
   (b)   experiments should be likely to produce results which could prove of general benefit unprocurable by other methods;
   (c)   an experiment should be properly designed and justifiable given the disease or problems to which it is addressed and the results of previous animal testing;
   (d)   all unnecessary pain, suffering or injury, physical or mental, should be avoided;
   (e)   no experiment should be conducted if there is reason to believe that injury, disablement or death may occur;
   (f)   the degree of risk taken should always be balanced or exceeded by the importance of the problem to be solved by the experiment;
   (g)   proper preparation should be made and proper facilities provided to protect the subject;
   (h)   only scientifically qualified persons should conduct experiments;
   (i)   the subject must be able to halt the experiment at any time;
   (j)   the investigator must be prepared to stop the experiment if he has reason to believe that to continue may lead to injury, disablement or death.

4   Association of the British Pharmaceutical Industry (ABPI) letter and guidelines on data to support the administration of new chemical entities to non-patient volunteers (1985) May 17 and Declaration of Helsinki basic principle number 12.

5 See, for example, Association of the British Pharmaceutical Industry (ABPI) Guidelines for Medical Experiments in Non-patient Human Volunteers (1988) and Clinical Trials Compensation Guidelines (1991); Royal College of Physicians Guidelines: 'Research on Healthy Volunteers' (1986) 20 RCP Journal, no 4, Research Involving Patients (1990) and Guidelines on the Practice of Ethics Committees in Medical Research involving Human Subjects (January 1990).

6 III/3976/88-EN.

7 Discussion Paper on the need for a Directive on Clinical Trials III/3044/91 (1991) January 23.

8 Medicines Act 1968, ss. 31–38. Trials involving healthy volunteers are not subject to regulation under the Medicines Act: products for supply only to healthy volunteers fall outside the definition of 'medicinal product' under the Act (s. 130(4)) and are therefore not subject to it.

9 Medicines (Exemption from Licences) (Clinical Trials) Order 1981 no 164.

10 Medicines (Exemption from Licences) (special cases and miscellaneous provisions) Order 1972 no 1200, Article 4.

11 Exemption from Licences (Clinical Trials) Order 1974 no 498.

12 E.g. Consumer Protection Act 1987.

13 The Association of the British Pharmaceutical Industry states in its *Report on the Relationship between Physicians and The Pharmaceutical Society* (October 1986): 'Formal arrangements are essential'.

14 See, however, guidance on what to consider in the Association of British Pharmaceutical Industry Circular 87/89.

15 Supply of Goods and Services Act 1982.

16 Unfair Contract Terms Act 1977.

17 *Report of the Committee to Investigate Medical Experiments in Staff Volunteers.*

18 'Research on Healthy Volunteers' (1986) 20 RCP Journal, no 4.

19 Legal 'persons' include corporate bodies and individuals.

20 J.K. Mason and R.A. McCall Smith, *Law and Medical Ethics* (3rd edn, 1991).

21 85/374/EEC OJ no L210/29.

22 Consumer Protection Act 1987, s. 4(1)(e).

23 At the time of writing, the Commission had not yet decided whether to institute further formal proceedings.

24 *Gold v Haringey Health Authority* [1987] 2 All ER 888; *Bolam v Friern Hospital Management Committee* [1957] 2 All ER 118.

25 The Medicines Act makes no provision for ethics committees although it recognises their existence. The refusal of a committee to sanction a trial must be reported by the sponsor to the licensing authority.

26 *Wilson v Pringle* [1987] QB 237.

27 Special care must be taken in this regard with those who are in a dependent or subordinate relationship with the sponsor or investigator or otherwise, e.g. employees, prisoners, existing patients.

28 Local Research Ethics Committees HSG(91)5.

29 *Gillick v West Norfolk and Wisbech Area Health Authority* [1985] 3 All ER 402, HL. Most codes of practice in fact advise that even in these circumstances parental agreement should be obtained.

30 *Re R (a minor) (Wardship: Medical Treatment)* [1991] 4 All ER 177.

31 Medical Research Council *Responsibilities in Investigations on Human Subjects* (Cmnd 2382) (1962–3).

32   HSC(IS)153 (June 1975), which states: 'Health Authorities are advised that they ought not to infer from this recommendation that the fact that consent has been given by a parent or guardian and that the risk involved is considered negligible will be sufficient to bring such clinical research investigation within the law as it now stands.'

33   *Re B (a minor) (Wardship: Sterilisation)* [1988] AC 199, [1987] 2 All ER 206, [1987] 2 WLR 1213.

34   *In Re F (Mental patient: Sterilisation)* [1990] 2 AC 1 and see also *T v T* [1988] 1 All ER 613.

35   *Reibl v Hughes* (1980) 114 DLR (3d) 1. 'Even if a certain risk is a mere possibility that ordinarily need not be disclosed, yet if its occurrence raises serious consequences, as for example paralysis or even death, it should be regarded as a material risk requiring disclosure'.

36   This is the approach followed in many jurisdictions in the USA: a patient's right to know overrides the need to know, unless disclosure would be detrimental to the patient's well being.

37   *Bolam v Friern Hospital Management Committee* [1957] 2 All ER 118; *Sidaway v Governors of Bethlem Royal Hospital* [1985] 1 All ER 643: '. . . although a decision on what risks should be disclosed for the particular patient to be able to make a rational choice . . . was primarily a matter of clinical judgment the disclosure of a particular risk of serious adverse consequences might be so obviously necessary for the patient to make an informed choice that no reasonably prudent doctor would fail to disclose that risk.' See also: *Gold v Haringey Health Authority* [1987] 2 All ER 888.

38   *per* Lord Bridge of Harwich in *Sidaway*.

39   N. 28, and see also HC(90)22 Consent to examination or treatment.

40   (Cmnd 7084) (1978).

41   See, for example, Ciba Foundation Study Group *Medical Research, Civil Liberty and Compensation for Injury* (1980).

42   Guidelines for Medical Experiments in Non-Patient Human Volunteers (1988).

43   ABPI Clinical Trials Compensation Guidelines (1991).

44   Letter to members, February 20, 1991.

Chapter 9

Product Liability

Introduction

Product liability claims over pharmaceutical products are a growth area in the UK. Currently in the English courts there are at least three active multi-plaintiff actions over drugs and other medical products – benzodiazepines, the contrast medium Myodil, and the Copper 7 IUD. Group action over human insulin, steroids, and human growth hormone is threatened. Claims involving faulty artificial heart valves are being settled by the manufacturers without litigation, and the government has settled claims by haemophiliacs infected with HIV by contaminated blood products.

As recently as 15 years ago there had been only one major multi-plaintiff action over pharmaceutical products – the thalidomide case. In the intervening period a number of such cases have been disposed of, including litigation over benoxaprofen (Opren), pertussis vaccine and neomycin. No UK court, however, has yet made a finding of liability against a drug company for injuries caused by a medicinal product. In some cases – thalidomide and Opren – the manufacturers have made out-of-court settlements, while in others – pertussis vaccine and neomycin – the court has found in the manufacturers' favour.

Inevitably such litigation will involve the medical profession as witnesses of fact. This is because any product which is pharmacologically active and liable to cause unwanted side-effects is likely to be available only on prescription, and non-pharmaceutical products are likely to have been used by a surgeon in an operation or administered or prescribed by a doctor. Where products give rise to litigation the physician or surgeon who has used them in the course of his treatment may be required to justify their use, either as a witness or even as a defendant. Accordingly, the increase in this area of litigation is as significant for doctors as the growth in medical negligence claims which it mirrors.

Types of liability

Producers of drugs and other medical products can be made responsible for their products under both tort law and contract law. In contract, producers may owe a contractual duty to any person with whom they make a contract for the supply or manufacture of the product. In tort (the word means a civil wrong) they owe a duty of care to those who may be affected by their negligence in the design or manufacture of the product – so-called 'fault' liability. In addition, since 1988, when the Consumer Protection Act 1987 came into force, producers may be liable for injuries caused by defects in their products whether or not they were negligent – so-called 'strict liability'.

A doctor may be liable in contract or in tort if he treats a patient privately for a fee, or in tort alone if the patient is an NHS patient.

Liability in contract

The manufacturer owes a number of duties relating to the goods which he manufactures and sells. The duties stem from the contract of sale and are therefore owed only to the immediate buyer. It would be unusual for the producer of a medical product to have a contractual relationship with the user of the product. In the case of prescription-only medicine, the manufacturer probably has such a relationship only with his wholesaler, who in turn has a contractual relationship with the retail pharmacist (or in country areas with the rural dispenser). The pharmacist has a contractual relationship with the patient only if the prescription is dispensed privately. Remedies under contract law are not likely to be important, therefore, in pharmaceutical product liability claims.

Implied terms are imported into the contract by statute, in the case of the product manufacturer by the Sale of Goods Act 1979, which requires the goods sold to be fit for their purpose and of merchantable quality. In a sense the obligation imposed on the seller is strict, because the presence of fault is irrelevant for the purposes of determining whether the contract has been breached. If the goods are unfit or unmerchantable, then the seller is liable for the damage which results to the buyer. This is relevant only in the case of non-NHS prescriptions or operations in which products are used; in most cases in the medical field the manufacturer and the person who sells the product to the consumer will not be the same. However, a surgeon who uses a defective prosthesis in an arthroplasty which he sells to the patient is in effect guaranteeing the quality and suitability of the product, and associated products used, such as adhesives.

Since the manufacturer will rarely have a contract with the ultimate user of the product, the reality is that the duty in tort is of much more importance in the field of product liability, given that the manufacturer is usually the target for the aggrieved patient when treatment involving a medical product goes wrong.

Fault liability

The other type of duty is that of 'fault' – the duty to take such care for the safety of the product user as is reasonably necessary in the circumstances. The strict liability brought in by the Consumer Protection Act 1987 has not replaced fault liability. The strict duty has been grafted on to the fault duty and it may in certain circumstances be necessary to fall back on fault duty if liability is to be established.

Failure to take care for the safety of the patient is negligence which, if it causes injury, gives rise to the obligation to pay damages. In this the obligation of the product maker is no different from that of the doctor, except in one important respect. It is now well established that a doctor is not negligent if he has acted in accordance with a practice accepted as proper by a responsible body of practitioners skilled in that art. Could a pharmaceutical company invoke the same test, given that its medical department will consist largely of doctors? There is a strong argument for saying that the same test applies. If the manufacturer can show that other responsible manufacturers would have done the same, then it would be difficult to contend that because some might have done differently negligence is established.

Mention must be made of the provisions of the Medicines Act 1968, which together with its subordinate legislation substantially controls the development, manufacture, sale and supply and import and export of medicinal products. That Act was passed as a direct consequence of the thalidomide disaster and was intended to remedy the inadequacies in the system for the control of medicinal products. The scheme of the Act is based upon an elaborate system of licensing, and a number of agencies are set up to assist in the licensing and subsequent control of medicines. Chief among these are the Medicines Commission and the Committee on Safety of Medicines. While subsection (2) of section 133 makes clear that breach of the Act or of regulations made under it does not give rise to a cause of action, any breach of its provisions (for example, those relating to the content of data sheets) will inevitably be relied on by those who allege that they have suffered damage as a consequence of a defective medicine.

On the other hand compliance with the provisions of the Act will (equally inevitably) be relied on by manufacturers whose medicines are being impugned. The stringent standards of testing and clinical trials imposed by the licensing authority (the Health and Agriculture Ministers), the Committee on Safety of Medicines and the Medicines Control Agency before a licence is granted for a new medicinal product and the control over post-marketing surveillance imposed through the terms of product licences can be relied on as evidence of compliance with the highest standards. It is perhaps for this reason that in recent cases it has become fashionable for the Government licensing and control bodies to be sued alongside the manufacturers.

Strict liability

The EC Directive on Product Liability, enacted in the Consumer Protection Act 1987, has altered the duty owed by a manufacturer of products put into circulation within the EC. The directive, intended to harmonise the law on product liability in the EC's member states, makes manufacturers strictly liable for injuries caused by their products. If the patient can show that the product caused the injuries then liability is established without proof of negligence. This has to be qualified, for not every injury will give rise to liability.

It is well known, for example, that treatment with some forms of cytotoxic chemotherapy carries the risk of serious side-effects. If the patient is warned of these and agrees nonetheless to undergo the treatment then plainly he cannot complain if such untoward effects ensue. He has agreed to take the risk of the side-effects as the price to pay for the benefit of the treatment. The significance of warnings provided by the manufacturer and the position of the treating doctor with regard to them are considered in more detail below. With this type of duty the question whether the manufacturer was negligent is irrelevant. It is enough simply to show that the product caused the damage complained of.

Section 2 of the Act states:

'Where any damage is caused wholly or partly by a defect in a product, every person to whom subsection (2) applies shall be liable for the damage.'

Subsection (2) applies to:

'(a)   the producer of the product
 (b)   any person who has held himself out to be the producer of the product
 (c)   any person who has imported the product into a member state in the course of any business of his to supply it to another.'

Subsection (3) makes the supplier of the product stand in place of the producer if the person suffering the damage asks him to identify the producer (as in subsection (2)) and he fails to do so. Thus if a doctor undertaking rural dispensing is asked by his patient to identify the producer of a pharmaceutical product which the patient alleges caused him damage and the doctor is unable to do so, the doctor may well have imposed upon him as the supplier of the product the same strict liability as would be imposed upon the manufacturer. In these days of the limited list and generic prescribing this is a matter of no small significance.

What constitutes a defective product? Section 3 states:

'There is a defect in a product if the safety of the product is not such as persons generally are entitled to expect.'

In determining what persons are entitled to expect by way of safety all the circumstances are to be taken into account. A number of matters to be taken into account are referred to expressly, the most important of which (at least for the purposes of this chapter) is:

'the manner in which and purposes for which the product has been marketed . . . and any instructions for and warnings with respect to doing or refraining from doing anything with or in relation to the product.'

Thus a very material consideration in assessing the safety of the product will be the nature of any warnings giving about it to the recipient.

Despite the strict nature of the liability imposed by the Act there are a number of defences, chief among which is the so-called 'development risk' defence. The European directive allowed member states to choose whether or not to include this defence in their domestic legislation and amid considerable controversy the UK chose to incorporate it in the Act. The relevant subsection provides:

'It shall be a defence for a producer to show –

(e)   that the state of scientific and technical knowledge at the relevant time was not such that a producer of products of the same description as the product in question might be expected to have discovered the defect if it had existed in his products while they were under his control.'

The scope of the defence has yet to be interpreted by the courts. There are those who argue that it allows manufacturers to escape strict liability and merely reverses the burden of proving negligence, requiring manufacturers to show that they were not negligent rather than requiring the product user to prove negligence. But notwithstanding that this defence was largely incorporated at the behest of the research-based pharmaceutical industry, on a strict interpretation it may be of fairly limited value so far as medical products are concerned. This can be illustrated by an example. The ability to cause phocomelia in the fetus characteristic of thalidomide was not discovered by the animal tests the product received prior to marketing. Indeed, for a considerable time after the tragedy was discovered, scientists were still unable to reproduce an animal model of the condition. It was only after many years that the condition was reproduced in a particular strain of the New Zealand white rabbit.

Applying the development risk defence, could it be said that Distillers (the licensed UK manufacturers of thalidomide) might have been expected to have discovered the defect in thalidomide? In one sense they certainly could have discovered it if they had conducted reproductive toxicity studies using the appropriate rodent. Was the state of scientific knowledge at the time such that they should have done? In this area there are those who argue that the risk of serious consequences is so great that a company with the resources of our major research-based pharmaceutical companies should discover such a defect, however obscure the tests required. It is unlikely that a court would impose so strict a standard, but until a case on the defence actually reaches the courts the correct interpretation of this provision can only be a matter of conjecture.

Common to liability in both contract and tort and to both fault and strict liability is the need to prove that the product caused the injury. It is erroneous for that reason (if for no other) to regard liability without proof of fault as a solution to the problems posed by the present system of compensation, particularly in the field of medical accidents. In most of the recent cases concerning defective products, causation has been a major if not *the* major issue. This was particularly so in the whooping cough vaccine case, *Loveday v Renton*,[1] in which Lord Justice Stuart Smith answered the question whether pertussis vaccine causes permanent brain damage in children in the negative. Without proof of causation there can be no compensation no matter how negligent a defendant may have been. Causation is likely to continue to be a major hurdle in the path of a plaintiff whatever changes are made to the system of compensation.

Product defects

We have considered above how the Consumer Protection Act 1987 defines a defect in a product. In the Sale of Goods Act 1979 goods are not described as defective, but tests are set out for determining whether goods are of merchantable quality or fit for their purpose which obviously have a considerable bearing on this question. What constitutes a defect for the purposes of tort is best considered in the context of the different types of defects that can arise in relation to medical products.

Manufacturing defects (quality)

When a medical product is under consideration it is often easy to overlook the fact that manufacturing or quality defects can arise and cause injury to patients. The feature of a manufacturing defect is that the finished product does not conform to the standard which the manufacturer has set for himself in relation to the product in question. In the field of medical products there have been remarkably few reported cases of such defects. While the manufacturers would no doubt point to the quality of their processes and controls by way of explanation, the statistician might be interested to investigate the readiness with which such cases are settled out of court before conceding the point. The most notable example of such a defect in the medical field was the supply of ampoules of hydrocortisone which had been filled with vecuronium.[2]

The difficulty in distinguishing manufacturing defects from the more common design defects is illustrated by the recent litigation brought by haemophiliacs who became HIV positive due to contaminated blood products imported from the USA, chiefly Factor VIII. Although the manufacturers were not parties to the litigation it serves to illustrate the point. The plaintiffs alleged that contamination would have been prevented by heat treatment. The manufacturing standard did not require heat treatment because the risk of such contamination was unknown. If, as stated above, a manufacturing defect is best confined to a failure to conform to the manufacturer's own quality standard, this would appear to fall more happily into the category of design defect.

This distinction is of more than academic importance. In the case of a manufacturing defect it is very difficult for the plaintiff to show precisely where the manufacturing process went wrong. On the other hand the court is more ready to infer negligence in such cases and to require the defendant to show that the defect occurred without negligence on his part.

As far as the Consumer Protection Act 1987 is concerned, a manufacturing defect is treated no differently from any other defect, assuming of course that the defect was present in the product at the time that the manufacturer put it into circulation. However, in such a case there can be no question of invoking the development risk defence; a defect caused by failure to adhere to the manufacturer's own standard can obviously be avoided.

Design defects

In liability for medical products in both the UK and the US litigants have focused upon defects in the design of the products. The list in this country might be regarded by some as long: thalidomide (1964), Eraldin (1974), hormone pregnancy tests (1975), oral contraceptives (late 1970s), Opren (1981), pertussis vaccine (1982), neomycin (1984), benzodiazepines (1988), blood products (1989), Myodil (1990), Copper 7 (1991). In fact, given the scale of the development of the use of pharmaceutical agents in the treatment of disease in the post-war years together with the parallel technological advances in surgical techniques, it could be argued with considerable justification that the incidence of design defects has been remarkably low. There is yet to be a full scale consideration by a UK court of the nature of the duty of care owed by a medical product manufacturer to the patient and the significance of the part played by the prescriber where the product is available only on prescription. This is not simply a reflection of the willingness of manufacturers to settle such litigation out of court. There have been relatively few such settlements. More properly it is a reflection of the high standards of scientific research prevailing in the industry coupled with the effectiveness of the control provided by government agencies under the Medicines Act 1968.

Not every adverse reaction to a drug or other medical product indicates a design fault. Idiosyncratic reactions and/or hypersensitivity reactions can occur in susceptible individuals without any defect in the product in question, and if a product were to be regarded as defective because it evokes such reactions in such patients there would be few medical products on the market which could claim not to be defective. If, rarely, such reactions occur then the prescribing information (in the case of prescription-only products) and the patient leaflet in the case of products available over the counter should contain a warning so that the patient can be made aware of this. Any propensity for such reactions to occur cannot always be ascertained before marketing, given the limitations of clinical trials and the comparative rarity of such reactions. Hence the importance of the special reporting provisions in the British National Formulary and MIMS for new products and the Committee on Safety of Medicines' yellow card system.

Another kind of adverse reaction which does not indicate a design defect is the type expected with the product in question and warned of in the prescribing information from the outset. This reaction does not depend on any idiosyncracy in the patient but is inherent in the pharmacological properties of the compound itself, for example, the toxic reactions associated with cytotoxic chemotherapy. Such products are usually available only on prescription and warnings for patients will need to be considered. This is dealt with below.

If a design defect is present in a medical product it is likely that it will come to light in the first few years of use. This is because the clinical trials to which the product has been exposed will not have identified it, and only the far wider use of the product in the population at large will provide adequate 'testing' to enable the defect to come to light. A very good example of this was the Eraldin oculomucocutaneous syndrome first identified in 1974, some two years after ICI first marketed the product. Although ICI chose to set up the Eraldin scheme to compensate those affected by the drug, prior to marketing Eraldin was submitted to the most extensive clinical trials without any indication of this propensity, and quite plainly ICI had available to it, had it chosen to defend the litigation, powerful arguments that the drug was marketed without any negligence on its part.

Thus if a manufacturer of a product can show that according to the state of the art at the time of development of the product he did all that could be done to ascertain the true properties of the product he will be exonerated from negligence and will have a reasonable prospect of establishing the development risk defence and thereby avoiding strict liability under the 1987 Act. The manufacturer of a medical product does not guarantee its safety, not even under the Consumer Protection Act's regime.

Sabotage defects

There is a further category of defect for which no blame can be attached to the manufacturer, but which may nonetheless give rise to strict liability. Mercifully there have been few instances of deliberate sabotage of medical products, but Johnson and Johnson's experience in the US with Tylenol, which was sabotaged as part of a blackmail conspiracy, should be borne in mind. Pharmaceutical manufacturers, particularly the research-based industry, are peculiarly at risk from this type of deviant conduct, especially from the animal rights movement, which objects to the industry's use of animals in testing products.

If products are sabotaged in this way after they leave the hands of the manufacturer no liability will attach for damage resulting. If the sabotage occurs 'in-house' no defence under the Consumer Protection Act 1987 would appear to be available and strict liability will be imposed. Provided there was no negligence in checking the product before it left the manufacturer's hands, fault liability will not attach, but the manufacturer could become negligent if he is not swift to issue appropriate warnings and recall the product once he becomes aware of the danger.

Directions and warnings

The directions and warnings provided by a manufacturer of a medical product, particularly a pharmaceutical product, form an essential part of the fulfilment of the manufacturer's duty to take reasonable care.

Medicinal products

If a manufacturer of a medicinal product wishes to promote the product, the Medicines Act 1968 and data sheet regulations made under the Act require him to publish a data sheet complying with the regulations. The current Data Sheet Compendium published by the Association of the British Pharmaceutical Industry (ABPI) contains all data sheets published by ABPI members.

The data sheet is approved by the Committee on Safety of Medicines on licensing and in practice alterations to it are made only with the committee's approval. So far as prescription-only medicines are concerned it is a document of fundamental importance, providing the manufacturer's guidance to the prescribing physician on the properties of the product, how it should be used and for what conditions. Most particularly it represents the manufacturer's opportunity to warn the prescriber about any dangers associated with the use of the medicine.

While a data sheet for a promoted medicine is mandatory, a patient leaflet (a leaflet inserted in or supplied with the packaged medicine and intended for the information of the patient) is not yet required (but see below). However, such leaflets are already common in cases where the directions for using the medicine are rather more complicated than the customary 'take two tablets twice a day'.

The duty of the careful manufacturer to provide essential information about his medicinal product so that it can be safely used does not, in English law, require him to provide that information to the patient. The law recognises that medicines available only through a prescribing physician form part of the treatment provided by the prescriber and it is sufficient for the manufacturer in fulfilment of his duty to provide the information to the prescriber and to leave to him the judgment as to what if anything he tells the patient about the medicine and its characteristics.[3] This is the concept of the 'learned intermediary', considered further below.

However he chooses to do so, the manufacturer remains under a duty to ensure through proper directions and descriptions that his product is used as safely as possible. In over-the-counter medicines this can be done only through the package leaflet or the packaging itself. Whether the patient leaflet or the data sheet is used (or both) it is essential that the information is adequate, and the fact that the leaflet has the approval of the licensing authority is no guarantee that it will not be found wanting if it falls under judicial scrutiny. As will be seen below, an EC directive will soon require a patient leaflet in most, if not all, pharmaceutical products. In this, Europe is following the lead given by the Food and Drug Administration in the US, where extensive patient leaflets containing everything found in UK data sheets, and a lot else besides, are the norm.

Other medical products

While the data sheet regulations apply only to medicinal products the necessity of providing proper information to the user of a medical product remains the same whether the product is a hip prosthesis, a pacemaker or a truss. In some cases the information will need to be directed at the patient, in others at the surgeon implanting the product and in other cases both. However it is achieved, the object is to ensure that the product can be safely used. The information will be judged according to the prevailing standards if subsequently things go wrong and the defect is alleged to relate to inadequate instructions for use or warnings.

Patient package leaflets

An EC directive is in preparation which will require patient information leaflets to be included in medicine packages except where the required information is on the outside of the package. The information which must be spelled out is of the sort currently found on data sheets, and includes the therapeutic indications, contraindications, precautions for use, interaction with other drugs or foodstuffs which could affect the medicine's action, any warnings necessary for special groups, such as the elderly or pregnant women, dosage, frequency of administration, risk of withdrawal effects, action to be taken in the event of an overdose, and undesirable effects which can occur with normal use. Leaflets will have to be written in terms which are clear and understandable to patients.

Member states must implement the directive by 1 January 1993, and from 1 January 1994 will have to turn down applications to market products not complying with the directive.

The 'learned intermediary' – the doctor's role

English law recognises that products can be marketed on the basis that they become available to the end-user only through the intervention of a third party who takes responsibility for their use. This fact is impliedly acknowledged in the Consumer Protection Act 1987 which states that the judgment to be made as to the safety of a product must take account of:

'the manner in which and purposes for which the product has been marketed . . . and any instructions for and warnings with respect to doing or refraining from doing anything with or in relation to the product.'

In determining what the duties of the product manufacturer and the intermediary are towards the end-user, it is essential to keep separate and distinct their different roles.

Historically the physician was also the apothecary. The concept of a pharmaceutical industry is of very recent origin; the oldest companies are little more than 100 years old. It is important to understand that drug companies have taken over only part of the traditional role of the physician in the devising and preparation of remedies. The role of the physician in treating the individual remains the same and he takes responsibility for his use of a particular remedy in treating the individual patient. This responsibility is one that cannot be shared by the manufacturer, who does not see the patient and cannot be expected to make judgments about the appropriateness of the use of his product in an individual case, nor is he able to monitor the progress of the patient when treated in that way. That is the function of the physician, who is or should have been properly informed by the manufacturer about the general properties of the product and its recommended uses. The responsibility of the manufacturer is to make the product properly and to provide adequate information about its properties to enable the prescriber to use it safely and appropriately in the course of his practice. Each has a distinct and complementary role to play in the treatment of the patient, the physician being concerned with individuals and the manufacturer with patient populations.

This helps to explain the importance of the physician's role in monitoring the success or otherwise of drug treatments, particularly when novel, and in reporting back to the manufacturer or the Committee on Safety of Medicines via the yellow card scheme when things go wrong. Sadly, this aspect of a physician's duty appears to be frequently neglected. It is estimated that only about 10 per cent of adverse reactions are reported in this way.

Notes

1   (1990) 1 Med LR 117.
2   See 'Patients get drug after mix-up' (1985) The Guardian, 29 June.
3   *Holmes v Ashford* [1950] 2 All ER 76, CA.

Chapter 10

Accountability and Discipline

One of the distinguishing features of the great professions, setting them apart from trades and businesses, is that they are self-regulating to the extent that those who transgress accepted standards of conduct may forfeit their right to continue in practice.

The medical and dental professions face a wide variety of sanctions and systems of accountability, more than any other professional group. The doctor and dentist may face the sanctions imposed by the criminal courts, the awards of compensation which may be given by the civil courts, the rigours of the professional conduct committees of the General Medical Council and the General Dental Council, the inquiries of the Health Service Commissioner, the complaints and tribunal procedures set up by Parliament, and the procedures for complaints and inquiries which form part of the hospital doctor's contract of employment. Additionally, those in partnership may face sanctions under the partnership deed if they fail to comply with the terms. Increasingly, press and media interest in professional practice produces yet another form of accountability for the doctor and dentist.

This chapter summarises the main systems of review and accountability, apart from civil claims for negligence, which are dealt with in Chapter 1.

Criminal law

Like any other citizen, the doctor or dentist is expected to obey the laws of the country in which he chooses to practise. Transgressions of the criminal law may lead not only to punishment by the courts but also to an inquiry by the General Medical Council or General Dental Council. This will be dealt with at greater length below.

The criminal law has been used against medical and dental practitioners on a number of occasions and remains a very powerful deterrent and a severe form of accountability. Theft and fraud charges may arise from misappropriation of public funds – for example, from false claims for fees and expenses. False certification – of sickness certificates or passport applications, for instance – may lead to criminal proceedings.

More rarely, doctors and dentists have been prosecuted for manslaughter and even for murder. Every practitioner is expected to achieve a reasonable standard of care, as judged by the '*Bolam* principle' (see Chapter 1), but if death results from a very serious breach of the duty of care or through recklessness, the practitioner may be charged with manslaughter. Examples in recent years have included the prosecution of the sole operator/anaesthetist or operator/sedationist following the deaths of patients, and prosecution of anaesthetists following operative deaths. Recklessness in the administration of drugs, usually associated with gross overdose, has led to prosecution for manslaughter. In 1991 two junior doctors were convicted of manslaughter over an intrathecal injection of a cytotoxic drug which should have been given intravenously.

To succeed in a charge of murder the prosecution must prove beyond reasonable doubt, to the satisfaction of a jury, that the intention (*mens rea*) of the doctor was to end the patient's life. Murder charges have been brought in the UK in recent years in cases of alleged mercy killing, where the prosecution claimed that the doctor's intention was to hasten death rather than simply to relieve pain and suffering. One doctor was acquitted in 1990 and a second is awaiting trial at the time of writing.

Euthanasia is fraught with danger if it is defined as taking steps deliberately and intentionally to hasten death. The penalty for murder is a mandatory life sentence. However, the caring clinician will be most unlikely to face criminal prosecution if it can be demonstrated that his intention was the relief of pain and suffering and no more.

Complaints procedures

There are no nationally agreed procedures to deal with complaints by patients against doctors and dentists working exclusively in the private sector. Individual institutions may have procedures for dealing with complaints, and it may be a term of the contract between the clinician and the institution that these are followed. Otherwise complaints in the context of non-NHS private practice are dealt with *ad hoc*. Within the NHS, formal and detailed complaints procedures exist, in hospital, community and general practice.

NHS hospital complaints

There are two complaints procedures for patients, one for complaints about the way a doctor or dentist has exercised his clinical judgment, the other for complaints about other aspects of hospital care.

Complaints involving the exercise of clinical judgment

Under this procedure, based on a voluntary agreement with hospital consultants, the patient first complains, orally or in writing, to the consultant, the health authority or one of its officers. The consultant is responsible for investigating the complaint, with the help of any other staff involved, and should try to resolve the matter by discussion with the patient.

If the patient is dissatisfied with the reply received at the first stage, he must put his complaint in writing. At this stage, the regional medical officer is informed. He discusses the matter with the consultant, who may wish to consult his colleagues. A further discussion between the consultant and the complainant may resolve the matter at this point.

If the complainant is still dissatisfied, the regional medical officer may decide to set up an independent professional review, asking for second opinions from two independent consultants, at least one from another region. This third stage is invoked only for serious complaints. The 'second opinions' will meet and examine the patient, who may be accompanied by a friend or GP, and see all the clinical records. The consultant responsible for the patient's care will not be present at the meeting, but should be available if required.

The 'second opinions' will produce a confidential report for the regional medical officer. They should attempt to relieve the patient's anxieties if they believe the medical staff have exercised their clinical judgment responsibly. If they have identified any inadequacies in care, they should write to the complainant explaining the steps they believe should be taken to prevent such problems recurring. When the review is completed, the regional medical officer writes formally to the patient, with a copy to the consultant.

Other hospital complaints

The Hospital Complaints Procedure Act 1985 obliged health authorities in England and Wales and health boards in Scotland to establish a complaints procedure for in-patients and out-patients in NHS hospitals and to draw this to the attention of patients. Department of Health circular HC(88)37 sets out advice on procedures to be followed. Each health authority is required to designate a senior officer to deal with complaints, who is to be given access to the relevant medical records. Any patient or ex-patient, parent of a child patient or relative or friend of a patient who has died may make a complaint, which need not be in writing. The designated officer is required to investigate the complaint, to seek comments from the hospital staff concerned and to reply to the complainant without delay.

Complaints against general practitioners

On entering general practice each new NHS principal is contracted to provide a range of medical services to patients in the family health services authority (FHSA) area. The terms of the contract are the doctor's terms of service which set out his clinical duties to patients and administrative responsibilities. An FHSA can institute a formal investigation only if it appears that a doctor or someone acting on his behalf has broken one of the contractual terms.

The vast majority of complaints against general practitioners are made by patients or their relatives, failure to visit or failure to diagnose accounting for almost half of these. Rarely an FHSA itself may act as complainant, usually when a doctor has failed to return medical records when requested or neglected to inform the FHSA of periods of absence and planned deputising arrangements.

If the doctor is found to be in breach of the terms of service the consequences may be far reaching, including withholding part of the doctor's remuneration, a reduction in his list size, and referral to the General Medical Council and/or the NHS tribunal (which can direct that the doctor's name be removed from the FHSA medical list if his continued inclusion is deemed to be prejudicial to the service).

GPs' terms of service

The doctor's clinical responsibilities extend not only to the patients on his own list, or those of other doctors for whom he is deputising, but to anyone within his practice area who requires urgent treatment and whose own doctor is not available. The doctor is responsible for patients outside his practice area (which should be clearly defined on the doctor's appointment) only if he has agreed to visit them at a specific address. While responsible for patients the general practitioner is required to provide them with general medical services 'of the type usually provided by general medical practitioners' and to exercise the degree of skill, knowledge and care expected from general practitioners as a class. In addition to providing general medical services doctors may also opt to provide maternity medical services, contraceptive services, child health surveillance and minor surgery services, all of which attract item of service fees in addition to the standard capitation fee.

Patients who fall out with their doctor can change practices by presenting themselves at the surgery of their choice and asking to be taken on to the practice list. Doctors who tire of their patients may remove them by giving notice to the FHSA provided that the patient does not require treatment more often than every seven days and has not been accepted for maternity medical services. Patients who are unable to find a new doctor can be allocated to a doctor's list by the FHSA.

Before the 1990 amendments to the GPs' terms of service doctors were required only to see and treat patients who were ill. One of the major changes in the new contract was the introduction of a variety of health checks for newly registered patients, patients not seen for three years and the over-75s. Patients in these categories must be issued with an invitation for a check up, which in the case of the over-75s may be in their own home. The fact that the invitation has been sent must be recorded in the notes as must the doctor's findings if the patient attends. The terms of service set out protocols to be followed for each category of patient, which for the under-75s includes life-style factors such as diet, exercise, use of tobacco, consumption of alcohol and misuse of drugs or solvents. Many doctors have criticised these health checks as being ineffective and wasteful of resources. Some have openly stated that they have no intention of carrying them out and it would appear that FHSAs have neither the inclination nor the resources to discover whether or not doctors are complying with this requirement. Patients too may be sceptical about the relevance of some of the questions. Most substantial applications for life insurance are accepted only after the medical attendant's report has been received and the prudent patient may well ask whether it is in his best interests to be completely open with his doctor.

The terms of service also set out the doctor's duty with regard to providing adequate premises and staff training, the maintenance of records, certification, when the GP can and cannot charge NHS patients, the provision of practice leaflets, the production of annual reports and reports for DSS medical officers and the FHSA's medical adviser.

The complaints procedure

FHSAs are obliged to investigate complaints which make a *prima facie* allegation of a breach of the terms of service and have been made within the statutory 13-week time limit. A copy of the complainant's letter is sent to the doctor and his written comments are invited. A copy of the doctor's response is passed to the complainant who may, if satisfied, withdraw the complaint. If the complainant remains dissatisfied he may make further comments on the doctor's letter before all the correspondence is placed before the chairman of the medical service committee (who may be a lawyer but in medical terms is a layman). The service committee chairman must decide if the case warrants an oral hearing before the committee. Committees can deal with a case on the papers alone, or hold a full hearing.

Medical service committees consist of the lay chairman, two or three lay members and two or three medical members. Hearings take place in camera, the parties may be represented but not by lawyers, evidence is not given on oath and witnesses cannot be subpoenaed. Hearsay evidence is admissible.

Following introductory remarks the chairman invites the complainant to make an opening statement. The complainant is then cross-examined by the doctor and then by the committee. If witnesses attend they appear only for the duration of their own evidence. At the conclusion of the complainant's case the spotlight turns to the doctor who presents his case in the same way. Both parties have a chance to sum up at the end of the hearing.

The service committee then enters its closed session to consider the evidence, make findings of fact and determine whether the doctor was or was not in breach of his terms of service. The service committee's findings must be ratified by the FHSA before the final decision is sent to the parties. This often results in a considerable delay. The disappointed party has a right of appeal to a central Appeal Unit at Harrogate.

The number of cases resulting in a hearing before medical service committees has risen steadily, from 750 in 1979 to 1761 in 1989. Of the 1989 cases only 242 resulted in a finding against the doctor and in 62 of these withholdings of £500 or more were made against the doctor's remuneration.

Complaints against dentists

The procedure for dental complaints is identical to that for medical complaints except that they must be made within six months of completion of the course of dental treatment or within 13 weeks of a patient's realising he might have grounds for a complaint, whichever is the sooner.

With the introduction of the new dental contract in October 1990, dental regulations changed and there has been a shift of emphasis giving patients considerably more rights than they had under the old contract. The continuing care commitments in relation to patients over 18 years of age, capitation arrangements for treatment of under 18-year-olds and new regulations to cover emergency treatment have all contributed to a new range of disputes between dentists and their patients. These changes, coupled with higher patient charges, have given rise to an increase in the numbers of complaints received by FHSAs.

Real efforts have been made to use informal conciliation procedures to reduce the number of complaints which progress to formal investigations culminating in dental service committee hearings. Statistical evidence is not yet available to show the effects of the new measures. The most common complaints concern allegations that treatment has proved unsatisfactory and relate to the appearance and fit of dentures, crowns and bridges. Failure of fillings and root canal treatment are also high on the list of causes, followed by complications arising after extractions, disputes about fees and, more recently, criticism of cross-infection control procedures.

During 1990 there were a total of 500 dental service committee hearings and 228 dentists were found in breach of their terms of service. The majority of these complaints were made directly by patients but another significant group arose as a result of the monitoring of general dental services by the Dental Practice Board. In 1990–91, 181 complaints were raised by the Board. In 80 per cent of those cases the dentists were found in breach of their terms of service. In 20 per cent of cases no breach of the terms of service was established and the cases were dismissed. In 37 of the DPB-inspired cases where breaches were established, prior approval requirements were imposed on the dentists concerned. This means that with the exception of dental examination and emergency treatment, approval has to be sought from the DPB before these dentists are permitted to undertake treatment plans for their NHS patients. The amounts which were withheld from dentists' remuneration varied between £40 and £1375. In cases where patients complained directly to FHSAs, withholdings sometimes reached even higher levels.

Criticisms of the complaints procedure

The service committee procedure has been strongly criticised by the Council on Tribunals, the independent watchdog on bodies, apart from courts, which exercises adjudicative functions. In its 1989/90 report the council said the procedure unfairly tilted the balance in the doctor or dentist's favour, by allowing representation by other doctors or dentists while barring patients from representation by lawyers, even if unpaid. Patients' representatives from Community Health Councils were no match for the skilled and experienced advocates – mainly doctors or dentists from the defence organisations – who appear on behalf of doctors or dentists, the council said. Doctors criticise the procedure for its delays – complaints can take up to two years to resolve – and for penalties which are seen as draconian.

NHS Tribunal

If, following the investigation of a complaint, an FHSA decides that continuing to include a doctor's name in the list of practice principals or continuing to allow a dentist to practise in the NHS would be 'prejudicial to the efficiency of the service', it can refer the case to the NHS Tribunal, set up under the National Health Service Act 1977. Only a handful of cases are referred each year, usually where the FHSA has received a string of complaints against one doctor or dentist. The FHSA must provide a concise statement of the facts and the reasons it believes the doctor or dentist should not continue to practise in the NHS. The doctor or dentist is entitled to legal representation at the inquiry. The tribunal may direct that the doctor's or dentist's name shall be removed from the FHSA's list and not included in any list kept by any other FHSA.

Health Service Commissioner

The National Health Service Act 1977 set up the office of Health Service Commissioner or 'ombudsman' to investigate complaints about maladministration within the health service. Although complaints about clinical judgment remain outside the ombudsman's remit, there is scope for argument over the definition and limits of the term. The Commissioner may, for example, take the view that a decision to discharge a patient from hospital or to transfer a patient to another hospital is an administrative decision, not a matter of clinical judgment, and so within his remit.

Many doctors and dentists have found themselves involved in the thorough and painstaking reviews carried out by officers appointed to assist the commissioner and some clinicians have found themselves criticised in his annual reports. The system provides a daunting method of accountability. Severe censure by the commissioner may even lead to an appearance before the parliamentary select committee which shadows him. At such hearings, held in public, there may be stringent criticism of individuals, reported in the press. In 1986 a consultant dental surgeon whose conduct was described as 'at best inept and at worst perverse' in the commissioner's report was summoned to appear before the select committee with health authority officials. The surgeon was asked why on three occasions it took him more than four months to respond to patients' complaints, in spite of repeated reminders and warnings. The complaints arose from two cases in which a large number of teeth were extracted from mentally handicapped children although their mothers had given consent only, in one case, to minor dental work and in the other, to an examination. The commissioner described the consents as 'travesties'.

Prevention of harm to patients

Accountability of doctors and dentists must extend to situations in which they may pose a risk to patients through physical or mental disability, including addiction to alcohol or drugs. In the NHS hospital and community services, the procedure colloquially known as the 'three wise men' procedure is designed to help prevent harm to patients resulting from sick medical or dental staff. Department of Health circular HC(82)13 advises each health authority to set up a special professional panel of senior medical and dental staff from which, on a case by case basis, a sub-committee can be appointed 'to take appropriate action on any report of incapacity due to physical or mental disability including addiction'. The sub-committee should make confidential inquiries to verify the accuracy of the report. If satisfied it has substance, they should give the practitioner the opportunity to be interviewed. If they feel that patients cannot be protected by the exercise of their influence with the practitioner, they should inform the regional medical officer.

In general practice, the National Health Service (General Medical and Pharmaceutical Services) Regulations 1974 grant powers to an FHSA manager, in consultation with representatives of the local medical committee, to take over the running of a practice. The powers may be invoked particularly where a sick single-handed practitioner is too ill or obdurate to agree to seek medical help, but cannot manage the practice nor attend to patients. Within a partnership it may not be necessary for the FHSA to invoke these powers if the partners can deal satisfactorily with the problems posed by a sick colleague.

The General Medical Council

The Medical Act 1858 established the General Medical Council and the medical register. The GMC is responsible for medical registration, education and discipline within the UK and its current powers derive from the Medical Act of 1983. The GMC is the body to which, above all others, the medical practitioner is accountable, since it alone has the power to suspend or erase a doctor's name from the medical register.

Disciplinary procedures

The Medical Act 1983 provides that a doctor convicted in the British Isles of a criminal offence or judged guilty of serious professional misconduct by the GMC's professional conduct committee (PCC) may, if the committee thinks fit, have his name erased from the register, his registration suspended for not more than 12 months, or conditions attached to his registration for up to three years. The committee has jurisdiction where a doctor has been convicted even if the offence did not involve professional misconduct. Medical practitioners' criminal convictions are normally reported to the GMC by the police.

In considering criminal convictions the GMC is bound to accept the determination of a court as conclusive evidence that the doctor was guilty of the offence. For this reason, it is important for doctors not to plead guilty if they believe they have a defence to the charge. A plea of guilty may expedite the case, limit publicity and reduce the sentence imposed. However, it is not open to a doctor who has been convicted of an offence to argue later before the GMC that he was not in fact guilty. Sixteen of the 55 cases considered by the PCC in 1990 were conviction cases. Convicted doctors appearing before the committee in 1990 had been found guilty of indecency, dishonesty, attempting to pervert the course of justice, improper prescribing or supplying of drugs, violence and abusive behaviour.

The other category of cases considered by the GMC are those where a complaint of serious professional misconduct has been laid against a doctor. This has been defined, somewhat vaguely, as 'no more than serious misconduct judged according to the rules, written or unwritten, governing the profession'.

Although cases of improper relationships with patients occupy many column inches in the tabloids, only eight out of 55 cases in 1990 involved such allegations. The largest category, with 18 cases, concerned disregard of professional responsibilities to patients.

Convictions, apart from trivial ones, and complaints alleging serious professional misconduct go first to the preliminary proceedings committee (PPC), which decides whether to refer them to the PCC for a hearing. But only about 10–15 per cent of complaints made each year to the GMC will even reach the PPC. All complaints are referred to a preliminary screener, a doctor member of the GMC who decides whether they come within the council's jurisdiction. A decision to refer a case to the PPC is taken by the preliminary screener, but no complaint is rejected without the agreement of a lay member of the GMC appointed to assist the medical screener. Where a case is to be referred to the PPC, the GMC writes to the doctor with details of the allegations inviting a written explanation for submission to the committee.

The GMC acts only when matters are brought to its notice. Allegations of serious professional misconduct reach the council from a variety of sources. The largest category is complaints by patients or their relatives, which may come in the form of a statutory declaration by the individual, a report from the manager of a family health service authority, or a report from a hospital manager following a committee of inquiry. Cases may also be referred by the Secretary of State following a finding that a GP has breached his terms of service, and complaints may be lodged by fellow doctors. Of 1087 complaints received in 1990/91, 807 came from the general public, 163 from a public authority and 117 from doctors. In response to criticism that GMC guidance discouraging doctors from making disparaging remarks about colleagues could deter them from reporting possible misdemeanours, the council revised its guidance in 1990. While making it clear that gratuitous and unsustainable comment which sets out to undermine trust is unethical and could itself give rise to disciplinary proceedings, the guidance states that it is a doctor's duty to inform the appropriate person or body where a colleague's 'professional conduct or fitness to practise may be called in question'.

The PPC, which has two lay members out of 11, sits in private and considers written information before deciding whether to refer a case to the PCC for a hearing. In 1990 46 out of 147 cases considered by the PPC were sent to the professional conduct committee. Instead of referring a case to the PCC, the PPC may decide instead to take no action, or to write a letter of warning or advice to the doctor. If it appears that the doctor may be suffering from a physical or mental illness which impairs his fitness to practise, the case may be referred to the health committee (see below).

The hearings of the professional conduct committee are open to the press and public. Evidence is given orally and on oath and doctors are entitled to legal representation by solicitors and counsel. The committee, six of whose 32 members are lay people, is subject to strict rules of evidence and has power to compel witnesses to attend. The PCC may also refer appropriate cases to the health committee.

Both the PPC and the PCC act as judicial bodies and may be advised in their deliberations by a legal assessor. The procedures and decisions of the GMC, like those of other statutory bodies, are increasingly being challenged in the High Court by judicial review. Doctors have a right of appeal to the judicial committee of the Privy Council – where appeals are heard by law lords – from a decision to erase their names from the register, suspend them or impose conditions on their registration.

Serious professional misconduct

Any abuse by a doctor of professional privileges and opportunities or any grave dereliction of professional duty or serious breach of medical ethics may give rise to a charge of serious professional misconduct. Traditional areas of concern for the GMC have been conduct derogatory to the reputation of the medical profession, the advertising of doctors' services and disparagement of professional colleagues. In recent years, however, there has been a shift in emphasis and the council now takes considerably more interest in standards of patient care.

Before 1985 the GMC did not normally concern itself with matters such as errors of treatment or diagnosis which could give rise to actions for negligence in the civil courts. In 1985 these cases were brought within its remit, but only where the doctor's conduct has involved such a disregard of professional responsibility to patients or such a neglect of professional duties as to raise a question of serious professional misconduct. In recent years, cases alleging disregard of professional responsibility to patients have formed the largest single category coming before both the PPC and the PCC.

In its 'Blue Book' (*Professional Conduct and Discipline: Fitness to Practise*, 1991) the GMC states that the public are entitled to expect good standards of medical care, which include taking an adequate history, making a sufficiently thorough professional examination, arranging investigations where indicated and then managing the case competently and considerately. There is also a requirement to deal promptly with conditions requiring urgent medical attention and a readiness, in appropriate circumstances, to consult colleagues. The GMC recognises that certain tasks may need to be delegated to nurses and others but insists that the doctor should retain ultimate responsibility for the management of his patients. Accordingly improper delegation or inadequate deputising arrangements may give rise to disciplinary proceedings.

Care is necessary in the prescribing of controlled drugs and in the completion of medical certificates and the GMC stresses the important duty of confidentiality. The council's views about advertising have been considerably amended in recent years following recommendations by the Monopolies and Mergers Commission in 1988/89. Distinctions are made, however, between advertising which is acceptable from a general practitioner and advertising which is acceptable from a specialist.

All advertising must be 'legal, decent, honest and truthful'. Medical advertising is subject to additional restrictions to ensure that the public is not misled. The doctor who intends to advertise (defined as providing 'information about services in any form to the public or other members of the profession') should take care to comply with the detailed guidance of the General Medical Council as set out in the 'Blue Book'.

The GMC considers that information about the services provided by general practitioners should be made widely available to the public in areas where those doctors practise. However, 'specialists may provide information to professional colleagues but not to the public' except for the inclusion of names, addresses, telephone numbers and professional qualifications in national and local directories and similar publications. The reason given for the distinction is to reflect the referral system on which general and specialist practice in the UK are based and which exists to protect patients.

Criminal convictions may lead to disciplinary proceedings even if the offence is not directly connected with the doctor's profession. The GMC is particularly concerned about personal behaviour involving the misuse of alcohol or other drugs, dishonesty or indecency or violence. Such criminal convictions are likely to lead to an inquiry by the GMC as to whether the facts and surrounding circumstances amount also to serious professional misconduct. The GMC will also be concerned about any improper financial transactions such as fraudulent claims for general practice allowances.

The 'sick doctor'

Until 1980 the GMC had no mechanism, apart from inappropriate disciplinary procedures, for dealing with doctors whose ability to practise was impaired through ill-health. It had no way of either protecting the public in such cases or helping the doctor towards rehabilitation. In 1980 the council set up voluntary procedures to deal with doctors referred because of serious health problems. A health committee was also established, but most cases never get that far. Most doctors accept treatment voluntarily, and the committee sees only those who continue to practise against medical advice or beyond their own capacity.

Virtually all the doctors who go through the health procedure suffer from alcohol or drug-related problems or mental illness, or a combination. Doctors are asked to accept medical supervision and limitations on practice while undergoing treatment.

Professional performance

The lack of powers to deal with doctors whose performance is not up to acceptable standards but falls short of serious professional misconduct has long been regarded as limiting the GMC's effectiveness and public credibility. For several years, in response to public and parliamentary pressure, the council has been investigating the possibility of introducing new procedures for dealing with complaints about poor performance by doctors. These would cover cases where a doctor's knowledge or skills are seriously deficient but there is no question of ill health.

Widespread discussion and consultation are under way at the time of writing. Any proposals approved by the GMC would require a new statute to amend the Medical Act 1983. The new procedure, if implemented, would not be disciplinary but would be modelled on the health procedures. It would seek to identify areas of practice falling below acceptable standards and encourage the doctor to improve practice performance through remedial advice and help. Only if a doctor refused to cooperate with the procedure is it envisaged that the GMC might take action to limit or suspend registration to protect the public. The procedure is intended to demonstrate how the profession can regulate itself effectively for the benefit of both the public and the profession.

General Dental Council

The statutory body which regulates the practice of dentistry is the General Dental Council. Like the GMC, it has a preliminary proceedings committee which decides whether to refer cases for a hearing, and a professional conduct committee which hears cases. In addition to erasure from the Dentists Register, the Dentists Act 1984 gave the PCC the option to suspend a dentist from the register for a set period, usually 12 months. The Act also established a health committee to investigate dentists whose fitness to practise may be impaired by ill health. The health committee may suspend a dentist's registration for up to 12 months, at the end of which it will review the case, and may impose conditions on a dentist's registration for up to three years.

All criminal convictions other than for minor traffic offences are referred to the GDC. The PPC decides whether the matter is sufficiently serious to refer to the PCC. Like the GMC, the GDC is bound to accept the findings of a criminal court as fact, and it is therefore unwise for a dentist to plead guilty to a charge if a defence can be mounted.

Chapter 11

The Employment Rights of the NHS Hospital Doctor

It is four o'clock on a Friday afternoon. It has been a heavy clinic, but the small sea of bored and anxious faces that you nodded your way past at one-thirty has now contracted to a handful scattered among the empty chairs and the off-call weekend is in sight. The telephone rings. It is the regional medical officer, a man you have met only once. He asks you to come and see him this afternoon at five-thirty.

'But I've still got six patients to see – can't it wait?'
'No, it cannot. It is imperative I see you today.'
'Why, for heaven's sake – what's this all about?'
'There have been complaints. I'm going to suspend you from duty.'

This is not some absurd fantasy or something that could only happen to someone guilty of gross misbehaviour: in recent years it has happened to a number of dedicated and competent consultants who have faced lengthy legal battles to hold on to their jobs. What is more, in the current state of play in the NHS, it is likely that more doctors than ever before will find themselves defending their employment rights. For example, on 28 February 1991 Dr Helen Zeitlin, a consultant haematologist at the Alexandra Hospital, Redditch, returned to her office after her morning out-patients session to find a letter sent by ordinary post from the regional medical officer. It gave her three months notice of redundancy (despite the fact that her post was newly-created in 1986), but asked her to cease attending the hospital immediately. At the time of writing, her appeal to the Secretary of State (see below) is pending.

The natural reaction of any doctor treated in this way is to feel: 'they can't do this to me: I must have legal rights that I can enforce'. The sad and little-understood truth is that the employment rights of the hospital doctor are so limited as to be nearly worthless, compared to the value of a wrecked career. This chapter will explore just what those few rights consist of and how best to use them.

Basic employment rights – the bare minimum of wrongful dismissal

Employment law is one of the infants of the legal system. Until 1971, the law of 'master and servant' (as it continued to be known) provided the employee with little beyond a right to receive the minimum period of notice – fixed by statute according to length of service – in the event of dismissal. An employer could sack an employee with 40 years service because he didn't like his tie or for no discernible reason at all, and incur no legal consequences beyond having to give him 12 weeks' notice or pay in lieu. An employee could be shamefully passed over for promotion, have his job radically altered or be subjected to grossly unfair discipline and yet have no redress beyond declaring himself 'constructively dismissed' (see below) and claiming his notice entitlement.

This remedy is called 'wrongful dismissal' and still exists, for what it is worth. It forms the background to the other two sources of legal remedies for hospital doctors – the 'unfair dismissal' jurisdiction of the industrial tribunal on the one hand, and the specific provisions of the contract of employment on the other. For practical purposes, these sources of remedy exist in separate watertight compartments and have to be examined in turn to see what rights a doctor has in any particular situation. I will deal with the special provisions of hospital doctors' contracts of employment below, but first it is important to understand the second component in the bare minimum of employment rights conferred by the general law – the industrial tribunal.

The slightly less than bare minimum – the industrial tribunal

The advent of the industrial tribunal together with the very limited remedies it provides for 'unfair dismissal' represented a major addition to the rights of employees generally. The first and perhaps most fundamental point is that apart from discrimination on grounds of race or sex the industrial tribunal, in practice, provides remedies for unfair *dismissal*. Other forms of employer behaviour, however unfair or unjustified, are simply not covered. Dismissal in the legal sense, however, is not confined to circumstances in which the employee is formally sacked, but can also include situations in which the employer behaves towards the employee in a way which entitles the employee to terminate the contract of employment and consider himself dismissed. This is called 'constructive dismissal' and has the same effect, for the purposes of the industrial tribunal, as outright dismissal in the usual way.

What can constitute 'constructive dismissal'? In essence, the employer must breach the contract of employment, but the breach has to be sufficiently fundamental to justify the employee in leaving. A few examples of each extreme may shed some light. If you are a neurosurgeon and the health authority instructs you to work in the hospital canteen, you have been constructively dismissed; if the district general manager interferes with the operating theatre rota and gives you the worst combination of sessions, you have not. If your contract of employment requires you to work in hospital A, and the health authority instructs you to work in hospital B, which is 50 miles away, you have been constructively dismissed; if the unit general manager decides that your excellent secretary will henceforth work for him and gives you an illiterate junior instead, you probably have not.

Assuming that you can get over that hurdle, you can get your industrial tribunal application off the ground provided that you have been employed for over two years and you make your application within three months of the date of your dismissal (constructive or otherwise). It is then up to the employer to show that you have been dismissed fairly, not for you to show the opposite. The employer can do this by satisfying the industrial tribunal that you have been dismissed by reason of:

(a)   your capability or qualifications for the job, or
(b)   misconduct, or
(c)   redundancy, or
(d)   a restriction imposed by statute (e.g. loss of registration), or
(e)   some other substantial reason.

Assuming that the employer fails to convince the tribunal that any of these is applicable and the tribunal therefore finds that you have been unfairly dismissed, what remedies are available to you? It is at this point that we come face to face with the fundamental inadequacy of the industrial tribunal as an effective channel of redress for the unfairly dismissed doctor, particularly the consultant.

Many people in this situation will simply want their job back, but although the industrial tribunal does have a power to order reinstatement, it is used very sparingly. But even if you manage to persuade the tribunal that it is practicable for you to return to your post, and that you have not contributed to your dismissal by your own conduct, there is still no guarantee that you will get your job back. This is because the industrial tribunal provides no legal 'teeth' to enforce an order for re-instatement: if the health authority is determined not to have you back, it can ignore the tribunal's reinstatement order. If this happens, the only penalty the tribunal can impose on recalcitrant employers is to 'fine' them by making them pay the employee an additional award on top of the normal compensation.

At this point it may be useful to mention what the normal compensation for unfair dismissal consists of. The figures are updated for inflation each year, but what follows is the tariff applicable between 1 April 1991 and 31 March 1992. Compensation is a combination of a basic award, arrived at, broadly speaking, by multiplying years of service (maximum 20) by weekly wage (maximum £198), together with a compensatory award limited to £10,000 for dismissals after 1 April 1990. The additional award, payable by employers who refuse to reinstate, is between £2574 and £5148 for ordinary cases, unless the dismissal has been for race or sex discrimination, when this component is doubled.

Thus, if your health authority or trust dismisses you unfairly for reasons other than sex or race, and you have 20 years service under your belt, the absolute maximum you can obtain from the industrial tribunal is the princely sum of £19,108. At a time when a consultant's basic salary without merit awards is more than £40,000, the powers of the industrial tribunal to provide compensation and redress for the destruction of a career are pitifully inadequate. Yet, if the special features of NHS employment contracts for the protection of doctors fail to save your job (and, as we will see below, they are far from being comprehensive or injustice-proof) then the paltry awards of the industrial tribunal are all you will have to fall back on to compensate you for loss of a job that most consultants consider wholly secure and impregnable. I shall return to the implications of this in my conclusion, but it should be apparent by now that hospital doctors, including consultants, really hold their jobs at the pleasure of the management, which nowadays is not something that any doctor can take for granted.

The rights provided by the NHS contract

Each health authority has its own standard form of employment contract, but each NHS doctor or dentist has 'written in' to his or her contract certain disciplinary and appeal procedures which provide limited safeguards for practitioners and guidance for health authorities who want to discipline or dismiss doctors in their employment. These may be summarised as:

(a)   The disciplinary procedure for cases of *personal conduct* (section 40 of the 'Blue Book'[1])
(b)   The procedure for dealing with allegations of *professional conduct* or *professional competence* (Department of Health Circular HC(90)9)
(c)   The procedure for appeals to the Secretary of State in all but personal misconduct cases (paragraph 190 of the 'Red Book'[2])

The voluminous labyrinth of national terms and conditions contained in the 'Red' and 'Blue' Books is part and parcel of the hospital doctor's contractual rights and thus section 40 and paragraph 190 will apply to everyone. The position of the HC(90)9 procedure for dealing with allegations of professional misconduct and incompetence – the basis of the Wendy Savage inquiry in 1986 – is slightly less clear. The circular, like its predecessor, HM(61)112, states itself to be *guidance* to health authorities, and in the High Court case brought by Dr Marietta Higgs against the Northern Regional Health Authority, the authority argued that the circular was not mandatory and that authorities were free to ignore it if they wished. In that case, the authority had imposed substantial disciplinary sanctions on Dr Higgs following the publication of Lord Justice Butler-Sloss' report on the Cleveland child abuse crisis of 1987, but without having any kind of disciplinary hearing and specifically avoiding using the procedure set out in the circular. In the High Court, the judge upheld this proposition, but Dr Higgs appealed to the Court of Appeal against that decision. In the Court of Appeal, the case was eventually settled on agreed terms and no formal decision was ever made on this point. In the course of argument, however, the Master of the Rolls, Lord Donaldson, expressed the view that the circular obviously represented custom and practice within the Health Service and that large employers within a national public service were therefore bound to observe the procedures laid down by the appropriate Government minister. The net result is that while this issue is tinged with grey, it is sensible to proceed on the basis that every practitioner employed by a health authority can insist that the procedure in the circular is used.

Somewhat less clear is the position of practitioners employed within the NHS trusts. Section 6 of the NHS and Community Care Act 1990 makes it clear that on day one of their existence the trusts take over all the employment duties and liabilities of the health authority, which must therefore include the disciplinary apparatus set out above. On the other hand, it has been stated repeatedly that trusts have the power to determine their own terms and conditions of service for staff and it is therefore open to a trust to introduce different systems by following the appropriate procedures for variation of contracts of employment. The net position for doctors employed by trusts is therefore that they are covered by the mainstream NHS procedures unless their own trust has introduced different procedures, in which case the latter are applicable.

Personal misconduct – section 40

Personal conduct is defined as:

> 'performance or behaviour of practitioners due to factors other than those associated with the exercise of medical or dental skills'.

The NHS procedure for dealing with allegations of this nature is set out in section 40 of the 'Blue Book' which comprises the entirety of the system for this category of complaint: there is no right to an HC(90)9 type of inquiry, nor is there any right to a paragraph 190 appeal to the Secretary of State against dismissal.

The section 40 procedure applies to all NHS employees accused of personal misconduct, from hospital porters to consultants, and consists mainly of a procedure for appealing to a committee of the employing authority against disciplinary action (including dismissal) taken at a lower level. The appeal is to a committee of three health authority members, at least one of whom should have a special knowledge of the work of the employee. Where this is not possible, and the appeal is against dismissal, the doctor's representative can ask for the appointment of a specialist assessor who will advise the appeal committee on matters of professional conduct and/or competence. Section 40 then sets out the standard procedure for the appeal hearing, including the usual provisions for the calling and cross-examination of witnesses, final addresses and mitigation.

The significance of section 40 is that since the removal, in March 1990, of the right to a paragraph 190 appeal to the Secretary of State in cases of personal misconduct, this procedure provides health authorities with a 'fast-track' method of dismissing doctors that they wish to be rid of. If your district general manager accuses you of illicit private use of the photocopier, for example, and his recommendation for dismissal is confirmed by the full authority, then only the section 40 appeal committee stands between you and the cold comfort of the industrial tribunal described above. If your contract is held at district level, there is a discretionary right of appeal to the region, but the discretion is theirs, not yours, and they cannot be compelled to hear your appeal at all.

Practitioners would be well advised, therefore, to contact their defence society as soon as any allegation of personal misconduct is raised, even if the subject matter appears to be trivial.

Intermediate procedure

In addition to updating the procedure for inquiries into allegations of professional misconduct and incompetence, Circular HC(90)9 introduced a wholly new procedure for dealing with allegations which were within those categories, but which fell short of the seriousness required for a full-blown inquiry procedure. Faced with such a case (which can include a 'clash of professional views') the Director of Public Health (DPH) of the employing authority may implement the new intermediate procedure.

His first step is to write to the Joint Consultative Committee (JCC) with brief details of the case, asking them to nominate assessors to conduct an investigation, while informing the practitioner at the same time. The assessors (normally two) will come from a different region and at least one will be of the same specialty as the consultant concerned. Once appointed, the assessors receive a written 'statement of the case' from the DPH which is also copied to the doctor concerned. The assessors can then decline to act on the basis that the case is either too serious or too trivial for them or because the case falls within the 'three wise men' procedure of Circular HC(82)13 (see Chapter 10), but if they decide to proceed within the intermediate procedure, their next task is to visit the district where the problem has arisen and 'undertake the necessary investigations'.

They then draw up a list of people they would like to see and copy this to the practitioner who may suggest additional names. Anyone who agrees to be interviewed (the assessors have no power of compulsion) will be asked to provide a written statement or to sign an agreed record of the interview. The practitioner will also meet the assessors either alone or in the company of a representative or friend, if he wishes.

Having completed their investigations, the assessors depart to write their report which will comprise a first part containing findings of fact and a second part containing details of which doctors (if any) are at fault and recommendations concerning organisational matters or advice to be given to the consultant. The DPH then receives the report (again copied to the practitioner) and then decides what action to take in accordance with section 40 if appropriate.

It is too early to say how this new procedure will work out in practice and certainly no aspect of its operation has been taken before the courts for review. The welcome aspect of the procedure is the way in which the procedure cannot be implemented behind the practitioner's back, as he must be informed from the very start. What is unwelcome, however, is the apparent inability of the practitioner to have any influence over the choice of assessors. There is nothing to stop the JCC appointing assessors who are either known to favour policies and clinical practices at the opposite end of the spectrum from the practitioner under scrutiny or individuals who are known informal associates of the practitioner's accusers or antagonists in the dispute under review.

Similarly, the inquisitorial method by which evidence is taken in private and in the absence of the practitioner provides abundant opportunity for unfairness, bias and malice. The procedure should provide for the practitioner to be seen twice, once at the outset to respond to the DPH's written statement of case and then again after all the other witnesses have been seen, to respond to any points or allegations which may have been made against him, which the assessors should be bound to disclose. It is a cardinal principle of natural justice, as enforced by the courts, that no information should be used against an individual in these circumstances unless that individual is given the information and an opportunity to rebut or comment. Practitioners who find themselves being made the subject of intermediate procedure should demand that the assessors adopt this method.

The full-blown HC(90)9 – preliminary steps

Where an allegation of professional misconduct or incompetence is too serious to be dealt with via the intermediate procedure – where the practitioner is in jeopardy of serious disciplinary action including (but not confined to, dismissal) – the full-blown HC(90)9 procedure must be used. The key figure in the early stages of this system is the health authority chairman, whose first task is to ascertain whether or not there is a *prima facie* case against the doctor concerned. Any preliminary inquiries must be conducted by the DPH who may also invoke the assistance of the authority's legal adviser. At this stage, the chairman is required to inform the practitioner immediately of the nature of the complaint made and that an inquiry, which could lead to dismissal, is under consideration. The practitioner is then given the opportunity to make representations to the chairman.

These 'early warning' provisions are less valuable than they seem. In the Wendy Savage case, which is the best documented example of the system in operation, the first 'complaints' were made over a year before Mrs Savage was notified in accordance with the above provisions. The first she knew that anything was afoot was when she was summoned out of a clinic to see the district medical officer in much the same way as in the imaginary case at the start of this chapter.

The significance of the Savage case is not just that so much of what is normally conducted behind closed doors was done openly and in the public spotlight, but that it also resulted in her complete exoneration from any suggestion of incompetence. In other words, it was a case that should never have been started at all and having started should have been stopped at the earliest opportunity. Nevertheless, it ran its full course, costing Mrs Savage a 14-month suspension with all the associated personal distress and Tower Hamlets Health Authority £250,000 which could otherwise have been spent on improving patient care. It is nothing less than a tragedy that the new HC(90)9 procedure which replaced the old HM(61)112 should embody none of the lessons which should have been learned as a result of that case. The opening paragraphs of the new procedure are an almost *verbatim* replica of the old procedure and still allow charges to be accumulated without the practitioner's knowledge.

Suspension from duty

The most immediate, humiliating and professionally damaging conse-quence of an allegation of serious incompetence or misconduct is suspension from duty. Mrs Savage was suspended on 25 April 1985, the day she was notified that the inquiry procedure was under way, and not reinstated until 24 July 1986, after the inquiry had taken place and the report had been produced. By the standards of other doctors in that position, however, she was fortunate: suspensions of three and four years are far from uncommon. The longest is believed to be that of Dr Bridget O'Connell, a consultant paediatrician working in East London who was suspended in December 1982 and remains so at the time of writing.

Despite the devastating impact of suspension, you will search in vain in the HC(90)9 procedure for any discussion of it. The only reference is a sentence which simply states that the inquiry procedure does not 'prejudice the right of the authority to take immediate action (e.g. suspension from duty) where this is required in cases of a very serious nature'.

The unpalatable reality is that employers generally have a very wide freedom to suspend employees from duty and the courts have shown a notable reluctance to intervene. The reason is that the law regards employment as a kind of commercial contract between the employer and employee – the employee provides services and the employer pays money in return. Suspension on full pay therefore is in the blinkered eyes of the law no more than the employer fulfilling his side of the bargain without requiring the employee to put in his or her side of it, rather like a shop giving away goods for nothing. Thus the law regards the suspended doctor not as someone who is undergoing the most professionally damaging experience it is possible to have short of outright dismissal, but as an unusually fortunate individual who is being paid without being required to work. As the law stands at present, therefore, the courts will intervene only if a doctor has been suspended in breach of an established local procedure, as there are none which bind health authorities on a national basis.

Suspension without due cause, or for an unreasonable length of time could constitute constructive dismissal, but where does that leave the practitioner? Once again the industrial tribunal with its inadequate remedies is the only recourse. Sooner or later, the courts are going to have to acknowledge that for highly skilled and dedicated professionals, suspension from duty is not a bonus but a devastating body-blow for which employers should be held fully accountable. For the moment, however, unjustified suspension is a wrong for which English law provides no meaningful or adequate remedy.

HC(90)9 – the inquiry

After hearing from the practitioner, the authority chairman decides whether a *prima facie* case still exists, and if he thinks that it does, he must proceed to the next stage in the inquiry. Note that he is not required to take any expert advice before taking this step and a distinguished consultant may find himself suspended and subjected to an inquiry on the grounds of incompetence without any expert medical opinion other than that of the Director of Public Health. Even if expert advice is taken, there is nothing to prevent its being obtained from a known opponent or antagonist of the practitioner or someone known for holding opposing clinical views. And even under the new procedure, the health authority chairman can suspend and proceed against any consultant without taking any outside opinion at all.

Once a decision has been made that there is a *prima facie* case, the chairman must proceed to hold a full inquiry unless the facts are undisputed, in which case the section 40 procedure is used. This is also to be used when the facts have been established by an official inquiry or a criminal case. If there is a dispute over whether an official inquiry has dealt with precisely the same issues as in the HC(90)9 allegation, an inquiry panel may be convened to decide whether a full hearing is necessary.

These stipulations about official inquiries are additions introduced by the new procedure and should serve as a warning bell to any practitioners who find themselves involved in such an inquiry. In the Cleveland inquiry, Lord Justice Butler-Sloss was at pains to reassure all concerned that her purpose was not to attribute blame and the normal procedure for warning individuals that they might be subject to criticism in inquiries was not used. Nevertheless, had the health authority decided to use the new procedure against Dr Higgs, they would have been able to attempt to by-pass the HC(90)9 inquiry altogether by invoking this clause. Any doctor involved in an official inquiry, therefore, should regard himself as effectively on trial, regardless of what is said to the contrary.

The inquiry panel specified by HC(90)9 consists of a legally qualified chairman, chosen from a list kept by the Lord Chancellor's Department, together with two side members – a doctor and a lay person in cases of professional misconduct, but two doctors in cases of alleged incompetence, at least one from the same specialty as the doctor accused of incompetence. The circular requires that terms of reference should be drawn up and that these together with copies of correspondence and any written statements made should be provided to the practitioner. He should also be supplied with a list of witnesses to be called for the 'prosecution' together with a note of the main points on which they can give evidence. This again is inadequate. For these proceedings to be conducted fairly, the allegations against the practitioner must be specified in as much detail as possible (there were 55 separate charges in the Savage case) and witnesses should be compelled to provide full statements so that the practitioner knows precisely the case he has to meet.

The proceedings follow the familiar adversarial pattern, save that the circular contains an exhortation to both sides to 'reduce the formality of the proceedings'. In my view, this encouragement should be resisted. Formality of the merely ceremonial or ritualistic kind is of course out of place in a hearing of this nature, but formality in the sense of orderliness of procedure and disciplined attitudes to matters of fact and opinion is essential if the practitioner is to obtain a fair hearing. As far as possible, allegations should be narrowed down, and evidence subjected to sensible but strict tests of relevance and admissibility. When a career is at stake (as it must be in these proceedings) it is not unreasonable for considerable care to be taken to guard against unfairness of any kind and experience shows that a casual, undisciplined approach to these matters is the enemy of justice and fair play.

At the end of the inquiry, the panel produce a two-part report to the authority on the same lines as that described for the intermediate procedure. The panel have no disciplinary powers themselves and the practitioner must be given a chance to make further representations to the authority before sentence is passed. One of the most welcome innovations of the new system is the introduction of a model timescale which envisages a complete HC(90)9 inquiry, from the time of the first decision that a *prima facie* case exists to the final report to the authority, taking no more than 32 weeks. As the Savage inquiry, then one of the fastest on record, took 14 months to make the same progress, there must be a degree of scepticism as to whether this time scale is realistic, but it nevertheless represents a major step forward.

The appeal to the Secretary of State – paragraph 190

A consultant or associate specialist dismissed for any reason other than personal misconduct has an automatic right to appeal to the Secretary of State for Health. This covers, for example, someone made redundant or dismissed after a full HC(90)9 inquiry, or after a section 40 hearing on professional conduct or competence. Notice of appeal must be lodged before the date the dismissal takes effect, but the full statement of case should be provided within four months of the date upon which notice was given, unless an extension is allowed by the Secretary of State. Thus a doctor who receives three months notice of redundancy on 1 January must give notice of appeal before 1 April, and get his statement of case in before 1 May.

On receipt of notice of appeal, the Secretary of State must ask the authority for its written views which must be provided within two months, subject to similar extensions if granted. The Secretary of State must also set up a professional committee to advise him on the case. This is chaired by the Chief Medical Officer of the Department of Health or his deputy and includes a representative of the Secretary of State and a representative of the practitioner's profession. It is assisted by a qualified solicitor or barrister and may, if it thinks fit, interview the practitioner and representatives of the authority, but is under no obligation to do so. The professional committee usually holds some kind of hearing, but can, if it wishes, conduct the entire procedure on the basis of the written statements and see no one in person.

Having conducted its investigation and deliberations, the committee reports to the Secretary of State, advising termination or continuance of employment or a third course, which is or might be acceptable to both the practitioner and the authority. Within three months of receiving the Committee's report, the Secretary of State must either confirm the termination or direct that the practitioner's employment continue or arrange some other solution acceptable to the practitioner and the authority. Thus the authority has a veto over any solution other than straightforward reinstatement.

Using the courts

The 'they can't do this to me' reaction of the suspended or disciplined doctor which was mentioned at the start of this chapter is usually followed by 'I'll sue – I'll take them to court', but the avenues for court action are few and offer very little. There have been a few attempts, however, to bring court action on behalf of disciplined doctors and it is worth examining what they have achieved.

Perhaps the most important in its effects is the case of Walsh[3] decided in 1984, which was concerned not with a doctor, but with a senior nursing officer employed by East Berkshire District Health Authority. Following a disagreement between Mr Walsh and a superior, the health authority dismissed Mr Walsh without going through the correct Whitley Council procedures, such as section 40 (discussed above). Mr Walsh applied to the High Court for judicial review on the ground that the health authority was a public body and that his case was therefore a matter of 'public law' and suitable subject matter for this type of remedy. The health authority argued, as a preliminary point, that judicial review did not apply to NHS contracts of employment and the Court of Appeal agreed, thus effectively shutting the door on all NHS employees using this remedy. It is sometimes suggested that this judgment does not operate to exclude a consultant using judicial review in a special case, but until such a case persuades the Court of Appeal to limit the ambit of the Walsh case, it remains a major obstacle.

The courts can be used, however, to take action based on contract law to compel health authorities to observe the procedures that we have examined above. In 1982, Mr Irani, an ophthalmologist in Southampton, quarrelled with his supervising consultant, a Mr Walker. The health authority responded by adopting an *ad hoc* investigatory procedure, setting up a panel of inquiry which saw Irani and Walker separately. This panel then reported that the differences between the two men were irreconcilable and the authority decided to deal with this problem by sacking Mr Irani, giving him his due period of notice and offering him an *ad hoc* appeal to the region with limited powers.

Mr Irani sued the health authority for breach of contract and applied to the High Court for an interlocutory (pending the full trial of the action) injunction, restraining them from sacking him until they had complied with either section 40 or section 33, which deals with the resolution of disputes between the employing authority and employees represented by a staff association or trade union.[4] The court granted the injunction, finding that damages would not be an adequate remedy for him if his employment were terminated by the time his breach of contract action came to trial and that if he lost his job in this way, he would be unemployable within the NHS.

This is therefore one of the very rare examples of the courts recognising the special nature of the NHS as a monopoly employer of dedicated professionals. A similar but equally rare moment occurred in the course of the Marietta Higgs appeal to the Court of Appeal. At the start of the second day's hearing, the Master of the Rolls, Lord Donaldson, described dismissal from the NHS as 'professional death' and made specific reference to the wholesale inadequacy of the legal remedies available to a doctor who suffers such a 'death'.

As if to underline the limited nature of this recognition, the Court of Appeal, in the case of Bliss [5] a few months after the Irani decision, held that the only damages for a palpably wrongful suspension was compensation for loss of private work as a direct consequence. Following another quarrel between colleagues, Mr Bliss, an orthopaedic surgeon at the Medway Hospital in Kent, was asked by the regional medical officer to undergo a psychiatric examination. When he refused, he was suspended and subjected to an HM(61)112 inquiry, which eventually exonerated him of all disciplinary charges. Bliss then sued the authority for breach of contract, claiming damages for distress, vexation and frustration during the period he was suspended on full pay. He was awarded £2000 for this by the High Court, but the Court of Appeal reasserted the classic principle that only financial loss directly flowing from the breach could be obtained. This case also established, interestingly, that the only power of health authorities to deal with consultants suspected of mental illness is the 'three wise men' procedure now contained in circular HC(82)13.

Conclusion – a suitable case for treatment

The law of England and Wales contains a gaping hole where the machinery for the adequate protection of doctors' employment rights ought to be. No recognition is given to the monopoly position of the NHS or the personal commitment that doctors make to it when they decide to make their careers in public medicine. Because of the inherent time limits on junior posts, consultant jobs are usually regarded as secure and at least indefinite, if not permanent; there is more interchange of consultant jobs than there used to be, but there is no recognised career structure other than that of obtaining greater seniority in the place of one's first appointment.

Yet most consultants would probably be shocked to learn that they hold their posts more or less at the pleasure of the health authority, which can suspend them with virtual impunity, subject them to potentially unfair disciplinary procedures and then expel them from the NHS, leaving them with a few thousand pounds to compensate for the loss of a career and a lifetime's dedicated work. Of course it happens to only a handful of doctors each year, but the signs are that the handful is getting larger and that trusts and health authorities are beginning to realise the extent of their powers.

Notes

1   The Whitley Councils for the Health Services of Great Britain, Conditions of service.
2   National Health Service Hospital Medical and Dental Staff (England and Wales), Terms and conditions of service.
3   *R v East Berkshire Health Authority ex p. Walsh* [1985] QB 152.
4   *Irani v Southampton and South-West Hampshire Health Authority* [1985] IRLR 203.
5   *Bliss v South East Thames Regional Health Authority* [1985] IRLR 308.

Index